ANSI C Keyword Command Reference

Here are the 32 ANSI Standard C keywords and their syntax. Terms in *italics* are placeholders (items that you replace with your own names or phrases), terms in brackets ([]) are optional commands that you may or may not choose to use, and the term `statement` should be replaced with the desired program code statements (not dependent upon the syntax being explained).

auto   Declares a variable local to a function or block within braces as temporary.
```
[auto] variable_name;
```

break   Exits from the body of a loop of a do, while, or for s
```
break;
```

case   Identifies case labels in a `switch` statement.
```
case [constant_expression]:
```

char   Declares a variable or an array of character elements
```
char variable_name;
```

const   Declares an object as nonmodifiable.
```
const declaration;
```

continue   Forces the loop execution to skip the remaining code and start the next loop cycle.
```
continue;
```

default   Used in a `switch` statement to identify the default code to execute when there is no matching case.
```
default:
```

do   Used with `while` to declare a loop with an ending control expression.
```
do
    statement;
while(expression);
```

double   Declares a double-precision floating-point variable or array.
```
double variable_name;
```

else   Used with `if` to declare an alternate path of execution.
```
if (expression)
    statement;
[else
    statement];
```

enum   Declares an indentifier with a list of enumerated constants and variables associated with each constant.
```
enum [tag] {enum-list} [variable_name];
enum tag variable_name;
```

extern   Declares a variable or function that is defined in a separate module.
```
extern variable_name;
```

float   Declares a single-precision floating-point variable or array.
```
float variable_name;
```

for   Declares three expressions, the initializer, the control, and the counter.
```
for([init_expression]; [control_expression]; [counter_
        expression]) statement;
```

goto   Forces a jump to a label located within the current executing function.
```
goto label;
label: statement
```

® 201 W. 103rd Street • Indianapolis, IN 46290 • (317) 581-3500
Copyright© 1995 Que Corporation

if	Used with a Boolean expression to allow or disallow execution of a statement.

if   Used with a Boolean expression to allow or disallow execution of a statement.
```
if (expression)
     statement;
```

int   Declares an integral integer data type variable or array.
```
int variable_name;
```

long   Qualifier for `int`, declares a variable data type of four bytes.
```
long [int] variable_name;
```

return   Forces termination of a function's execution. When used with an argument it returns the argument to the calling function.
```
return [expression];
```

short   Qualifier for `int`, declares a variable data type of two bytes.
```
short [int] variable_name;
```

signed   Qualifier which enables any integral type to represent a negative number.
```
[signed] char variable_name;
[signed] int variable_name;
[signed] long variable_name;
[signed] short [int] variable_name;
[signed] long [int] variable_name;
```

sizeof   Returns the size in bytes for the storage requirements of a data type or structure.
```
sizeof expression;
```

static   Declares that a data type or structure should be stored permanently in memory even when the function is not active.
```
static variable_name;
```

struct   Declares an identifier that represents a group of data types that are stored contiguously in memory.
```
struct [tag] {member_list} [variable_name];
struct tag variable_name;
```

switch   Followed by an argument, declares a set of case expressions where each expression has an associated statement(s) that will be executed.
```
switch (expression)
{
        [case constant_or_expression]:
            statements;
        [default:]
                statements;
}
```

typedef   Declares a data type to be associated with a new identifier.
```
typedef type_declaration synonym;
```

union   Declares several variables or structures and specifies their storage at the same memory location.
```
union [tag] {member_list} [variable_name];
union tag variable_name;
```

unsigned   Qualifier declares integer data types to be positive numbers only.
```
unsigned [int] variable_name;
unsigned long int variable_name;
unsigned short int variable_name;
```

void   Used as a specifier that declares a function that returns no value, a function that takes no parameter, or a nonspecific pointer that can be used with any other data or pointer type.
```
void declarator;
```

while   Declares a loop with a controlling expression.
```
while(expression)
     statement;
```

Using

C

NEFYN JONES
ZENECA

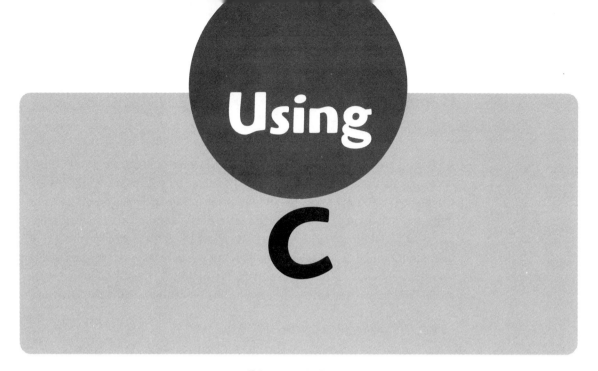

Using

C

Clint Hicks

Using C

Library of Congress Catalog No.: 95-70634

ISBN: 0-7897-0267-3

97 96 95   6 5 4 3 2 1

Interpretation of the printing code: the rightmost double-digit number is the year of the book's printing; the rightmost single-digit number, the number of the book's printing. For example, a printing code of 95-1 shows that the first printing of the book occurred in 1995.

Credits

President and Publisher
Roland Elgey

Associate Publisher
Joseph B. Wikert

Editorial Services Director
Elizabeth Keaffaber

Managing Editor
Sandy Doell

Director of Marketing
Lynn E. Zingraf

Senior Series Editor
Chris Nelson

Title Manager
Bryan Gambrel

Acquisitions Editors
Lori Jordan
Fred Slone

Product Director
C. Kazim Haidri

Production Editor
Patrick Kanouse

Editors
Mary Anne Sharbaugh
Hugh Vandivier

Assistant Product Marketing Manager
Kim Margolius

Technical Editor
Brian Blackman

Technical Specialist
Cari Skaggs

Acquisitions Coordinator
Angela C. Kozlowski

Operations Coordinator
Patty Brooks

Editorial Assistant
Michelle R. Newcomb

Book Designer
Ruth Harvey

Cover Designer
Dan Armstrong

Production Team
Steve Adams, Angela D. Bannan, Becky
Beheler, Joan Evan, Jason Hand, Darren
Jackson, Daryl Kessler, Damon Jordan,
Clint Lahen, Bob LaRoche, Julie Quinn,
Laura Robbins, Bobbi Satterfield, Craig
Small, Michael Thomas, Kelly Warner,
and Todd Wente

Indexer
Mary Jane Frisby

Composed in *ITC Century*, *ITC Highlander*, and *MCPdigital* by Que Corporation.

Dedication

About the Author

Clint Hicks has been writing about computers and computer software since 1984. A 1982 graduate of Rice University in Houston, Texas, Clint worked as a technical writer in a number of engineering and software development firms. In 1988 he joined the staff at Peter Norton Computing, Inc. By 1989 he had taken over as Manager of Technical Publications; later, he was promoted to Senior Editor. In this capacity he oversaw all aspects of software documentation at PNCI, including writing, editing, layout, and production. Clint has been working as a freelance technical author and editor since 1990.

Clint's specialties include operating systems, utilities, and programming languages. His software documentation and trade computer publications on these subjects have consistently won high praise. The Society for Technical Communication singled out in particular his manual for Version 1.0 of the Norton Utilities for the Macintosh. More recently, a work of his on MS-DOS was favorably recommended in the *New York Times*. Other publications include Que's *Visual Basic CD Tutor*.

Currently, Clint lives with his wife, daughter, and son in Santa Fe, New Mexico. Outside interests include physics and astronomy, cooking, gardening, and anthropology; he's currently at work on an advanced degree in the latter subject, focusing on the history of technology in general and the culture of computers in particular.

Acknowledgments

It has really been a joy to have seen how this book came together. Many thanks to Patrick Kanouse and Chris Haidri at Que for ensuring that it did so. I must also thank Fred Slone for all his help and most especially for his patience. Thanks to Matt Wagner at Waterside Productions for handling the details.

Contents at a Glance

Table of Contents

3 A Sample C Program

4 Places To Store Data

5 Paying Constant Attention to Data

6 Expressing Yourself with C Statements

7 Getting Information from the Keyboard and Putting It On-Screen

8 Performing Mathematical Calculations in C

9 Finding the Truth of Expressions

12 About Data Streams

13 Some Optional Ways To Store Data

14 Call Several Variables by the Same Name

15 String Variables as Places for Characters

16 Structure Storage To Meet Your Own Needs

17 How To Indirectly Access Data Storage with Pointers

18 Turning One Data Type into Another

19 Get Strings To Do What You Want

20 Controlling a Program—Where It Goes, What It Does...

21 What Else Can I Do with Functions?

22 Cool Things To Do with Pointers

23 Messing Around with Bits and Bytes

What You Need To Know about Disks and Their Files

25 Make Your Work Easier with the C Function Library

26 Make Memory Work for You

27 How Do I Find and Fix the Errors in My Program?

28 Programs That Update Themselves

29 Use Code That You or Somebody Else Has Already Written

A Answers to Review Questions and Exercises 437

Introduction

I wrote this book for myself. You see, although I know a fair bit about computers, I'm not a professional programmer. So I asked myself, "What kind of book would I have liked to have had available when I was learning C?" To the extent possible, I wrote that very book.

If you're like me, you're comfortable with computers, but your life doesn't revolve around them. Mine revolves around my kids and my garden, although lately I've been exchanging lots of information on how to get rid of pesky bugs with my Dad over the Internet. I like to think that I use my computer but that it doesn't use me. There are entire days—weeks, even—when my computer sits silent.

I know something about programs and have written a few useful programs of my own but not, until relatively recently, in C. Yet for the last ten years all I've heard from my programmer buddies is "C, C, C." "So what is C," I kept asking, "and what makes it so special?" Having learned the answer to these questions, I next wondered, "How do I use C to write programs I'd want to use?"

What I found out, I put in this book. I have to assume that you, too, are curious about C: what is it, and what makes it hot. Otherwise, you'd be over in the bookstore's gardening or automotive sections, looking up stuff about peonies or piston rings. What I think you want to know about C is what I wanted to know: how do I use C to write programs I'd want to use? That's what this book is all about.

Why is this book different?

There are literally dozens of different books on programming in C. I have several of them in my office at this moment. Some are better than others, yet none really gave me what I wanted. Some presupposed a lot of technical programming knowledge on the reader's part. Others had to be read practically from cover to cover before you could really use what was in them. Others relied too much on trivial and useless examples that, though they worked, told me nothing about how the features they purported to illustrate could be harnessed for use in the real world.

This book is meant to address these shortcomings. To the extent possible, we at Que have tried to organize the book so that you can open it to an interesting topic and begin reading there. Naturally, there are some topics—pointers, for instance—that require some background knowledge on your part before you can really delve into them. Still, we like to think that, if you know enough to ask a question, you know enough to understand the particular chapter that deals with it. To help you, we've included numerous cross-references to other chapters, where you can turn for more information.

We've also tried to use as many real-life examples as possible, always keeping that question in mind: how do I use C to write programs I'd want to use? In addition to making our example programs relevant, we try to let you know some real-world uses for each aspect of C that you learn.

Above all, we strive to present information in a way that doesn't assume you're already an ace programmer but doesn't insult your intelligence either. The book has numerous features to make learning C easier, features you'll learn about in the next part of this Introduction. Before we move on, though, I can promise you one more thing: you won't find a single dumb joke or bad pun about C in the entire book.

How can I use this book in the real world?

How does this book work? You'll find information divided into a number of chapters, with the easiest material coming first and the more difficult stuff saved for later. Later chapters build upon work done in early ones. What's more, within each chapter there are a number of important features to help you in your quest to learn C. Let's look at each of these aspects of the book in turn.

Structure of each chapter

I've tried to keep each chapter as short and focused as possible, without glossing over or omitting important information. Within each chapter, you'll find several important features designed to make your learning experience easier.

Plain English, please!

Outside of the government and military, computer programming must be the most jargon-infested area on the face of the Earth. **RAM**, **ROM**, **GUI**, **OOP**—the list of terms and acronyms seems to go on forever. In this book, whenever I have occasion to introduce a new term or concept, I do it in a section marked "Plain English, please!," which is where I define the item in question without jargon or bad English.

 Whenever you see this icon, you know that the previous code will be explained: how it was put together, what each part of the program does, and why it does it that way.

 # Speaking C

In these sections, we show you exactly how to phrase things in C. We show you what C expects when you use one of its features, and give you at least one example.

How can I use this in the real world?

Another way adults torment children is to teach them how to swim by tossing them into the lake. This is an example of the "learn by doing" theory of instruction, which holds that you learn how to do things—swim, build houses, write computer programs—by plunging right in and doing it. I also believe that you learn by doing. To that end, I've included in each chapter at least one section that shows you how to apply what you've learned to something you'd really want to do. The "How can I use this in the real world?" sections show you how to apply what you've learned to tasks that a real person might really want to accomplish using a computer.

Catch the bug

As a kid, did you ever make a major goof-up on something, only to be told patronizingly by some adult, "Well, that's how we learn." It's true, you know. We can learn a lot from our mistakes. What's more, we can learn almost as much from mistakes made by others. For your benefit, I've adopted the latter idea for this book. In "Catch the bug," you are presented with a brief C program or a section from a program. Each "Catch the bug" contains a critical mistake that keeps the program from functioning correctly. I ask you to locate this mistake. I also tell you the correct answer and explain why the bug in question keeps the program from working.

Q&A   *I have questions, like what is this section?*

Here we try to anticipate questions you might have about C and provide answers for them.

CAUTION   **Cautions like this one alert you to potential pitfalls and dangers—** things you should avoid when writing programs of your own.

TIP   **Tips draw your attention to nifty aspects of the current topic or** provide hints for using aspects of C most effectively—things you probably wouldn't have thought of on your own.

Review questions and exercises

At the end of each chapter, after a point-by-point summary of the chapter's contents, I give you the opportunity to test and apply what you've learned. Each chapter has a brief set of questions on the subject matter. Most chapters also feature exercises that challenge you to apply what you've just learned in writing programs of your own. Answers to the review questions and exercises are found in appendix A. For the programming exercises, I usually provide hints and suggestions for solving them, rather than providing complete programs.

1

What Is C?

● **In this chapter:**

● Why would I need to use a
  programming language?

● What is C all about?

● How does C compare to other
  languages?

*Once you learn C, the sky's the limit. You can write programs
to fulfill all your business and personal needs . . . .* ❯

All the good jobs require a fair amount of computer literacy these days. When comparing computer-literate workers, those who know how to make computers do new things tend to have the edge over those who merely know how to use existing computer applications. In fact, over the next couple of decades government economists expect computer programmers and systems analysts to experience the best job growth of any profession. Even in jobs outside the computer industry, employees with solid computer skills will find themselves at a considerable advantage over their colleagues who don't know how to program computers.

Now, when comparing the merely computer-literate with those who are computer-savvy, I think the difference boils down to between using an existing computer application to search computer records for needed information and fashioning such a tool to meet the exact needs of yourself, your employer, or a client. What I'm talking about is writing your own computer programs.

 Plain English, please!

A computer **program** is just a set of instructions that tells a computer how to do a certain group of tasks. You're undoubtedly familiar with large, complex computer programs such as word processors, databases, and spreadsheets. **,,**

Commercial software programs represent years of work by dozens—sometimes hundreds—of programmers. On the other hand, there are many smaller tasks that are also good candidates for turning into computer programs. Almost any job that can be broken down into a set of steps, you can turn into a program if you speak your computer's language.

Your two-minute guide to programming languages

To start writing programs, you have to deal with programming languages. A programming language is very much like an ordinary human language such as English or French. A programming language consists of the words, phrases, and syntax you need in order to tell your computer how to do something. Compare this with French. French consists of the words, phrases, and syntax you need to tell your waiter to bring more mineral water. You can't order from a French waiter if you don't know French, and you can't tell a computer how to do things if you don't know a programming language.

There are several programming languages in active use today and many more that have fallen by the wayside in the forty-odd years since the first programming language was invented. Each computer language has had its own focus, usually dealing with the kinds of problems it's meant to help solve. All computer languages, however, share some important characteristics that you need to understand in order to write effective programs.

What are languages used for?

At first glance, it might seem as if I've already answered this question: A programming language is what you use to write computer programs—sequences of instructions that tell a computer how to accomplish a specific task. Why is such a specialized vocabulary necessary, though?

At its heart, the problem-solving part of your computer, usually called its central processing unit (CPU), does not speak English or any other human language. Instead, it accepts instructions in machine language.

 Plain English, please!

> **Machine language** is a set of very fundamental instructions unique to each type of computer. A typical machine-language instruction might tell the CPU to add two numbers together and store the result in a specific place. A typical CPU recognizes several dozen such commands, each intended to accomplish a small and very specific task.

It's quite possible to write a computer program entirely in machine language; indeed, the very first computers were programmed in this way. The process, however, is very tedious. Machine language isn't written with words and phrases, but in long strings of 0s and 1s—the binary numbers—that are the only form of information the CPU really understands. For example, at times it's necessary to have the CPU wait while other parts of the computer finish up certain tasks. At such times, the CPU must be explicitly told to do nothing! Now, the command to do nothing at all on one particular kind of CPU is expressed as

```
0100111001110001
```

Imagine having to keep track of hundreds of these codes! What's more, programming directly in machine language requires you to know exactly how your computer works, something that's difficult for anyone. Early programmers didn't like all this, so they quickly developed a kind of short-hand, in which each machine-language instruction was represented by a brief word or abbreviation. The shorthand code for "no operation" is

```
NOP
```

This early way to program computers was called **assembly language**. It is still in limited use today. While assembly language is readable by you and me, it's still difficult. Even the simplest tasks, such as performing arithmetic with two numbers, require several steps to accomplish.

Because many important tasks had to be done frequently, it became common practice to write a separate little program for an operation—say, addition—and to give the little program a name that it could be referred to in the main program. From there, someone got the idea of writing an entire, computer language consisting of these little, named procedures. With the right names for certain operations, such a language would read almost like English. Because they exist at a greater level of abstraction than assembly languages—representing complex operations with single words—these computer languages came to be known as **high-level languages**.

Thus, the high-level languages were born, and they have ruled the computer roost ever since. In fact, some of the very first high-level programming languages are still in use, although subsequent innovations like C are supplanting them more and more.

Speaking computerese

Among the first important programming languages were **COBOL** and **FORTRAN**. COBOL (it's full name is Common Business-Oriented Language) was intended for business use. FORTRAN, which stands for Formula Translator, was intended for use in scientific and engineering calculations. The following is a line of COBOL programming code that divides one number by another and stores the result.

```
COMPUTE AVERAGE_SCORE = SCORE_TOTAL / NUMBER_TESTS
```

The same line of code works in FORTRAN if you leave out the word
COMPUTE.

Although useful for computer professionals, neither of these languages was considered ideal for teaching novices how to program. BASIC, which stands for Beginner's All-Purpose Symbolic Instruction Code, was developed at Dartmouth College in the mid-1960s as an aid for teaching computer programming. BASIC became very popular, especially for use on small computers. If you're working with PCs, chances are that you have a version of BASIC installed on your machine. Other programming languages you might encounter include Pascal, PostScript, and LISP.

For more information on compilers, see chapter 2, "Specifying, Designing, and Implementing a C Program."

All these high-level languages make it easier for the non-expert to program a computer, but this ease-of-use has its cost. Paradoxically, the further away you get from machine language, the more machine-language instructions it takes to perform the same task. This is because a program written in a high-level language must still be translated into machine code, using a special program called a **compiler**. The overhead involved in translation means that programs translated from high-level languages always have more statements than equivalent programs written directly in machine language. What this all means is that such programs take longer to do their work and take up more computer resources while doing it.

What about C? C was developed by Dennis Ritchie at AT&T Bell Laboratories in 1972. (C was a third try; the first two attempts were named A and B.) Although it's a high-level language like FORTRAN and BASIC, C preserves a number of features more commonly found in assembly language. Thus, C was meant to provide the power and flexibility of machine-language programming, without sacrificing the ease-of-use of high-level programming languages. C has a number of other powerful features and advantages, as you'll see shortly.

What C has that others don't have

With so many programming languages available, why should a person choose C? C has a number of advantages over other programming languages. Sure, C has its disadvantages, but those are greatly outweighed by the advantages.

C's advantages are...

What has the C programming language got going for it? Four major things. C is powerful. C programs can accomplish a lot of computing in a small number of steps. C is portable; you'll find it available on lots of different computers. This power and portability have made C popular, meaning that lots of folks use C these days. Finally, C is constantly progressing; new and exciting features are being made available to C programmers all the time. You'll look at the importance of each of these virtues in turn.

...power...

Everybody wants to get the most for the least, whether you're talking about cars or computer programs. C has features that make it one of the most powerful programming languages available. Again, being powerful means getting a lot accomplished in a few steps.

For example, in most programming languages, if you want to increase the value of some quantity by one, you must write a statement to add 1 to the quantity:

```
RESULT = RESULT + 1
```

This statement tells the computer to take the value stored in RESULT, add 1 to it, and then replace the previous contents of RESULT with the new value. In C, on the other hand, you write

```
++RESULT;
```

Though this is only a savings of six characters, this saving requires less machine-language activity within the computer. However, it achieves the same result: increasing the value stored in RESULT by 1.

C also lets you program *close to the ground*, which means that you can directly manipulate aspects of your computer's memory. For example, rather than referring to a place where data is stored with a name like RESULT, you can refer to the location directly, much like assembly language is capable of. Again, this lets you perform powerful manipulations in a very few steps. This probably doesn't make much sense now, but it'll be made clear in chapter 17, "How To Indirectly Access Data Storage with Pointers." Doing more work in fewer steps makes your programs run faster and lets them do more and better things for the end user.

...portability...

Ralph Waldo Emerson said, "Build a better mousetrap, and the world will beat a path to your door." The world has certainly beat a path to

Dr. Ritchie's programming language. There are versions of C available for just about every computer system in existence. This includes PCs, Apple Macintoshes, and UNIX systems. (In fact, the UNIX operating system was rewritten in C and has been maintained in C ever since. Microsoft Windows and Windows NT were also developed mainly in C.) For you as a programmer, this means that you can easily expand your horizons beyond one type of machine.

The C programming language is maintained by the **American National Standards Institute** (**ANSI**). Although ANSI doesn't "own" C in any sense, the organization publishes a precise specification of what the C language should contain—and what it should be able to do—no matter what computer system it's running on. Because there are versions of C that don't adhere to the standard, the versions that do are called **ANSI Standard C**. This book deals almost exclusively with ANSI Standard C.

Because of the portable way that C is designed in, a program that runs in C on an PC, generally runs with little or no modification on another system, such as an Apple Macintosh. However, this portability is restricted in cases where the program interacts extensively with the operating software of the computer it's running on. However, relatively simple programs that don't use a lot of graphics should require few, if any, changes when they're **ported**, or moved, to another machine.

...popularity...

C's power and portability have made it very popular. More commercial programs for PCs are written in C than in any other language. Popularity, of course, is not itself necessarily a virtue. In the case of programming with C, however, popularity produces additional virtues.

The number of programmers working in C makes the market of C-related products a force to be reckoned with in the computer world. Because folks who want to sell stuff tend naturally to gravitate towards large markets, you'll find there are many C-related programming tools available, certainly more than there are for Pascal or FORTRAN. In like manner, you'll find that, with so many C programmers out there, it's quite likely someone else has solved some pressing problem before you and that it doesn't take much for you to locate and adapt that work to your own purposes, as you'll see in chapter 29, "Use Code That You or Somebody Else Has Already Written."

...and progress

C is growing and changing all the time, usually from additions and extensions. The original part of the language doesn't change because C's portability would be jeopardized. The additions to C are usually special libraries of ready-to-use programs that, among other things, can be worked into programs meant to run with graphical user interfaces (GUIs)—Microsoft Windows, the Macintosh, and OS/2 are the most common GUIs.

For more information about OOP, see appendix D, "C++: the Object-Oriented C."

C has also expanded into the realm of **object-oriented programming** (**OOP**), which has become the dominant force in programming. Rather than going into the details at this point, I'll just say that it's much easier to program under a GUI using OOP. As you might expect, there's an object-oriented form of C called **C++**. Learning C is a great step to learning C++ because everything in ANSI Standard C is still useful in C++. Under the covers, C++ is still C.

C's disadvantages are...

For the most part, C's disadvantages result from deliberately-designed aspects of the language. Although at first they present obstacles, you'll find in time that these aspects of C are part of its power.

...rigid structure...

C is not a language that lends itself to careless programming. Programs written in C tend to be very formal in structure; C compilers won't have it any other way. To take but one example: in most computer languages, a single step in a program appears on a line by itself, like

```
Taxes = Rate * Balance
```

In C, you must add a semicolon at the end of most (but not all) steps in a program:

```
Taxes = Rate * Balance;
```

The semicolon is very important to C and, as you'll read later in the book, isn't there merely to mark the end of a line. If you're coming to C from another programming language (like BASIC), you'll find yourself forgetting the semicolon frequently and apt to find it a bit of a nuisance, at least for a while.

There are other formal aspects of C programming, which will be introduced as the book unfolds. Keep in mind that each of these has a purpose and that all of them actually contribute to the language's power. The French author Marcel Proust wrote that good poets find their greatest lines because of the tyranny of rhyme. In like manner, the precise structure of C forces you to do things a certain way, and out of that, great programs can arise.

...some data is difficult to handle...

Although I like to regard many of C's vices as virtues, the language does have shortcomings that are true deficiencies. Of particular note is the way that C handles character data such as names and addresses. In computer idiom, we call such data (a person's name, for instance) **strings**. C does not handle strings as gracefully as most other computer languages, particularly later forms of BASIC.

For example, if you want to combine two strings into one in BASIC, you can use a statement like

```
FULLNAME = FIRSTNAME & LASTNAME
```

This is an operation that looks and works just like addition. In C, however, you can't use the addition operator for strings. The C equivalent to the preceding line of programming is

```
strcpy(Fullname,FirstName);
strcat(FullName,LastName);
```

You can see that the C version of this operation takes two steps, whereas the BASIC version requires only one. There are other peculiarities in the ways C deals with strings, which you read about it chapter 15, "String Variables as Places for Characters."

...and C is difficult to learn

Given C's rigid structure and its quirkiness with some data, that many people consider the language difficult to learn, especially those who've never programmed before, is no surprise. Languages such as Pascal and BASIC are the languages of choice for teaching computer programming.

With the right guidance, however, C can serve as a first language for the novice programmer. That kind of guidance is provided in *Using C*. As someone interested in learning how to write computer programs in C, you'll benefit greatly from this book.

Summary

This chapter covered the following:

- A programming language is a special vocabulary for talking to a computer and getting it to do what you want.

- C, COBOL, BASIC, and Pascal are examples of programming languages. (There are many more.) Each has advantages and limitations.

- The C programming language was developed in 1972 at AT&T Bell Labs, to combine the best features of high-level and assembly-language programming.

- C is powerful, portable, popular, and progressive.

Review Questions

1 In what way were the first computers programmed? Why did this method prove difficult?

2 Name two of the first high-level programming languages developed.

3 Which computer operating system was rewritten entirely in C?

4 What do I mean when I say that the C programming language and programs written in it are *highly portable*?

5 Name a kind of data that is more difficult to handle in C than in BASIC.

Exercise

Before you can write programs in C, you need to have a C compiler on your computer. This is a program, usually accompanied by other tools, that translates your C programs into machine-language programs that your computer can understand. Several very good C compiler packages are available. Your task is to acquire one, if you haven't already, and to familiarize yourself with its use. You should consult your compiler's documentation for how to install it on your computer, and how to run it. Chapter 2 gives some general instructions on this subject.

2

Specifying, Designing, and Implementing a C Program

● In this chapter:

- Steps for creating a computer program

- What is an algorithm, and where does it fit in?

- After I type in the code, what do I do?

Writing a computer program is much like drafting a set of plans and using those plans to build a structure . . . . ▶

To construct a building requires considerable organization on the builder's part. Building a good, solid computer program is no different. We can divide the process of creating a C computer program into three broad steps: specifying, designing, and implementing.

In the first step, the programmer determines what the program should do (and perhaps as importantly, what it shouldn't do) and what kind of data it uses. In the second step, the programmer uses the specifications to create a sequence of steps to follow for solving the problem. Finally, this set of steps is translated into a full-blown program, using the C programming language and its associated tools. In this chapter, you look in detail at the steps of specifying, designing, and implementing a C program.

Specifying a program

Computers are only useful for providing answers to problems that you already know how to solve. If this sounds confusing, consider balancing your checkbook each month. This is a problem you know how to solve (one hopes!), yet each month the exact solution to the problem—how much money is left after all deposits and withdrawals are accounted for—is unknown until you compute it. For this sort of task, writing a program is useful: the task happens regularly, and you know how to solve it, but the exact solution is unknown each time you perform it.

Not all solvable problems are worth programming, however. If you only write a computer program to solve a problem you already know how to solve, then when does it make sense to have a computer do the work? Simple: when it saves you time. Computers can perform calculations millions of times faster than you and I can; thus, problems that involve doing math on lots of numbers are natural candidates for writing computer programs to solve them. This presumes, however, that the amount of time saved over the long haul ends up being greater than the time it takes to write the program.

The first question—the very first—you should ask yourself when contemplating a new program is, "Is this a problem worth solving by computer?" Keep in mind that the more times you can use a program to solve different versions of the problem (balancing your checking account each month, for example), the more time you'll save by programming.

It's all right to spend some time and effort on small problems when you're first learning how to program in C, but even in this book I'll try to keep trivial examples to a bare minimum. I want you to learn how to do useful things as soon as possible.

What will the program do?

In order to decide it was worth doing with a computer, you had to have at least a vague notion of what you want your program to do. Now that you've decided it's worth programming, it's time to sharpen your focus on what it'll do. Suppose you've been looking at cars and are overwhelmed by a variety of prices and financing rates. You wonder how much each deal will cost you per month, and you think this is a good candidate for a computer program. What next?

Think about it some more. What you need here is a program that can take the changeable parts of this problem—the prices of different cars, the amount of the down payment you're going to make, the interest rate on loans of varying lengths—and calculate the payment on a given vehicle. Now, you're ready to ask yourself some specifics:

- Should the program do all these calculations in a batch, or should it do them one at a time?

- Do I need to calculate the interest rate as an annual or monthly figure?

- Do you want the program to provide an amortization schedule—that is, a table that shows for each month how much money goes to interest and how much goes to pay the balance on the loan?

Answering these kinds of questions will give you the broad outline of your program. I find it extremely useful to jot the questions and answers down as they come to me. The results might be something as simple as this:

Calculates the payment on a loan

Calculates one loan at a time

Uses annual interest figure

Does not provide an amortization schedule

A really useful and complex program has many more points than this, but you get the idea.

By the way, almost as important as deciding what a program will do is determining what it won't do. You might build the internal structure of a program differently if you know that you need to add a feature later or that you will definitely never include it.

What data will the program use?

Having sketched with a broad brush what a program will do, your next task is to determine what it will do it with. That is, what kind of data does the program need, and what form should the data take? Again, there are nitty-gritty questions you need to ask:

- Will the data be numbers or words?

- What does each piece of data mean, and how should it be treated within the program?

- How will the program obtain this data—will they be put in by the user at the computer keyboard, or will they come from some other place?

Asking these questions about the loan payment example gives more or less the following answers:

- The program needs the amount of the car loan, the interest rate per year, and the number of months before the load is paid.

- All this data is in number form, with dollars to the left of the decimal point and cents to the right.

- The user enters the data from the computer keyboard.

Knowing exactly what data your program needs isn't always possible until you've determined a little more about how to solve the underlying problem. In the case of making payments on a loan, for instance, you would only come up with the preceding points if you already knew that calculating a loan payment requires the loan amount, the interest rate per period, and the number of periods before the loan is paid. If you weren't aware of those facts at first, they'd become clear as soon as you started to research the problem.

You can always go back and modify your notes based on new discoveries regarding your program's data requirements. You'll find that writing a program is an evolving process that involves lots of this kind of feedback.

Designing the program

With a good idea of both the outline of your program and of the data it needs, you can proceed to the next step: designing the actual program. Here, you need to decide the steps involved in getting your program to do its work, and you need to determine how the program will interact with its users.

Design a step-by-step procedure

It's in a computer's nature to work through a problem one step at a time, performing a distinct operation on data at each step. Once you've formulated a programmable problem, your next task is to design a step-by-step procedure that, given the data your program has to work with, manipulates that data and comes up with the correct answer to your original question. This step-by-step procedure is called an algorithm.

 Plain English, please!

An **algorithm** is an orderly, unambiguous sequence of steps to compute a certain desired result given certain information at the start. The word "algorithm" comes from Arabic and refers to a kind of narrative, or story. **99**

At the heart of any algorithm is some sort of relationship among the data that you can obtain the desired result from. For example, when multiplying a two-digit number by a one-digit number, the important relationship states that a number times the sum of two numbers is the same as the sum of that number times each of the two numbers in turn. (You may have heard this rule referred to as the Associative Property of Multiplication when you were in school.) In symbols, this turns out to be

$$A \times (B + C) = (A \times B) + (A \times C)$$

Think of 6×47, for instance. We can write that as

$$6 \times (7 + 40)$$

The Associative Property rule says that this is equal to

$$(6 \times 7) + (6 \times 40)$$

which equals 282. If you think about it, this is just how you solve the problem when working it out on paper:

$$
\begin{array}{r}
47 \\
\times 6 \\
\hline
42 \\
+240 \\
\hline
282
\end{array}
$$

The real trick in developing an algorithm for a program is determining what relationship to use and determining how to "massage" that relationship into yielding the answer you want.

The beauty of an algorithm is this: having worked it out once, you can then apply it to any data you want. The preceding algorithm works for just about every conceivable combination of balance, interest, and checking-account fee. Thus, having solved a problem once, you can proceed to create a computer program that solves it again for new data, as many times as you want. That's how you save time and labor using a computer program.

So I've designed a program...but how do I use the design?

A final thing to consider when designing a computer program is how people are going to use that program. This part of the program is called the user interface.

 Plain English, please!

A program's **user interface** determines how data gets into a program and how a user tells the program what to do and when to do it. For example, the drop-down menus, command keys, and movable screen elements found in programs like Microsoft Windows are elements in a **graphical user interface** (**GUI**). These elements define how a user works with Windows. **99**

How can I use this in the real world?

The possible applications of algorithms are numerous; the preparation of a to-do list counts. You might think of such a list as an algorithm for getting through your afternoon. Usually, though, computer algorithms involve numbers.

Suppose you have a choice between two banks: First National and Second National. At First, they pay 3% simple interest on your end-of-the-month checking balance, but they also charge a flat fee of $10 for the first 40 checks processed each month. Second National doesn't pay interest on checking accounts, but they also don't charge a fee. Which is the better deal?

It's a question of cost. The Second National account costs nothing. The First National account costs $10, minus whatever you earn in interest. You could even end up on the winning side. But when?

The essential relationship in this case is that giving simple interest. Supposing the interest rate is expressed in percent, you know that the formula for simple interest is given by

InterestEarned = AccountBalance × PercentInterest ÷ 100

Now, interest is always advertised in percent per year, not per month. So you have to further divide by 12 to get the monthly interest earned.

InterestEarned = AccountBalance × PercentInterest ÷ 1200

From this formula, it's clear that the dollar amount of interest earned by the account at First National depends strictly on your monthly balance since the interest rate and the amount of time interest is earned both stay the same (one at 3% and the other at one month). With this information, you can specify an algorithm for determining which account is the better deal.

1 Take your end-of-month bank balance, multiply it by 3 and divide that result by 1200.

2 Subtract $10—the checking account fee—from this result.

3 Compare this result with 0. If the step 2 result is less than zero, then the account at Second National is a better deal. If the result is more than 0, the First National account is better.

You can verify with a calculator that it takes a closing balance of $4,000 to offset the $10 per month First National account fee. In my case, at least, the Second National account is the better deal.

Although different computer systems are becoming more and more alike, at the programming level there are still as many kinds of user interfaces as there are kinds of computers. GUIs such as Microsoft Windows, the Macintosh, and Sunsoft Solaris may look very similar, but each is programmed quite differently. Because this book is meant to be a general treatment of ANSI Standard C on all computer systems, it is impossible for us to discuss most aspects of user interface design.

In this book, a program's user interface is limited to some kind of character-based design rather than a GUI. All input consists of keystrokes from the keyboard, and all output is characters on-screen. You should simply keep in mind that such an interface is generally not acceptable for professional purposes; that is, if you want to sell a program to a client or to the public. To get into GUI design, you'll have to learn more about programming with the specific computer or computers that you want to work with. That's a subject for another book, at least. However, what you learn about C programming in this book will make it possible to move on to GUI programming if you choose.

Implementing the program

So you have a specification, a description of the data, and an algorithm for your programming project. What next? Now, you write the program. This means preparing a text file containing C language steps that correspond to the steps in your algorithm. In effect, this is the point when you take the plans you've prepared—the algorithm and specifications—and use them to "build" your program.

Translating an algorithm into code

A great deal of time and effort has been expended over the last 40 years to make the language used to program a computer correspond as closely as possible to the language one uses in writing an algorithm. In a perfect world, we'd write both algorithms and programs in plain English. Perhaps you've noticed that the world isn't perfect.

Still, existing computer languages in widespread use don't tend to differ in their structure very much from the way you express an algorithm. The task becomes translating the step-by-step algorithm into a step-by-step program written in a specific programming language. Here, you need enough familiarity with the language to know what words and phrases to use to express the parts of your algorithm.

Where do I write the program?

When it comes to preparing a program, handwritten notes obviously won't do. Very few computers are set up to read such notes—and even those that do, don't do it well. So translating an algorithm into a program—building your computer program structure out of your plans—involves not only translating the algorithm into a programming language but transforming the results into a form your computer can handle.

This form varies from language to language. In the case of C, you need to prepare a simple sort of computer document consisting only of text. You do this using an existing computer program called a **text editor**.

Every computer sold today has some sort of text editor included with it. Such a program behaves basically like a typewriter, allowing you to enter text and see it on-screen. Most text editors have features that have made typewriters obsolete, although such features tend to vary from editor to editor, and moreover are generally *not* important to your C programming.

Using a text editor, you type in your program code, translated from the algorithm. This is your program. Before you can use it, you must save this program, meaning that you create a named copy of it on some sort of long-term storage medium, usually a computer disk. This keeps the program from disappearing from the face of the earth when power to the computer is interrupted, either intentionally (you press the on/off switch) or accidentally (the power company blows up). On most computer systems, the program's name includes an extension: a period followed by one or more letters which indicate what kind of file it is. C program files usually have the extension C.

Regardless of where it's saved, a text file produced by a text editor pre-serves data in a very specific form. This form is sometimes called **ASCII format**.

 Plain English, please!

ASCII is a special computer standard that associates each character (letter, numeral, and punctuation mark) with a different number value. The name ASCII itself is an acronym for **American Standard Code for Information Interchange**.

The great thing about ASCII text files is that they're usually readable on just about any computer system with a minimal amount of translation. (Making PC ASCII files available to a UNIX system, and vice versa, does require translation.)

By the way, a C program needs to be in ASCII form. This is why you need to take care if you rely on a word processor to edit your program text. Most word processors store their data in a form other than ASCII. Storing a program in such a form is likely to render it unreadable later in the process, as you'll soon see. Fortunately, every decent word processor lets you store files in ASCII form. Usually this option is described as text only.

To make a program run... compile, link, and go

Having prepared an ASCII text file of your program, you have built a computer program out of your set of plans. What can this program do, now that it's built? Absolutely nothing. Before you can use it, the program must be transformed by a couple of special software programs whose job it is to make your programs intelligible to your computer. Making a program usable involves three steps, generally described as compile, link, and go.

 Plain English, please!
Compile, link, and go is programmer's lingo for what you do after you've typed in the code. In other words, compile, link, and go describes what you do to run the program.

What is a compiler?

Recall from chapter 1 that computers take instruction in the form of 1s and 0s, and that computer languages were developed to make it simpler for human beings to communicate in this machine language. This is done with the help of a special program called a **compiler**.

Plain English, please!

A **compiler** is a computer program written for a specific computer system. The compiler's job is to translate computer programs written in a specific programming language, such as C, into machine-language programs that the computer can run directly. **"**

And compilers do what?

Compilers are very finicky eaters. First, the compiler goes through the program line-by-line making sure everything's in the correct form. Most compilers expect the program to be written in ASCII form. If not, the program is unintelligible and the compiler rejects it. If the compiler finds so much as a single error, it stops processing and spits the program back out. As a rule, the compiler displays a message on your computer screen telling you whatever it knows about the error it found. This may not be much, but at the very least it should tell you which lines of your program caused problems and what the compiler thinks went wrong at each trouble spot.

If the program doesn't contain any errors of form, the compiler proceeds to translate it into machine language. At this point, the compiler takes your source program and turns it into an object program. A compiler translates source code into object code.

 Plain English, please!

A program's **source code** is just what you have written: an ASCII text file in a specific computer language. **Object code** is a partially translated version of your program; it's meant to be intelligible to your computer. **"**

By the way, you need a different compiler for each programming language on each computer system that you want to program in. This is because a compiler must prepare machine-language code, and this code is different for each type of computer. The object code prepared to run on an IBM compatible is useless on a Silicon Graphics workstation and vice versa.

Submitting to an urge to compile

No matter what system you program for, compiling a source program into object code is roughly the same. Programmers say that you submit a program for compilation. In essence, you "tell" the compiler you want it to run and compile a program, and you tell it where on your computer to find that program.

The specifics of submitting a program for compiling vary somewhat from compiler to compiler, and (what's more) among computer systems, most particularly on the Apple Macintosh. On a system that works with command-line input, such as DOS or Solaris, you typically enter the name of your compiler followed by the name of the program you want to compile and press the Enter key.

Catch the bug

Suppose I have a C compiler on a PC-compatible named MYC.EXE and a program in the same directory called MYPROG. I propose to submit this program for compiling by entering:

```
myc.exe myprog.doc
```

Can you see anything wrong with submitting the program in this way?

Answer: *Check out the program file's extension—the three letters following the period. The extension DOC usually indicates a file belonging to a word processor. Such a file is most likely not in ASCII form. The compiler will probably reject it. Presuming a plain ASCII form of the program file exists and that it's named in a typical manner, you need to enter either*

```
myc.exe myprog.txt
```

or

```
myc.exe myprog.c
```

The latter form is much preferred. Be sure to get in the habit of saving your C programs in ASCII form and giving them the extension C.

Now you link and go

Even after a program has been translated from source code into object code for a specific computer system, it isn't ready to use. Certain additional, system-specific information must be incorporated or linked into the object program. This is performed by another special program called a **linker**.

A linker provides your program with all the extra information it needs to work with a particular type of computer system. Sometimes a program is compiled and linked in a single step; in other cases, you must submit an object program to be linked, after you submit the source program to be compiled. The procedure you have to follow depends on the specific compiler package you're using. You'll need to check your compiler's documentation for details.

The end result of all this is an executable program. (This is the "go" part in compile, link, and go.) You computer system can now run the program, and you can use it to obtain results.

Summary

This chapter covered these points:

- To create a C program, you should first specify what the program should do and what data it will work with.

- A program's specification may be turned into an algorithm, which is an orderly and unambiguous sequence of steps that specifies how to solve a given problem.

- An algorithm, in turn, can be translated into steps in the C language. This becomes a computer program to solve the same problem solved by the original algorithm.

- The process of turning a program into something a computer can use is called *compile, link, and go*. A compiler translates a program into machine language. The linker provides it with additional information it needs in order to run on a specific computer system. Go refers to actually running the program.

Review questions

1 When is a problem a likely candidate for solving with a computer program? Would multiplying two specific eight-digit numbers—a process a computer can do in fractions of a second—be a good candidate?

2 Define *algorithm*.

3 In what form should a C source program be?

4 Suppose you own an Apple Macintosh and an IBM PC-compatible. How many C compilers do you need?

5 What do you call the output from a compiler? Is this output ready to run?

Exercises

1 Write an algorithm for multiplying two three-digit numbers.

2 Determine the data required to find the interest returned on a savings account, and the form that data should take.

3 Develop a specification, a description of the data, and an algorithm for a program that finds the volume of either a cube or a sphere, whichever is chosen by the user of the program while the program's running.

A Sample C Program

● In this chapter:

- **Show me an example of a real C program**

- **The parts of a C program**

- **What does each program part do?**

Your program specification provides a sort of scaffolding upon which you can erect the actual C statements that constitute your program . . . . ❯

n this chapter you look at taking what you learned in the previous chapter and applying it to the creation of a real C program. You'll look at specifying and implementing a short program that accomplishes a real task, rather than just printing a message on the screen like the majority of introductory examples do. In the process, you'll see some specific things you need to know about how a C program is structured.

Specifications for a sample program

So you want to know how to develop a C program. The first step is to state the problem and write the specifications for it, using these in turn to develop an algorithm.

Determine the problem

Suppose I deposit a sum of money in a bank account at a fixed rate of interest. How much will my deposit be worth at the end of a certain span of years? That, in a nutshell, is the compound interest problem I propose to solve using a C program. The specifications for such a program are quite simple:

- The program accepts the appropriate values as input from the user. Text appears on-screen to indicate what the user should enter.

- I looked up a standard formula from mathematics to calculate the growth in a balance left to compound interest. Unfortunately, what I found may seem a bit complicated at first. The formula is

  future balance = (present balance) $\times 2.7183^{(\text{rate})\text{x}(\text{time})}$

- The program runs through only once; to input a different set of conditions, the user must run the program again.

- As for data, the program requires a present balance, a rate of interest expressed in percent per year, and a length of time the interest accumulates, expressed in years. These values are entered by the user and are in numeric form. The program also needs a place to store its result.

Create the algorithm for the problem

Working through the points shown above, I came up with the following algorithm:

1 Have the user input the values desired for the present balance, the rate, and the time.

2 Calculate the future balance using the following formula: divide the rate by 100 to obtain a percent, multiply this by the time, and then raise the number 2.7183 to that power; multiply this result by the opening balance, and store the result as the future balance.

3 Print the future balance along with a brief message.

4 Stop the program.

TIP **Whenever I've developed what I hope is a satisfactory algorithm** for a result involving numbers, I test it with my pocket calculator. I try to find a known set of results to test against. In this case, I used a bank account statement.

Implementing the C program

Listing 3.1 shows a completed C program to determine compound interest, based on the specifications developed previously. I show you the program in its entirety right away so you can get a feel for what a C program looks like. Don't be concerned that you can't interpret most or all of the individual lines in the program. I'll explain the program's basic parts next. Of course, certain things done by individual lines of the program are covered in the next several chapters.

Listing 3.1   A program to find compound interest

```
/*A program to find compound interest*/

#include <stdio.h>
#include <math.h>

/*Declare variables*/

float balance, rate, future, years;
main()
{

/*Have the user input the values desired */
```

continues

Listing 3.1   Continued

```
/* for the present balance, rate, and time */

printf("\nEnter the opening balance: ");
scanf("%f",&balance);
printf("\nEnter the interest rate in percent per year:  ");
scanf("%f",&rate);
printf("\nEnter the number of years the balance is held: ");
scanf("%f",&years);

/*Calculate the future balance using the formula*/

future = balance * (pow(2.7183,(rate/100)*years));

/*Print the results*/

printf("\nThe future balance is %f",future);
}
```

The parts that make up a C program are...

Can't make heads or tails of listing 3.1? Don't worry; I'll take you through it. You'll find that all C programs are similar in that they're broadly organized into parts in the same manner. We'll look at each of these parts in turn.

...header...

A typical C program begins with a **header**. The header tells the C compiler about the program's overall requirements. In the interest example, the header is

```
/*A program to find compound interest*/

#include <stdio.h>
#include <math.h>
```

In addition to a line meant for a person (also known as a comment; more on these a bit later), this header contains two lines that tell the compiler that this particular C program needs two special files in order to run correctly. These files are called stdio.h and math.h. They give the program the capability to accept input from the keyboard and perform certain mathematical calculations. A typical C program has at least one #include line in the header. The exact file or files included in this way depend on the program's needs. The opening comment line is not required, but it does clue a person into what the program is meant to do.

...variable declarations...

A C program needs places to store data, whether it's parameters entered by the program user or program results. The next section in the interest program creates these storage places, which are called **variables**.

```
/*Declare variables*/

float balance, rate, future, years;
```

This part of the program creates four numeric variables, intended to contain the present balance, the interest rate, the future balance, and the number of years the balance is left to accrue. You'll learn more about using variables in chapter 4, "Places To Store Data."

...main function body...

Every C program has a `main()` **function**; this is the part of the program that does the real work.

 Plain English, please!

> A **function** is a named section of C programming code that accomplishes a specific task.

The `main()` function starts like

```
main()
{
```

The `main()` function always has the open brace on the line following the `main()` function. This brace is very important in C; among other things, it marks the beginning of a function.

...statements...

The body of the program consists of lines written in the C programming language. We call these individual lines **statements**. Statements do the program's work; they correspond roughly to the steps in the original algorithm.

```
/*Have the user input the values desired */
/* for the present balance, rate, and time */

printf("\nEnter the opening balance: ");
scanf("%f",&balance);
printf("\nEnter the interest rate in percent per year:  ");
scanf("%f",&rate);
printf("\nEnter the number of years the balance is held: ");
scanf("%f",&years);
```

```
/*Calculate the future balance using the formula*/

future = balance * (pow(2.7183,(rate/100)*years));

/*Print the results*/

printf("\nThe future balance is %f",future);
}
```

These statements accomplish the three tasks of inputting values from the keyboard, calculating the future balance, and printing that balance on the computer screen. Notice how each of the statements ends in a semicolon; this is how C marks the end of a statement, and it cannot be omitted except in special circumstances (see chapter 10, "Control the Way a Program Runs," for those cases). Note the close brace that ends the program.

...and comments

Perhaps you've noticed the statements marked with /* and */ in the preceding examples. These statements seem to contradict what I've said all along about C not being equivalent to common English; however, these lines seem to be written in common English. It's true, they are, but they're not for the program, they're for the programmer.

Lines of a program enclosed with the symbols /* and */ are called **comments**. (Note that comments don't require a semicolon at the end.) They're meant to label parts of the program, to explain to a person what they're meant to do. Your C compiler doesn't care one bit about comments; in fact, it ignores them entirely.

I encourage liberal use of comments; they can be of immense benefit during the development of a program, especially when you have to leave your work (over lunch, overnight, or over the weekend) and then return to it. Comments can make it much easier for you to pick up where you left off. Comments also make it much easier to adapt existing programs to new uses later.

By the way, you'll find (as I have) that the lines from your algorithm make handy comments. You could even use the file containing your algorithm as a foundation for your program: save the file as text only and make sure each line in the algorithm is enclosed in /* and */ symbols to make it a comment. In this way, your program specification provides the scaffolding for erecting the actual C statements that constitute your program.

Catch the bug

What's wrong with the following block of three C statements?

```
scanf("%f",&Age);
AgeInDays=Age*365.25
printf("Your age in days is %d", AgeInDays);
```

Answer: *The semicolon is missing at the end of the second statement. If you try to compile a program containing these three statements, the compiler prints an error message. Why doesn't the compiler simply put in a semicolon for you? Because there are actually times when it makes sense to omit it. This isn't one of them, but the compiler has no way of "knowing" that, so it takes the safest route and tells you there's an error.*

Walking through the sample program

Let's go through the compound interest program line by line to see what it does. I've repeated the program listing so you don't have to flip back and forth.

```
/*A program to find compound interest*/

#include <stdio.h>
#include <math.h>

/*Declare variables*/

float balance, rate, future, years;
main()
{

/*Have the user input the values desired
/* for the present balance, the rate, and the time */

printf("\nEnter the opening balance: ");
scanf("%f",&balance);
printf("\nEnter the interest rate in percent per year:  ");
scanf("%f",&rate);
printf("\nEnter the number of years the balance is held: ");
scanf("%f",&years);

/*Calculate the future balance using the formula*/

future = balance * (pow(2.7183,(rate/100)*years));
```

```
/*Print the results*/

printf("\nThe future balance is %f",future);
}
```

code

1 The first three lines set up the program. The first line is a comment, which the compiler ignores. The next two lines, each starting with `#include`, tell the compiler to include information from two other files.

2 The fourth line, starting with `\* Declare`, is a comment introducing the line that follows, which creates the variables for the program. The variables are named `balance`, `rate`, `future`, and `years`.

3 The next three lines, starting with `main()` and ending with the comment beginning `\* Have`, set up the main body of the program.

4 The next line prints a message on the computer screen, `Enter the opening balance:`. The line following reads the number entered by the user and puts it into the variable named `balance`.

5 Next, the line beginning `printf("\nEnter` prints a message on the computer screen, `Enter the interest rate in percent per year:`. The line following this reads the number entered by the user and puts in into the variable named `rate`.

6 The next line prints a message on the computer screen, `Enter the number of years the balance is held:`. The line following reads the number entered by the user and puts it into the variable named `time`.

7 The next line is a comment introducing the line that follows, which does the program's real work. This line is a C translation of the mathematical relationship

future balance = (present balance) × 2.7183$^{(rate)x(time)}$

Again, don't worry if the exact way this statement works is unclear to you; you've the remainder of this book to find out what such things are all about.

8 The line beginning `/* Print` is a comment introducing the line that follows, which prints the results obtained in step 7 on the screen. The last line marks the end of the `main()` function—hence, the end of this program.

Typing the program into a text editor isn't enough

To repeat an important point from the last chapter, the program shown in the preceding section is capable of doing nothing at this point. Having been saved under the name `interest.c`, it must be transformed from an ASCII text file into an executable one.

Compile the program

I happen to be working on a PC, keeping my fingers crossed every time my Pentium chip, which I never got around to exchanging, does a long division. In my case, I compile the interest program by entering the name of my compiler and the name of the program file on the DOS command line, like so:

```
myc.exe c:\myfiles\interest.c
```

Note that I've included the complete path name of my interest program file. That's because it isn't in the same directory as my compiler. The result of this operation is an object program that my compiler names `interest.o`.

Q&A *Why do I get warnings from my compiler when I try to compile `interest.c`? Are these warnings important?*

The `interest.c` program does a couple of things that some C compilers mildly object to but don't prevent the program from working. Eliminating these slight defects would have been easy but would also make the example harder to read. Any warnings you might get when compiling `interest.c` aren't important. You learn what you need to know to eliminate these warnings in chapters 11, "The Functional Structure of C Programs," and 18, "Turning One Data Type into Another."

Compiler warnings are different than compiler errors. Errors prevent your programs from being compiled; they usually result from your mistyping a statement or omitting something important like a semicolon. Warnings, on the other hand, are just your compiler's way of asking "Do you really want to do this?" Many times, the answer is "Yes, in fact I do."

Link the program

Having compiled the source code for `interest.c` into an object program, I now have to link that object program to get it into executable form. Again, on my DOS machine I enter

```
mycl.exe c:\myfiles\interest.o
```

on the command line. My C linker adds stuff that my program needs to know when working under DOS. The result is an executable program called INTEREST.EXE. Note that some C compilers, such as Microsoft's Visual C++, can compile and link in the same step. You'll have to consult your compiler's documentation to find out how to compile and link with your particular C compiler.

Run the program

So does it work? It does, in fact. The following shows what happens when I enter **INTEREST.EXE** on the DOS command line, with an opening balance of $1,000, an interest rate of 3.5%, and a term of five years.

```
Enter the opening balance:  1000
Enter the interest rate in percent per year:  3.5
Enter the number of years the balance is held:  5
The future balance is 1191.247559
```

This tells me that after five years, an account of $1,000 left to accrue at 3.5% interest will be worth about $191.25 more. But suppose the interest rate is 7.25%? I run the program again with this new number.

```
Enter the opening balance:  1000
Enter the interest rate in percent per year:  7.25
Enter the number of years the balance is held:  5
The future balance is 1436.920654
```

The balance is now significantly more. Suppose I leave such an amount to accumulate for 30 years, the life of the U.S. Treasury's so-called "long bond"?

```
Enter the opening balance:  1000
Enter the interest rate in percent per year:  7.25
Enter the number of years the balance is held:  30
The future balance is 8802.313477
```

My initial investment is multiplied almost nine-fold in this case. I can run this program over and over with different combinations of opening balance, interest rate, and term. That's the real beauty of a computer program.

Summary

In this chapter you read about the following:

- The general process of creating a computer program involves writing program and data specifications, translating these into an algorithm, translating the algorithm into a C program, and then compiling and linking the program into an executable file.

- A program to calculate compound interest requires the user to input the opening balance, interest rate, and length of time the balance accumulates. The calculation of the future balance is based on the mathematical relationship

    $$\text{future balance} = (\text{present balance}) \times 2.7183^{(\text{rate})\text{x}(\text{time})}$$

- A typical C program includes a header, variable declarations, a `main()` function, statements, and comments.

- Comments make a source program more intelligible to you and me. Comments are enclosed in the symbols `/*` and `*/`; they are ignored by the C compiler. If saved in a text file, an algorithm can serve as the basis for comments.

Review questions

1 What symbol should most C program statements end with?

2 At which part of a program would you find the statements marked `#include`?

3 Name two uses for comments. How would you take a line from the program specification and turn it into a comment?

4 What's the final step in preparing a C program to run?

Exercises

1 The following is a repeat listing of the `interest.c` program. However, some changes have rendered it useless. It also has changes that make it less readable. Without referring to the original program earlier in the chapter, can you spot the three errors in the new listing, as well as the changes that affect readability?

```
#include <stdio.h>
#include <math.h>
float balance, rate, future, years;
{
printf("\nEnter the opening balance: ");
scanf("%f",&balance)
printf("\nEnter the interest rate in percent per year:  ");
scanf("%f",&rate);
printf("\nEnter the number of years the balance is held: ");
scanf("%f",&years);
future = balance * (pow(2.7183,(rate/100)*years));
printf("\nThe future balance is %f",future);
```

2 If you haven't done so already, type in the code for the INTEREST program (that is, the example that works from earlier in the chapter) into a text editor on your computer, compile and link it, and try executing it with different values on your system. Ignore any warning messages you may receive from your compiler; they aren't important.

3 Can you modify the INTEREST program so that the term is given in months, while keeping the interest rate entered in percent per year?

Places To Store Data

● **In this chapter:**

- **How do I store data that my C program uses?**

- **What kinds of data are there, and how do I work with them all?**

- **What kind of data housecleaning should my programs do?**

Develop the vacant acreage that is your computer's memory—
survey and zone it—then the data can move right in . . . . ⊚

A s claimed in chapter 1, "What Is C?," computers perform operations on data. Think of your own computer as you sit with your word processing software up and running, your mind a vast and undifferentiated blank. (Except for perhaps Michael Crichton and Barbara Cartland, this is the state that typically all writers are found.) Eureka! A thought occurs. You type a few words. The action of your fingers is transmitted to the innards of your computer, fed to your word processing software, and echoed back to your screen. At this point, you can delete your words, edit them, save them, or leave them to go grab a Diet Coke.

So where are your words in the meantime? If you've worked with computers at all, you know there's a place in the computer to hold data while your work is in progress. The fundamental need for what we call **working storage**—that place to hold information that is in progress—is met by the computer's **random-access memory** (**RAM**). Because you're interested in writing your own programs, and in doing so with C, you need to learn how to make your C programs store working data in RAM.

Use variables to store program data

What capabilities must a program's data storage have? For one thing, as certain operations are apt to be repeated with different information (or else what's the point of having a computer program do the work?), this storage place ought to be capable of handling different items of data at different times, just as a shop within a strip mall might at one time hold an optometrist and later host a cafe.

Data storage must also be organized like a city or a subdivision. Because all data looks the same in RAM—it's all 1s and 0s—there's no way to know what a given chunk of data is supposed to be just by looking at it. So a computer program must have some way to keep track of stored data: where it's located, how much there is, and what kind of information is there. You can think of this sort of information as analogous to a city's zoning rules.

The chunk of RAM taken over by your program is at first a featureless and empty landscape, like undeveloped land. Your program has to develop it for data storage. In a C language program, as in all others, variables meet this need.

Plain English, please!

A computer **variable** is a named storage location, usually maintained within a computer's RAM, for storing data of a specific kind. In programming, a variable provides a placeholder within a program for data that may change. This could be various things: data input by the user, the results of intermediate calculations, or the final results of an operation.

How do I make a variable?

You create a variable at the beginning of a C program by **declaring** it. Declaring a variable dedicates a piece of RAM for use by your program and gives that area a special name that your program can remember. Variables are declared in **variable declaration statements**, which appear after any #include statements. (Their exact location can vary, and for good reason, as you'll learn in chapter 13, "Some Optional Ways To Store Data.") The following programming code shows three variable declaration statements that create four variables:

```
char MyInitial;
int x,y;
float NationalDebt;
```

 The first line of code creates a character variable named MyInitial. This variable can hold a single alphanumeric character, such as R or 9. The second statement creates two integer variables named x and y. These variables store whole number values. The last statement creates a floating-point variable named NationalDebt. This variable can handle large numbers (well...you need large variables for large debts), including fractional parts.

Just from looking at the preceding example you can see that a variable declaration statement has two parts. The first, introduced by a word such as char or int, tells the computer what kind of data is to be stored and how large it will be. You'll find out exactly what char, int, and other such words do in a bit when data types are discussed. Whatever word appears, this part of the statement surveys and zones RAM, setting aside storage space of a certain kind and restricting its use to a certain type of data: characters, integers, etc. The second part of a variable declaration statement gives the storage area a name.

What's in a name: the dos and don'ts of naming variables

Although the keyword indicating a variable's type comes first in a declaration statement, the first thing to think about when creating a variable is what name to give it. Although the exact number varies from compiler to compiler, most versions of C support variable names up to 31 characters long.

You have lots of room to be creative with your variable names, which is a good thing. You can assign meaningful names, like RateOfInterest, AgeInYears, and so on. Such names are clearly preferable to cryptic designations like R or A.

On the other hand, you can go overboard with the naming thing. Consider a variable name like AgeOfBankLendingProspectInYears. The name is 31 characters long, so it's legal. But suppose you use the variable in several places in your program. Imagine having to type out all those letters every time. In addition, the more letters you have to type, the more opportunity you have for making typographical errors. Naming variables requires you to balance clear and readable programs with a reasonable amount of work.

Perhaps you've noticed that all the sample variable names have been made up of separate words run together. There's a good reason for this: C doesn't allow you to use spaces in a variable name. There are two accepted alternatives in the programming world for giving variables multiword names. You can capitalize each word in the name, as in the examples in this book. Or you can separate each word with an underscore (_): InterestRate or Interest_rate in this scheme.

TIP   **You can use whichever of the two ways of naming variables is** easiest for you to read; your C compiler does not care. I do think it's a good idea to pick a way of doing it and stick with it; either always capitalize or always use underscores.

Q&A   *What points do I need to keep in mind as I name variables?*

- The first character in a variable name must be a letter or the underscore character.

- After the first character, you can use any combination of letters and numbers in the variable's name. You can't use nonalphanumeric characters such as # and $.

- In C, a letter's case is significant. The variable names Cost and cost are two different variables.

- You can't use certain words as names for variables. Many of these words are commands that indicate to your C compiler that you want to perform a certain task. Refer to appendix C for a complete list of words that can't be used as variable names.

Just my type: variables for different kinds of data

The other important part of a variable declaration statement is the variable's **data type**. Remember, a variable's data in RAM cannot be interpreted solely on the basis of its contents because all of RAM looks like long sequences of 0s and 1s. Why does this matter? Because the same sequence of 0s and 1s that represents a certain number can also represent a specific character. A variable's data type must be known before data is retrieved so that the computer knows how to interpret it.

Speaking of spaces in variable names

C doesn't let you use spaces in variable names because to C a space indicates that one item has ended and the next is about to begin. C treats

```
word1_word2
```

as a single word, but it treats

```
word1 word2
```

as two separate words. If you try to declare a two-word variable, as in

```
int word1 word2;
```

your C compiler gives you an error message. C thinks you want to declare two variables but accidentally omitted the comma.

C has six fundamental variable data types:

Keyword	Variable type and purpose
char	Character data; letters and numbers
int	Integer data; whole numbers only
short	Short integer; (no difference between int and short on some systems)
long	Long integer; for larger numbers than int or short
float	Floating-point number; fractional or large values; up to seven digits
double	Double-precision floating-point number; up to nineteen digits

In addition, C supports the use of the unsigned keyword in variable declarations. This means you can create variables that hold only positive values. The unsigned keyword can precede or follow the variable type keyword in the declaration statement. You cannot create unsigned floating-point variables.

Now that you know something about naming variables and giving them data types, you can look at the way variables are created.

There are some things to know about the different variable types. Each variable type has a range of data it can store. Data outside this range cannot be accommodated. For example, integer variables can handle data from –32,768 to 32,767. Long integers can handle more than this amount squared (that is, up to about two billion).

A floating-point variable can handle from about 1.2×10^{-38} to 3.4×10^{38}, along with equivalent negative values. Double-precision floating-point variables work with data in the range 2.2×10^{-308} to 1.8×10^{308} and with equivalent negative values. (I'll point out here that the total number of subatomic particles in the known universe is thought to be less than 10^{100}; thus, a double-precision floating-point variable ought to be sufficient to handle any conceivable number you'd want to use in a program.)

The unsigned equivalent of a number variable can handle about twice the maximum value of the signed version but won't accept values less than zero. In addition, you can only use unsigned with integer-type variables: int, long, and short but not float or double. Finally, a character variable holds a numeric value equivalent to a single ASCII character.

Catch the bug

Can you tell what's wrong with the following three variable names? There's one error in each name.

```
92FederalWithholding
float
part#
```

Answers: *The first variable's name begins with a numeral; variable names must begin with a letter or underscore. The second variable uses a C language keyword; C keywords are reserved for use as instructions only. The third variable's name contains a nonalphanumeric character, the pound sign. Variable names can only contain letters, numerals, and the underscore character. Corrected versions of these three variable names follow (keep in mind that many possible corrections exist):*

```
FederalWithholding92
FloatingPoint
PartNum
```

Okay...I know how to create a variable... now what?

How do you put it all together to create variables in your C programs? Recall that you declare all variables at the beginning of a program, after `#include` statements. Also, it's a good idea to give a variable an initial value before your program attempts to use it. You look at both processes in more detail in the following sections.

How to use declaration statements

You know that most C language statements must end in a semicolon. Variable declaration statements follow this rule as well, in addition to some others of their own.

You should houseclean your variables

When you declare a variable in a C program, your computer sets aside space for it in RAM. However, it doesn't do any housecleaning in that space. There may have been data stored there previously from another program that ran before yours did. Because of this, your variable may contain some sort of "garbage" value at first. If your program attempts to get data out of the variable before this garbage is cleaned out (with the mistaken impression that a new variable ought to contain zero, for example), your program won't run as you expect.

To take care of this problem, you can immediately give a variable a specific value after creating it. This is called initializing the variable. You can think of initializing as equivalent to the kind of housecleaning a landlord might order for an apartment that's been vacated and is getting new tenants.

 Plain English, please!

> To **initialize** a variable is to assign it a specific initial value immediately after it's created. Number variables are usually initialized to 0; character variables can be initialized to a blank (' ').

Speaking of declaration statements

The general form of a C language variable declaration statement is

```
typename [unsigned] variablename1[,variablename2,...];
```

Note that the brackets shown in the preceding line indicate optional parts of the statement; they don't appear in the real C statement. `typename` must be a valid C data type: `int`, `char`, and so on. `unsigned` indicates that a number variable should only store positive values. Omit this `unsigned` if you want to store negative numbers. `variablename1` is the name of the first variable you're declaring—remember the rules for variable names in C. You have the option of creating additional variables of the same type if you want; just separate each variable name with a comma. The following statement, for example, declares three unsigned integer variables named `age`, `weight`, and `height`:

```
int unsigned age, weight, height;
```

To initialize a variable, you write an assignment statement that puts the initial value into the variable; this statement can be part of the variable declaration statement itself. **Assignment statements** are how you move data into and out of all variables, both during initialization and later in your program.

Whenever a value is assigned to a variable, the old contents are destroyed. You might say the variable's old tenants are permanently evicted the moment the new tenants move in.

How can I use this in the real world?

One semester during my early grad school days, I taught remedial college algebra. I was constantly being asked, "How am I going to use this stuff in real life?" Perhaps you're wondering the same thing about variables, a concept that is, after all, borrowed from algebra.

The fact is, you're going to end up using variables in any sort of program that does any kind of useful work whatsoever. Variables provide places to store the results of interim calculations in, and they also let you store data entered by a program user. This last item is critical; without variables, a program can't accept input. It could only work with data you put into it when you wrote it. To vary the data, you have to change the program. Using variables, your program can work with any value of data a user might want to enter.

Speaking of assignment statements

The general form of a C assignment statement is

```
variablename1 = [variablename2 = ] value;
```

variablename1 is the name of the first variable to be assigned a value. You have the option to assign other variables the same value if you want; include an additional equal sign for each such variable. *value* is the actual value to be assigned to any and all variables in the statement. The following statement declares an integer variable named age and assigns the value 0 to a variable:

```
int age = 0;
```

Catch the bug

The following three variable declaration statements each contain an error. Can you spot them?

```
integer Repetitions;

single LargeNumber;

double HugeNumber, HugNumber=1000000000000;
```

Answers: *The keyword to create an integer variable is* int, *not* integer. *Although there is a type of variable named* double, *there's no such thing as* single. *In the last statement, you can initialize a variable in the same statement that you create it in, but this isn't the way to do it.*

Here are corrections for the problems:

```
int Repetitions;

float LargeNumber;

double HugeNumber = 1000000000000;
```

Summary

In this chapter you learned about variables. You saw that variables are named storage locations for maintaining a program's working data in RAM. You learned how to create various types of variables in declaration statements.

Review questions

1 Define a *variable*.

2 What is the purpose of initializing variables, and how is it done?

3 Where do you create variables in a program?

4 What is a *floating-point number?*

Exercises

1 Find and correct the problems with the following three declaration statements:

```
int $Salary;

AvogadrosNumber float;

character Name;
```

2 What errors can you find in the following short program? Concentrate on the variables.

```
#include <stdio.h>

int radius;
float pi = 3.14159

main()
{
printf("Enter the circle's radius: ");
scanf("%d",Radius);
Area = (radius)^2 * pi;
printf(\n"The circle's area is %d",Area);
}
```

3 Write a group of statements that create two unsigned long integer variables named Deficit and Revenues and a character variable named YesOrNo.

5

Paying Constant Attention to Data

● In this chapter:

● Use the same number over and over again in a program

● How do I create and use constants?

● What kinds of constants are there?

Constants are like shorthand symbols for words or phrases; however, unlike variables, they're meant to represent numbers or words that don't change . . . . ❯

I n the preceding chapter, I showed you how to create storage locations for your variable program data. Just as important is creating places to store data that doesn't change but gets referred to at different times within a program. In fact, we tend to do the same thing in mathematics.

Consider finding the area or circumference of a circle. You use a special mathematical symbol, π, in your calculations. The symbol π actually represents a number—it's the ratio of the circumference of any circle to its diameter. π is approximately equal to 3.1415928, although the digits to the right of the decimal never end and never repeat. Writing a significant part of this number down every time you need it is tedious, and it can even obscure what you really mean in a formula. So it's been assigned a symbol in mathematical shorthand.

There are a multitude of symbols that are used to represent longer items that don't change. Stenographers are required to learn lots of them. You can define and use the same sort of thing for your C programs, using a special kind of variable called constants. **Constants** are like shorthand symbols for words or even phrases, only they're meant to represent numeric or character values that don't change, unlike ordinary variables, which can.

What are constants good for?

Well, consider this math formula:

$$3.1416 \times r^2$$

It isn't necessarily apparent what this formula represents. However, suppose you introduce the constant that equals 3.1416 in the preceding formula:

$$\pi \times r^2$$

Now, the formula becomes clear: it's the area of a circle. Everybody's heard of "pie are squared." It's easy to forget that when you say π, you're really talking about a numerical value—you're just using a symbol for simplicity's sake.

Constants make code easier to read

Constants make your C code easier for you to read and understand. What's more, because you can give a constant a short name, such as e or pi, you can save yourself some typing. Using constants for such values within a program also ensures that you use the same value wherever the constant appears.

Without constants, it's easy to mistype the value in one or more places, making your program's results faulty or even causing it to fail altogether.

Constants make code easier to change

Another advantage when using constants is that maintaining and updating your programs is easier. For example, you use the constant pi in a program in several places, originally giving it the value 3.1416. At a later time, if you find that this value of pi isn't accurate enough, you can replace it with 3.141593. If you haven't represented pi with a constant, you have to find and change every instance of pi. Even if you have a search-and-replace feature on your text editor, you might miss a value you mistyped since it won't match the value you're looking for. Using constants gets you around this potential problem.

If you need to change pi's value, you need to change it in only one place: the statement where the constant pi is declared.

Where do I use constants?

There are two types of constants, which are discussed later in this chapter in "Two different types of constants." Suffice it to say for now, you use one type of constant when you have a non-changing value that is used more than once in your program. For numbers and other data that you use only once in a program, you use the other type of constant.

For example, there's a good use for one of the types of constants, whose utility becomes more apparent in chapter 9, "Finding the Truth of Expressions." There are certain operations in C that are meant to yield an answer of True or False. In C, True is represented by 1, False is represented by 0. Using 1 and 0 in these cases results in programming code that's less readable than it could be. So you can define two constants, named True and False, setting the first equal to 1 and the second equal to 0. You can then use the constants True and False in your program, and your C compiler knows what you mean.

Creating a constant is easy

You must declare a constant before you can use it. How you declare a constant depends on what type of data it represents, and how you mean to use it.

Two different types of constants

There are two types of constants in C. **Symbolic constants** are used to represent one value by a variable name. The second type of constant, a **literal constant**, is used when you want C to interpret exactly what you type as a value and where the constant occurs.

For example,

```
printf("Enter the circle's radius: ");
```

everything within quotes is a character literal constant; at the appropriate point within the program, C prints the characters Enter the circle's radius: on the screen. Without the quotes, C thinks you're using several variables' names in succession, names that you never declared. You'll get an error message at compilation time.

You can't include a quotation mark as part of a character literal constant without causing some confusion. If you do, C thinks you're ending the constant and won't be able to interpret anything after that. There's a way around this, however. You precede a quotation mark with a backward slash when you want to use it within a literal constant, as in:

```
printf("Mother says \"Eat your spinach.\" I agree.");
```

Any numbers you use directly in your programs are also considered to be literal constants. You don't enclose number constants in quotes. If you do, C thinks you're referring to the numbers as characters—that is, as numerals, not as number values. This is problematic if you attempt to use them in mathematical calculations.

So literal constants are created more or less in place, either by simply using them in the case of numbers or by enclosing them in quotes in the case of characters. Symbolic constants, on the other hand, are created the same way as variables, with some slight additional work.

Use const to declare constants

For a refresher on variable declarations, see chapter 4, "Places To Store Data."

In C, you create symbolic constants using the **const** keyword at the beginning of what would otherwise be a variable declaration statement. You declare constants in the same place within a program that you declare variables: at the beginning.

Catch the bug

Can you tell what's wrong with the following four constant declaration statements? There's one error in each.

```
const integer Maniacs=10000;

const float unsigned NationalDebt=4000000000000;

const char Initial=R;

const int Age;
```

Answers: The first statement creates an integer constant called Maniacs. However, the keyword is wrong: it should be int, *not* integer. *The second statement attempts to create an unsigned floating point constant; unfortunately, there's no such thing. The* unsigned *keyword is invalid when used with* float. *The third statement accidentally omits the necessary quotes around the literal constant* R. *The last statement purports to create an integer constant named* Age *but fails to include the value for this constant. Corrected versions of these four statements are:*

```
const int Maniacs=10000;

const float NationalDebt=4000000000000;

const char Initial='R';

const int Age=35;
```

Speaking of constant statements

The general form of a C constant statement is:

```
const type_name constant_name = value;
```

type_name is the data type for the constant; you use the C variable type keywords here, such as int for integer data and char for character data. The following statement assigns the value 0 to three variables. *constant_name* is the name of the constant. *value* is the value assigned to the constant. The following example creates a single, floating-point constant called pi and sets it equal to 3.141593.

```
const float pi = 3.141593;
```

How can I use this in the real world?

Let's go back to the old friend, π. There are many times when you might use the value of π in calculations—for example, finding out how much paint is needed for the bottom of a circular swimming pool or how many cubic feet of helium it takes to fill a spherical balloon. It's easier to perform any such calculation using the symbol for π, rather than having to remember and type its decimal value. The following program listing performs three calculations using pi, yielding the circumference of a circle, area of a circle, and volume of a sphere, all using the radius. However, the program uses a literal constant for π.

```
#include <stdio.h>
float radius;
main()
{
printf("\nEnter the radius: ");
scanf("%f",&radius);
printf(("\nThe circumference is %f",3.1416*radius*2);
printf("\nThe area is %f",3.1416*radius*radius);
printf("\nThe spherical volume is %f",
➥4/3*3.141159*radius*radius*radius);
}
```

There are two problems with this program. First, with all those numbers and decimal points hanging around, the program isn't as readable as it could be. Line 9 contains the second problem: a different value of π is used, and an inaccurate one, at that. The program yields an incorrect result for the volume of a sphere with a set radius, and its values for the circumference and area of a circle won't be as accurate as they could be.

How do you mend this situation? Let's use a symbolic constant for π. In that case, the program becomes:

```
#include <stdio.h>
float radius;
const float pi=3.141593;
main()
{
printf("\nEnter the radius: ");
scanf("%f",&radius);
printf(("\nThe circumference is %f",pi*radius*2);
printf("\nThe area is %f",pi*radius*radius);
printf("\nThe spherical volume is %f",
➥4/3*pi*radius*radius*radius);
}
```

Summary

This chapter looked at the following points about constants:

- Constants are symbolic shorthand for values that don't ever vary.

- Literal constants are meant to be taken literally; they mean exactly what they represent. A literal character constant is enclosed in quotation marks. A literal number constant is simply typed out.

- Symbolic constants represent a value by a name, just as variables do. However, the value of a symbolic constant doesn't vary. You create symbolic constants at the same time you declare variables—at the beginning of the program, immediately following any #include statements. The declaration statement includes the const keyword, then an equal sign, and then the constant's value.

- Symbolic constants make your programming code more readable and easier to input, and they also make your programs easier to update whenever you need to substitute a new value for the constant.

Review questions

1 What is the difference between a variable and a constant?

2 Distinguish between a symbolic constant and a literal constant.

3 What is required to change a statement declaring a variable into one declaring a constant?

4 Where in a C program should symbolic constants be declared? What about literal constants?

Exercises

1 Write three lines of C code to create three constants; an integer constant named Weight equal to 185, a floating-point number constant named e equal to 2.718282, and a character constant named Ampersand equal to &.

2 Figure out what changes you'd make to the example program in this chapter's "How can I use this in the real world?" if you wanted to use 3.1415928 for π, rather than 3.1416.

3 The density of water is about 62 pounds per cubic foot. Write a short program to calculate the weight of water in a circular pool with the radius and depth of the pool entered by the user. The volume of such a pool, by the way, is given by $\pi \times r^2 \times h$, where r is the radius of the pool and h is its depth. Use symbolic constants for π and the density of water.

6

Expressing Yourself with C Statements

● **In this chapter:**

● **I've heard about this thing called an expression, but what is it?**

● **There are three different types of expressions**

● **Statements are made up of expressions**

● **How do I get data into a variable?**

Get ready to make a statement—in fact, lots of them!
C programs are built one statement at a time. . . . . ▶

Computer programs are all about manipulating data. As a programmer, you must have ways to tell a computer what to do with certain data and how to do those things. These capabilities lie at the very core of a programming language such as C. This chapter introduces you to the ways that you can use expressions and statements to get C to manipulate data.

Expressions are the building blocks of statements

The concept of an **expression**, like that of a variable, is borrowed from algebra. An expression is a group of symbols representing a specific value. An expression may contain numbers, characters for mathematical operations like addition and division, and even the names of variables.

You can think of each separate character in an expression as a step in a recipe. The expression's final result is its value. Expressions **evaluate** to the value in question. In the following example, the expression evaluates to 25.

```
(4 x 5) + 5
```

Reading this expression from left to right and character by character, you can deduce the following:

(Perform the next calculation first, before any other

4   The number 4

x   Multiply the previous number or result by the next

5   The number 5

)   This part of the expression is finished; calculate it

+   Add the previous number or result to the next

5   The number 5

If you take the trouble to follow this recipe, you'll see that it indeed cooks up the number 25 as its result.

An expression always evaluates to a single value. The exact value depends on the contents of the variables in the expression if any. The type of data contained in these variables is also critical to the evaluation of an expression. The following expression evaluates to 25, if the value contained by the variable `Multiplier` is 4.

```
(Multiplier x 5) + 5
```

There are, of course, an infinite number of ways to arrange an expression and still have it evaluate to the same result. The previous example, for instance, can be rewritten as

```
(Multiplier + 1) x 5
```

and still evaluate to 25. The point is exactly how you arrange an expression isn't important; what's important is that single value which an expression evaluates to. It's that value your program uses in subsequent calculations.

The three types of expressions

Just as there are types of data that can go into variables, there are three types of expressions to deal with that data.

- A **mathematical expression** resulting in a number (integer or floating point)

- A **text expression** resulting in a character string

- A **logical expression** resulting in either 1 or 0 (interpreted as True or False)

I'll have a lot more to say about each of these kinds of expressions in subsequent chapters. For now, you'll take just a limited look at each of them.

Mathematical expressions

A mathematical expression always evaluates to a numeric result. Mathematical expressions in C are composed of numbers and variables, along with symbols representing math operations such as addition, subtraction, multiplication, and division. Parentheses can also be a part—frequently a crucial part—of a mathematical expression. You learn much more about mathematical expressions in chapter 8, "Performing Mathematical Calculations in C."

The following is an example of a mathematical expression:

```
(2 + Value) × Rate
```

Text expressions

Text expressions evaluate to sequences of characters. These sequences are called character strings.

 Plain English, please!

> A **string** is simply a sequence of characters—numerals, letters, punctuation, and other symbols—that are being considered together as a single entity. Your name, whatever it may be, is an example of a character string—including the period after your middle initial.

A literal constant representing a character string, as in the following example, is a simple text expression:

```
"Clinton R. Hicks"
```

A char-type variable, which represents a single character, represents the very simplest and shortest text expression possible.

Unfortunately, C has never been the easiest language to manage text expressions in. For this reason, it'll be a while before you've accumulated enough C experience to tackle character strings. You can learn about them beginning with chapter 15, "String Variables as Places for Characters."

Logical expressions

The last kind of expression evaluates to an "either-or" kind of answer: Strictly speaking it's always 1 or 0, although it's conventional to regard these values as representing Yes or No or True or False. Because these expressions follow the long-established rules of logic, they are called logical expressions. The rules of logic are much like the unwritten rules in a cookbook—for example, baking soda combines with the acid in a batter to produce gas that leavens the dough. Knowing the rules of the kitchen, you can construct recipes that yield delicious food. Knowing the rules of logic, you can construct logical expressions that answer useful questions.

Indeed, thinking of a logical expression as an expression that poses a question is quite helpful in understanding this type of expression. Working step-by-step through the expression according to the rules of logic yields the answer to that question. Consider the following example:

```
CheckingBalance < 0
```

You can read more about logical expressions and the rules governing them in chapter 9, "Finding the Truth of Expressions."

This is a logical expression. It asks the question: Is the value in the variable CheckingBalance less than zero? The answer, of course, depends on exactly what's in CheckingBalance at the time the expression is evaluated. If the value of CheckingBalance is a negative number (as it all too often is in my case), then the preceding expression evaluates to 1, which is True in C shorthand. (Recall from chapter 5, "Paying Constant Attention to Data," that you can define a symbolic constant named True and set it equal to 1; using the word True instead of the number 1 later in the code can make your program easier for a person to read and understand.)

What's in a statement?

Expressions don't exist in a vacuum. Just as the symbols in an expression add up to form the final expression, as a sort of data recipe, expressions are combined to form the fundamental unit of a C program: the **statement**, which is a single line of C programming code that accomplishes one specific task.

Statements represent steps in cooking up a program, just as expressions represent the steps in a statement, and the symbols within an expression represent the steps within that expression. The expression "a beaten egg," for example, is a cooking expression; obviously there are steps involved in beating an egg. This expression can be incorporated into a statement, as in "Fold a beaten egg into the batter." C expressions and statements combine in the same manner, as the next sections demonstrate.

Words that hold the key to statements

At the core of every C language statement there is a word or symbol telling C what the statement is meant to do, which are called instruction keywords.

 Plain English, please!

A **keyword** is a specific word or symbol that tells C to perform one specific task. Keywords are considered **reserved**, which means that within a C program you cannot use any keyword in another way (for example, as the name of a variable or constant).

Consider this line from a recipe: "Fold a beaten egg into the batter." Here, the keyword is the verb "fold." This word sums up what the whole step is about, which is exactly what C keywords also do.

You can use expressions in statements

If keywords are the "verbs" in a statement that tell C what has to be done, then you can think of expressions as the nouns—they tell C what the operation specified by the keyword should do to the expression. In the last example, the expression "a beaten egg" is what's getting folded.

Not every C language statement has one or more expressions attached to it, but most do. The value of the expressions in a statement—that is, what they evaluate to—generally plays a crucial role in determining exactly what the statement does and which data it does it to.

How can I use this in the real world?

Frequently, a short C program that you write will contain one essential statement that does much of the program's work. Being able to isolate such a statement from an existing program can help you learn how to construct your own. Go back to the example algorithm in chapter 2, and the example program in chapter 3. You can isolate the statements in them that did the fundamental calculations in each instance—that is, the statement that sets the payment on a loan with a given balance, interest rate, and number of payments, and the statement that finds the value of a savings account that is left to accrue a fixed rate of interest for a given number of years.

In the loan payment algorithm example, the fundamental statement, which is not phrased in C, can be given as

$$payment = (rate \times amount \times e^{rate \cdot time})/(e^{rate \cdot time} - 1)$$

In the compound interest example, the statement is:

```
future = balance × (pow(2.7183,(rate/100) × years));
```

There are three types of statements

Just as there are different types of expressions to work with different data types, there are different types of statements to perform different program tasks:

- **Variable Declaration Statements** A variable declaration statement creates one or more variables, with specified names, of a given variable type.

- **Assignment Statements** These statements move data into (assign data to) variables. You can recognize them by the presence of an equal sign.

- **Program Control Statements** These statements perform a variety of tasks, such as controlling the order that a program's statements execute in.

Variable declaration statements

In C, variable declaration statements are important because you must create variables explicitly before you can use them. This isn't true in other programming languages; in BASIC, for instance, you can explicitly declare a variable simply by using it in a statement.

I talk about the exact form of variable declaration statements in chapter 4, "Places To Store Data."

Variable declaration statements come toward the beginning of a C program, after any `#include` statements. Each variable declaration includes a keyword that indicates what data type the variable is and an expression that is generally the name of the variable to create.

Assignment statements

After you create variables, you need ways to move data into and out of them. This is done using assignment statements, a subject touched upon briefly in chapter 4.

You can recognize an assignment statement by the equal sign. This symbol tells C to evaluate the expression to the right of the equal sign. It also tells C to move the expression's value into the variable to the left of the equal sign.

Catch the bug

Is there anything wrong with the following compound assignment statement?

```
Balance = (Royalties × 0.85) = 1000 × 24.95 × 0.04;
```

Answer: Yep. The part between the two equal signs isn't a variable name; it's an expression. C expects a variable name to the left of any equal sign. Your C compiler won't be able to interpret this statement.

You should note, however, that C lets you include an equal sign as part of an expression. The following statement is formed correctly, although it does not achieve the same result as the erroneous one shown previously:

```
Balance = 0.85 × (Royalties = 1000 × 24.95 × 0.04);
```

In this statement, the expression 1000 × 24.95 × 0.04 is evaluated, and then moved into the Royalties variable. This variable's contents (now equal to the value of the expression) are then multiplied by 0.85 and moved into the Balance variable.

Program control statements

Perhaps the most powerful class of statements in C are those that control how your program is executed. Among other things, these statements can give your programs the power to make decisions and take action based on current conditions. For example, you can formulate a statement that tests the value of a variable and then executes either one group of statements or another based on the value of that test.

You'll learn much more about program control statements in chapter 10, "Control the Way a Program Runs."

Program control statements can also perform single, specific actions no matter what the current conditions are. An example of this class of program control statement are those that read input from the keyboard or perform output on the screen.

How can I use this in the real world?

Imagine paying a bunch of bills and suddenly discovering you're out of money. Does that change the way you deal with the next bill? Of course—you hold off on paying it until you get some more money.

It's necessary to transfer the same kind of decision-making over to your programs. For instance, in a program to calculate compounding interest on a savings account, you don't want to try to add interest when the balance is below 0. In a program that plays blackjack against the user, you need to make the program deal cards to the user when necessary...but not when the user doesn't want a hit.

Program control statements are the key to making sure your programs carry out the right set of actions in any given circumstance. You'll put the power of these statements to work in virtually every program you write.

Summary

In this chapter you learned about expressions and statements in C language programming. I defined what an expression is and looked at different types of expressions. Next, you saw how expressions are combined into statements. Finally, you looked at different types of statements, including those to move data into a variable.

Review questions

1 Define *expression*.

2 What are the three main types of expressions? What distinguishes them?

3 What is a statement?

4 What is meant by the term *keyword*? Can a keyword also serve as the name of a variable?

Exercises

1 Write a block of statements to create variables corresponding to your age, weight, and height in inches, and then use each of these in an assignment statement to give them the appropriate values.

2 Given the following short program, can you identify the keywords in each of the statements in that program? Ignore the lines containing `main()` or braces.

```
/* Calculating simple interest */
float AcctBalance, Rate, Term;
main()
{
puts("Enter your balance, the rate, and the term:");
scanf("%f %f %f", &AcctBalance, &Rate, &Term);
AcctBalance = AcctBalance * (1 + Rate/100) * Term;
printf("\nYour new balance is %f", AcctBalance);
}
```

3 Again referring to the example program for exercise 2, go through each line of the program and determine what kind of statement each one is. Ignore the lines containing `main()` or braces. (These can be considered program control statements.)

Getting Information from the Keyboard and Putting It On-Screen

● **In this chapter:**

- **Using info that a user types**

- **Showing the user text on the screen**

- **What functions are there for showing text on the screen and for letting the user enter data?**

Using just three different C functions, your programs can accept information from users and display results in return . . . .

Before your C programs can work with data, you have to provide a way to get that data into the computer. Although you could do this by having all the data present as literal constants when you create the program—editing and recompiling it every time you change the data—such a method is tedious. It also wastes computer resources. What's more, you'll still be left with no way to determine your program's results. Clearly, your C programs need statements that take in data and display readable results. Collectively, these functions that take in data as the program is running and that give you back results are called **input/output** or simply **I/O**.

C is a highly portable language—one that creates programs to run on a variety of computer systems. This characteristic can pose problems when it comes to working on I/O. To keep C programs portable, it's necessary to "insulate" them from the peculiarities associated with how every different computer handles data when either coming in or going out or when both situations are in process. This means that any functionality within C associated with I/O has to be very general, unless you're willing to give up portability. In that case, it becomes possible to use special, add-on capabilities meant to be used with a particular computer. However, to make programs that run across the board, you must stick to general capabilities.

Every computer has a keyboard and a monitor attached to it. Although some computer systems can return some pretty impressive output, all systems can send back to the screen the same characters that you can type on the keyboard. It makes sense, therefore, for fundamental I/O in C to address itself to what the user can type; this kind of I/O is referred to as **character-based I/O**. A C program using character-based I/O is very similar to a typewriter that can be programmed. Such a typewriter accepts keyboard input from the user and produces output on the page, varying that output's position depending on where it's been instructed to put it: centered, double-spaced, etc. This kind of input and output might not seem very glamorous. However, it's effective and still portable.

Characters from the keyboard and on the screen

With character-based I/O, it is important to be aware of both the keyboard and the screen. However, there is a particular capability (or lack of) to consider. Strictly speaking, the main or core part of the C programming language doesn't have any I/O capability (again, for portability). Any kind of I/O, including character-based, must be included into a C program at compilation time. Although the type of I/O you can include varies from one computer system to another, there's a standard set of character-based I/O capabilities that you can include on virtually every system. This set of I/O capabilities is discussed later. First, you must consider some important facts about the keyboard and screen that these capabilities are designed to work with.

What you need to know about the keyboard

The standard computer keyboard closely resembles that of a typewriter. The symbol keys (that is, letters and numbers) on such keyboards are laid out in that absurd QWERTY layout that you'll never—I repeat, never—be able to get rid of. In addition to the symbol keys, you find editing keys such as Enter, Backspace, Home, Page Down, and the arrow keys. These control where the next typed symbol appears. Finally, there are the control keys, such as Esc, Break, and the function keys. These keys are usually used to issue commands to a computer or to a program running on it. Figure 7.1 shows some common layouts for a computer keyboard.

Fig. 7.1

These are three common computer keyboard layouts.

For more informa-
tion on the function
keys, see chapter 12,
"About Data
Streams."

For now, the only key on the keyboard that should be pointed out, except for the symbol keys, is Enter. With character-based input, the user must press the Enter key so that the computer processes anything that was typed as the computer paused for input from the user.

What you need to know about the screen

Computer screens come in a variety of sizes. Most display numerous colors. However, some are monochrome (this means black-and-white or black-and-amber or black-and-green). For purposes of character-based I/O, however, all screens are the same. They behave similarly to a piece of paper scrolling out of a typewriter. Figure 7.2 shows character-based I/O on a typical small-computer screen.

Fig. 7.2
Character-based output appears on a computer screen.

```
C:\1using.c\examples: type hello.c
#include <stdio.h>
#include <math.h>

double x, root, sum=0;
int z,y=0;
main()
{
for ( x=1; x<1000; x++)
{
root = pow(2.000000,-x);
sum = sum + root;
}
printf("\nThe root is %f, the binary sum is %f", root, sum);
return 0;
}
C:\1using.c\examples:_
```

For character-based I/O, it's useful to think of the screen as being divided into vertical rows, with each row further divided into columns (usually 80). Imagine a sheet of paper in a typewriter with the same row-column configuration. Now, if that sheet of paper contained a grid of boxes of just the right size, every character typed would fit neatly into one box of that grid. Pressing the Enter key both finishes the current line and sends the typewriter back to the first square on the next line.

Character-based output in C works in exactly this way. You build such output line-by-line, in the same way you type it. On every line, each character within the line falls into one of the columns on the screen (usually 80). Also, just as a typewriter has a spacebar and a Tab key with which you can adjust where the characters appear—for example, leaving additional space between words—C gives you the capability to determine exactly which box a given character appears in.

To use I/O, you need to tell the computer

Before one of your C programs can work with I/O in this way, however, you must tell your C compiler that you want to include such capability. You do this by making sure you have the file `stdio.h` in the same directory on your computer as your C compiler (all commercial compilers take care of this for you) and by featuring it in an `#include` statement at the head of your program, as in

```
#include <stdio.h>
```

Essentially, this file contains information that tells your C compiler how to perform character-based I/O on your particular computer. It then makes certain functions available to your program that you can do such I/O with. The information in this file never changes; that's why it's maintained in a file separate from your program's source code. You must have the line of code shown in the previous paragraph in your program before you can use the I/O capabilities that form the subject of the remainder of this chapter.

Getting numbers from the user

So far you've mainly learned about number data (a deficiency that I will begin to expand on in chapter 15, "String Variables as Places for Characters"). How do you go about getting numbers into a C program so that it can crunch them? `stdio.h` gives your programs a statement that lets users input numbers in much the same way as a pocket calculator works.

The `scanf()` statement

To have a program accept numeric input from the keyboard, you must use the `scanf()` function. `scanf()` causes your program to pause, waiting for the user to press keys and then Enter. After the user presses Enter, whatever else was typed is stored in a specified variable. The `scanf()` function isn't limited to numeric input; you also can use `scanf()` to input letters and symbols. `scanf()` is only one of many C functions that we learn about in this book.

A single `scanf()` statement can input more than one number. At the time a program is run, each such number must be separated by at least one blank space when entered by the user. Note that the parentheses, the quote marks, and the characters % and & are all required in their proper place for `scanf()` to work. You focus next on % and & and what they mean.

You have to tell `scanf()` what you expect from the user

As part of using `scanf()`, your program must tell the function what kind of data it should expect to have inputted. You do this using a **conversion specifier**. `scanf()` requires a separate conversion specifier for each value to be input. Conversion specifiers always begin with the percent sign. Multiple conversion specifiers are separated by commas; all are enclosed within a single pair of double-quotes. The entire sequence of characters within quotes is referred to as a **format string**.

Speaking of `scanf()`

The general form for using the `scanf()` function is

```
scanf("%conversion_specifier[s]",&variable1[,&variable2...]);
```

conversion_specifier is a single-character code that tells C something about the data that's to be input. *variable1*, *variable2*, and so on, are the names of variables that the data the user enters are to be stored in. An ampersand is required before each variable name. For example, a statement using `scanf()` to read a decimal value into a variable named Age looks like

```
scanf("%d",&Age);
```

and a statement to read decimal values into the variables Weight and Height looks like

```
scanf("%d %d",&Weight, &Height);
```

There are other conversion specifiers available that you can read about in chapter 12, "About Data Streams."

The most common conversion specifiers are

%c   Character

%d   Signed Integer

%f   Floating-Point Number

%s   Character String

%u   Unsigned Integer

Variables with scanf()

A scanf() statement also requires one or more variable names, each preceded by an ampersand. You should use a separate conversion specifier for each variable name. Multiple variable names are separated by commas; again, each variable name must be preceded by an ampersand.

What is the purpose of the ampersand? In C, we refer to it as the **address-of operator**. Paired with a variable name, it refers to the location in memory where the data is stored. C functions frequently require the memory address of a variable, rather than the variable itself—that is, the variable's location, rather than its contents. In scanf()'s case, you're telling C the place in memory where C should store the data that the user inputs. This location happens to be associated with a variable.

For more on the address-of operator, see chapter 17, "How To Indirectly Access Data Storage with Pointers."

Further discussion of the address-of operator enters uncharted territory. For now, it is sufficient for you to know that each variable name in a scanf() statement must have the address-of operator prefixed to it.

Syntax Error

Catch the bug

What's wrong with the following scanf() statement?

```
scanf("%d, "Age);
```

Answer: Not only is the variable Age missing its address-of operator, but the comma separating the format string from the variable is inside the quotes; it should be outside. The corrected statement reads

```
scanf("%d",&Age);
```

Time to use `scanf()`

The following three statements represent calls to the `scanf()` function as they might appear in a typical program

```
scanf("%f",&balance);
scanf("%f",&rate);
scanf("%f",&years);
```

Each of these `scanf()` statements uses the conversion specifier `%f`; this lets the user input fractional values. The first reads a value into the variable `balance` (or more properly, into the place in memory where the `balance`'s contents are stored). The second reads the value that the user inputs into the variable `rate`. The last reads a value that the user inputs into the variable `years`.

There is another interesting way to use `scanf()`. Because a program pauses for input when a `scanf()` statement is encountered, you can use the statement to do just that—pause. A statement using `scanf()` and one of your program's variables suffices, as in

```
scanf("%d", &Age);
```

The only problem with using `scanf()` to pause a program is that you don't tell the user that they must enter data and then press the Enter key before the program stops running. The reason is that you have yet to learn how to write a message onto the computer screen, the place where the user sees it.

Functions for showing text on-screen

While there is one C function to read input from the keyboard, two functions let you write output to the computer screen. One outputs simple text

Speaking of `puts()`

The general form of a statement using `puts()` is

```
puts(character_string);
```

character_string is any valid C string, especially including literal string constants. A statement using `puts()` to display "This is what I really call a message!" looks like:

```
puts("This is what I really call a message!");
```

messages to the screen, and the other outputs such messages along with the formatted contents of program variables.

The `puts()` function

You can use the `puts()` function to output a text string onto the computer screen. This is the only purpose that `puts()` is used for. Like `scanf()`, you must include the standard I/O header file `stdio.h` in any program that uses `puts()`.

Each separate statement using `puts()` outputs its characters on a new line.

The `printf()` function

The `puts()` function prints simple messages, but suppose you really want to output the results of calculations? To do this, you need a function that can print the contents of the variables that these results are stored into. The `printf()` function does just that.

How can I use this in the real world?

Just about all the C programs you write require some sort of input from the user. A program might ask for some financial figures, for example, to perform some sort of calculation with, like the payment on a loan. While you do use calls to the `scanf()` function to let the program user enter data, `scanf()` itself does nothing to inform the user what sort of data is expected. Having your user rely on hand-written instructions for what data to enter when might work but isn't very friendly. And what happens if the user loses your instruction sheet?

It's much better to have the program itself tell the user exactly what kind of data it's expecting and when it expects it. Programmer types calls this **prompting the user for data**. An on-screen statement that asks the user to enter data is likewise called a **prompt**.

You can use calls to the `puts()` function to prompt the user to enter data. You can pair a call to `puts()` with each call to `scanf()`, first prompting the user to enter information and then using `scanf()` to let the user do the actual data entry. This also applies to your using `scanf()` as a means of pausing a program before quitting. A couple of lines like the following should do the trick:

```
puts("Enter any number to quit");
scanf("%d", &AnyVariable);
```

Notice that, unlike with `scanf()`, you don't use the address-of operator with variable names in `printf()`. The reason is that you are not concerned with the variable's location but with its contents.

The `printf()` function uses conversion specifiers

The `printf()` function uses the following conversion specifiers:

`%c`	Character
`%d`	Signed Integer
`%f`	Floating-Point Number
`%s`	Character String
`%u`	Unsigned Integer

TIP Notice that `printf()` **uses the same conversion specifiers that** `scanf()` uses.

Speaking of `printf()`

The general form of a call to `printf()` is

```
printf("format_string",expression1[,expression2...]);
```

You saw how to use *format_string*s when you learned about `scanf()`; `printf()` uses the same sort of *format_string*s, with some useful additions. *expression1* and *expression2* refer to valid C expressions, including simple variable names. Because you can use expressions, you can do calculations directly within a `printf()` statement, without the need to move the results of such a calculation into a variable.

A `printf()` statement to print the contents of a variable named Age, in decimal form, resembles this

```
printf("%d",Age);
```

To print half the value of Age, you could have a `printf()` statement, such as

```
printf("%d",Age/2);
```

`printf()` lets you include more than just conversion specifiers as part of the format string. You can include literal constants as well. These print exactly as they appear. With an important exception, noted next, anything within a `printf()` format string that isn't preceded by a percent sign is simply printed.

Special characters for doing special things

Early in this chapter you learned that you can control C output as you would a typewriter; it's now time to back that up. In the process, I identify the exception mentioned in the preceding paragraph.

The `printf()` statement supports the use of **escape sequences**; these are basically just instructions telling C what to do next—perform a special action like sounding a beep, place the next character at a certain position, or just print a certain character. An escape sequence consists of a backslash (\) followed by a single character. The following includes some common escape sequences:

\a	Sound a beep
\b	Backspace the insertion point
\n	Move to beginning of next line
\t	Tab over
\\	Print a backslash
\?	Print a question mark
\'	Print a single quote
\"	Print a double quote

Again, you embed these escape sequences within the `printf()` format string. You should know that a call to `printf()` doesn't necessarily print on the next line; it may pick up where the last such statement left off. To have `printf()` print on a new line, you need to include the new-line escape sequence \n.

The following statement uses `printf()` to print the contents of the variable Age, along with a message, on a new line on the screen and sounds the beep.

```
printf("\nYour age is %d\a", Age);
```

You can also use escape sequences with the `puts()` statement. You just insert them into the string that you want `puts()` to print. For example, listing 7.1 is a program for calculating compound interest. The program sounds a beep when it is first run and when the result is displayed, using the escape sequence \a along with puts(). The program listing follows:

Listing 7.1 This program computes compound interest and lets you know when it's done with a beep

```
/*A program to find compound interest*/

#include <stdio.h>
#include <math.h>

/*Declare variables*/

float balance, rate, future, years;
main()
{

puts("\aA program to find compound interest");
/*Have the user input the values desired */
/* for the present balance, the rate, and the time */

puts("\nEnter the opening balance: ");
scanf("%f",&balance);
puts("\nEnter the interest rate in percent per year:  ");
scanf("%f",&rate);
puts("\nEnter the number of years the balance is held: ");
scanf("%f",&years);

/*Calculate the future balance using the formula*/

future = balance * (pow(2.7183,(rate/100)*years));

/*Print the results*/

printf("\nThe future balance is %f\n",future);

/*Pause for the user to press Enter before Quitting*/
puts("\a\nEnter any number to quit");
scanf("%f",&rate);
}
```

code

The escape sequence \a appears in the first and last calls to puts() to sound the beep. The escape sequence \n appears in every call to the puts() function. The program uses puts() to prompt the user to enter data and scanf() to read this data in. Results of the interest calculation are shown using printf().

Figure 7.3 shows the output from this program to calculate compound interest.

Fig. 7.3

You can't hear the beep. However, you can see all the prompts and messages, each separated from the preceding by an additional blank line.

```
A program to find compound interest

Enter the opening balance:
1000

Enter the interest rate in percent per year:
5

Enter the number of years the balance is held:
5

The future balance is 1284.027588

Enter any number to quit
```

Expressions with `printf()`

With `scanf()`, you tell C where to store data entered by the user, using the addresses of one or more variables. With `printf()`, on the other hand, you simply tell C what to print, using either variable names or expressions. Expressions appear after the format string and are separated by commas.

CAUTION You must have a separate expression in `printf()` for each conversion specifier. If you include a conversion specifier that doesn't match with a variable or expression, `printf()` won't put the appropriate output on the screen.

Time to use the `printf()` function

The preceding program to calculate compound interest used one `printf()` statement. This statement, to print the results of the interest calculation, is

```
printf("\nThe future balance is %f\n",future);
```

This `printf()` statement prints the contents of the variable `future` along with the message `The future balance is`. The way this statement's format string is written, the value of `future` is printed before an additional line is skipped.

Summary

This chapter gave you an introduction to working with input and output (I/O) in C. Topics covered included limitations for I/O in C. The material also introduced you to the concept of character-based I/O. You learned how to use scanf() for input and puts() for text message output. Finally, you now know how to output program results using printf().

Review questions

1 Define *character-based I/O*.

2 What is a *format string*, and where and when is such a string used?

3 What are *escape sequences*? Which escape sequence do you use to sound the system beep?

4 What do conversion specifiers do?

5 Name two differences in the way printf() and scanf() handle variables.

Exercises

1 Write a single statement to output your name, street address, and phone number on the screen, each on a separate line.

2 Modify the following program to use puts() statements instead of printf() in places where this is possible. Try to arrange it so that program output is exactly the same. (Hint: Pay attention to line spacing.)

```
#include <stdio.h>
float Age;
main()
{
printf("\nA program to find your age in days");
printf("\nEnter your age in years; fractions allowed");
scanf("%f", &Age);
printf"\nYour age in days is %f", Age*365.25);
}
```

3 Write a simple C program that asks the user to input an integer and then echoes that integer back to the user with the message `You entered the number`. Include an opening message, `Input a number`, and a pause at the end, with the message `Press the Enter key to quit`.

Performing Mathematical Calculations in C

● **In this chapter:**

- **Do you remember your math?**

- **What's basic arithmetic like in C?**

- **Show me a slick way to add and subtract by one**

- **Parentheses order your math**

You can give away your pocket calculator because there isn't any kind of math C can't handle better and faster . . . . . ➤

Y ou can think of computers as number-crunchers. That's the work they were born and bred to do. One of the original uses for a computer was calculating ballistics tables for guns and missiles, work that had previously been done by hand. This was back in the days when the entire world market for computers was estimated to be about six units—thus not worth IBM's time. Subsequently, computers have in many cases become part of everyday life, although many of the systems in operation today still spend most of their time crunching numbers. Some of the most common number crunching involves your bills. Your gas bill, how much credit is left on your SuperCharge card, and whether increased percentages of CO_2 in the atmosphere will make Tucson even warmer this summer—all of these are calculated using computers. This makes mathematical operations critical to any computer programming language.

C comes equipped with the typical set of **mathematical operators** (addition, subtraction, and so on) found in most programming languages. These are just symbols to represent the different operations of arithmetic. With these operators, you can formulate mathematical expressions to solve any problem in arithmetic, just as if you used a pocket calculator. In fact, the mathematical operators in C are similar to the keys on a calculator, and you form mathematical expressions in the same way you punch out a problem to be solved.

Mathematical expressions in C

Chapter 6, "Expressing Yourself with C Statements," introduced you to expressions in general and to mathematical expressions in particular. That introduction did not consider the different operations available in C. This chapter reviews and expands on the concept of mathematical expressions and then shows you the different operations available.

Parts of mathematical expressions

A mathematical expression has some parts that represent data, others that represent operations to be performed on that data. You'll recall that an expression evaluates to a particular result. The exact result depends on the data values in the expression and on the order that operations are performed in.

Consider this simple example:

```
Balance + Tax
```

In this expression, some data is contained in the variables `Balance` and `Tax`. The operation to be performed on this data is indicated by the plus sign, which represents addition. The value in `Balance` is to be added to the value in `Tax`.

Expressions can contain literal numeric constants, as in

```
Whole/2
```

an expression representing the value in the variable `Whole` divided by 2, which is a literal constant. Finally, expressions can contain several operators and many pieces of data, as in

$$\text{Balance} + \text{Tax} \times \text{Whole} \div 2 + 3.14159 - A \times B \times C$$

How such long expressions are evaluated—and how to phrase them so that you get the value you want—is discussed later in the chapter in the section, "Yes, there is order in math." In each of these examples, though, the expression tends to be evaluated just as you enter it using a calculator. In the preceding example you do the following:

1 You punch in the value for Balance, press the + key, and then punch in the value for Tax.

2 Then you press the multiplication key, enter the value for Whole, press the division key, and enter 2.

3 Then you press the plus key again and enter 3.14159. (Remember to press the decimal key after the three.)

4 After this, you press the minus key, enter the value for A, press the multiplication key, and then enter the value for B.

5 Then you press the multiplication key one last time and enter the value for C.

6 You then press the = key to indicate that you are done and want to see the result.

Those of you (like, unaccountably, my wife the architect) who favor Hewlett-Packard calculators and others that rely on so-called RPN logic will not recognize the above description as the way your calculator works. C uses algebraic logic, like Texas Instruments and Sharp calculators.

When, where, how to use expressions

As a rule, you can use a mathematical expression in C many places that you use either a numeric constant or a variable, with certain exceptions. One exception, for example, is that an expression can't appear to the left of the equal sign in an assignment statement. Expressions commonly appear to the right of the equal sign in such statements, however, as in

```
GrandTotal = Balance + Tax;
```

where contents of the variable `Balance` and of the variable `Tax` are added, and the result stored in the variable `GrandTotal`.

You can also use expressions within a `printf()` statement, in place of variables. This can prove to be efficient in some cases—you save a step and a variable to hold the calculation. For example, a statement to both calculate and print the area of a circle, given its radius, might resemble

```
printf("The circle area is %f", pi*radius*radius);
```

This assumes that the constant `pi` has been declared, as well as the variable `radius`. Compare this with the two-step method of performing the same process:

```
area = pi*radius*radius;
printf("The circle area is %f", area);
```

Both of these pieces of C code accomplish the same task. However, the first does it in only one step and doesn't require a variable named `area`.

What about using expressions with `scanf()`? You can't; it would be similar to trying to use an expression on the left side of an equal sign. You can use expressions in just about any context in which data is read out of a variable. However, you can't use them in places where data is written into a variable.

Q&A *So I can use expressions and not just variables in calls to functions like* printf( )*. Just because I can, does that mean I should?*

Some experts would say, "No, you should avoid using expressions in the place of variables." The usual reason given is that creating such complicated statements makes your code hard to read. Later on, it might not be obvious what calculation the expression you're using is meant to perform.

For more information on addresses and working with data using addresses, see chapter 17, "How To Indirectly Access Data Storage with Pointers."

Personally, I don't see much harm in substituting expressions for variables when appropriate. I think it's particularly handy if the result obtained is only going to be used in that one place—in a call to printf(), for instance. Since a call to printf() usually includes text that describes the result being printed, you don't really run the risk of having an unintelligible calculation to worry about later. And you end up saving two statements: one to declare a variable to hold the result and another to do the calculation and move the results into the result variable.

Syntax
Error

Catch the bug

The following line of code is meant to read half the value of a number input by the user into a variable referred to as Half. What's wrong with it?

```
scanf("%f",&Half/2);
```

Answer: You can't use an expression in the preceding statement and expect it to work correctly. Unfortunately, in this case you won't get a compiler error telling you it's wrong. Your compiler assumes you want to store the entire value read in by scanf() at an address in memory that is equal to half the address of the variable Half. Who knows where this place actually is. However, trying to store data there is sure to cause you a lot of grief. To store half the input value, you really need two variables and two statements, such as the following:

```
scanf("%f",&Whole);
Half = Whole/2;
```

Back to school—fundamentals are essential

Having now learned some places that you can use mathematical expressions in, it's appropriate to study them more closely to see what kinds of operations they can contain. If you have programming experience other than that involving C, you'll find some differences between C and other programming languages in this regard.

C has the following basic arithmetic operators:

Unary Operators

++   Increment variable

--   Decrement variable

Binary Operators

+   Addition

-    Subtraction (also Negation)

*   Multiplication

/   Division

%   Modulus (integers only)

The **unary operators** work with a single piece of data; the **binary operators** work with two pieces of data.

Addition and subtraction

The operators for addition and subtraction work as they always have. The two pieces of data joined by either of these operators can be literal constants, variables, symbolic constants, or even expressions. The addition operator adds the value of whatever is to its left to the value of what is to its right. The subtraction operator subtracts the value of the expression to its right from the value of the one to its left. These concepts are illustrated in the following expressions:

        5 + 3

is equal to 8, and

        5 - 3

is equal to 2.

The increment and decrement operators also perform addition and subtraction, respectively, but in a more limited and compact way than + and –. You can use only variables—not constants or expressions—with the increment and decrement operators. Also, these operators are good for only one type of calculation: either adding 1 to or subtracting 1 from the variable that the operator is affixed to. The operator does this immediately, without your having to include the variable in an assignment statement. Therefore,

```
X++;
```

is the same as

```
X = X + 1;
```

while

```
X--;
```

is the same as

```
X = X - 1;
```

The placement of the operator with respect to increment and decrement is also important. You can actually place the operator either to the immediate left or right of the variable you're modifying. The place in which the operator appears affects when the increment/decrement operation is performed. When the operator is to the left, the operation is performed immediately; to the right, the operation is performed after the variable has participated in the rest of the statement. Therefore,

```
Y = X++;
```

puts the current value of X into Y, then increases the value of X by 1. If X holds 5 before this statement is executed, afterward Y holds 5 and X holds 6. On the other hand,

```
Y = ++X;
```

immediately increases the value in X by one and then puts that result into Y. If X holds 5 before the statement is executed, both variables afterward contain 6.

Multiplication and division

Multiplication and division are just as simple as addition and subtraction, except that the symbols C uses (* and /) might not be those that you are familiar with, such as × and ÷. Like addition and subtraction, the two pieces of data joined by either of these operators can be literal constants, variables, symbolic constants, or even expressions. The multiplication operator takes the value of whatever is on its left and multiplies it by the value of what is on its right. The division operator divides the value of whatever is on its left by the value of what is on its right. Therefore, the expression

```
6 * 3
```

evaluates to 18, while the expression

```
6 / 3
```

evaluates to 2.

How can I use this in the real world?

While incrementing or decrementing might seem trivial, there are actually lots of places within programming where you need to increment or decrement a variable. C gives you a much more efficient way of performing these calculations than do other programming languages. You can read more about this subject in chapter 10, "Control the Way a Program Runs."

The increment and decrement operators turn out to be very useful, although this won't become completely apparent until chapter 10, when you begin to learn about how to change the way a program is run. It turns out, you can have a group of statements within a program execute multiple times. Within such a block, you can use the increment operator along with an integer variable, to keep track of how many times the block is actually run.

For example, if you're allowing a program user to enter as many individual data items as desired, until some specific ending value is entered (for example, enter −1 to stop data entry), you can use increment along with a variable to keep track of exactly how many data items were entered.

There are some things you need to keep in mind when you're working with these operations. With division, be aware of the possibility of fractional results. If you move the results of an expression containing a division into an integer variable, fractions are lost. With multiplication, be sure the variable you use to store results has enough storage space to handle every possible result. Again, beware of using integers; on most systems a standard int-type variable can't hold a number greater than about 64,000. It's easier to multiply two numbers and get a result greater than that. Consider using long integers or floating-point variables instead.

I don't want remainders?

There's an operation related to division that always yields an integer result. The **modulus operator** finds the remainder when one number is divided by another. Modulus is represented by the percent sign. Therefore, the expression

    6 % 4

evaluates to 2 (4 goes into 6 once, leaving a remainder of 2), while the expression

    6 % 3

evaluates to 0 (3 goes into 6 twice, leaving no remainder).

Exponents in C

Those of you with experience programming in other languages might have seen operators to raise a number to a power. In this operation, a number referred to as the base is multiplied by itself the number of times shown in the exponent. In BASIC, for instance, this operator is represented by a carat, ^. Therefore, 3 * 3 is represented as

    3^2

while 2 * 2 * 2 is represented as

    2^3

Unfortunately, there is no such operator in C. Instead, you must use the pow( ) function to raise a number to a power.

How can I use this in the real world?

The modulus operator resembles some arcane mathematical trick. Can you really use it to carry out processes that matter? Yes, you can. It is of particular use when working with nonfractional decimals; for example, in situations where exactly 10 units of something are not required to make a larger unit. Two examples are time and English measurements. There are sixty minutes in an hour and 12 inches in a foot. This can result in some messy division operations when you're trying to find the number of hours and minutes or the number of feet and inches.

Think of trying to find the number of feet and inches in a given number of inches, for example 189 inches. If you do

```
189 / 12
```

the result is

```
15.75
```

The result includes a decimal fraction, and any building contractor will tell you that this complicates matters considerably. What you really need is the whole number of inches left over. You can use the modulus operator to find this result. The following is a brief program to input the whole number of inches. It also prints out the feet and inches represented by this number. Naturally, it uses the modulus operator to determine this result.

```
/* A program to find feet and inches */
/* in an integral number of inches*/

#include <stdio.h>
/* Declare variables */
int inches, feet;
main()
{

puts("A program to find feet and inches
in an integral number of inches\n");
/* Have the user input the number of inches */
printf("\nEnter the number of inches: ");
scanf("%d",&inches);

/* Calculate and Print the results */
feet = inches/12;
printf("\n%d inches represent %d feet and
%d inches", inches, feet, inches % 12);
```

```
                    /* Pause for the user to press Enter before quitting */
                    puts("\n\nEnter any number to quit");
                    scanf("%f",&inches);
                    }
```

The calculations are performed in the two lines starting with `feet = `. The first of these finds the whole number of feet in the given number of inches; the result is moved into the integer variable `feet` so that the fractional part is lost. You don't need it at this time, anyway. The next line prints the results, including the modulus of the number of inches divided by 12. This gives the number of inches left over after 12 is divided evenly into the total number of inches. The figure below shows the results of running this program with 189 as the number of inches.

Running the FEETINCH program gives the number of feet and inches in 189 inches.

```
A program to find feet and inches in an integral
number of inches

Enter the number of inches:  189

189 inches represent 15 feet and 9 inches

Enter any number to quit
```

Speaking of `pow()`

The general form of an expression using the `pow()` function is

> `pow(base,exponent);`

base is the number to be raised; *exponent* is the power to raise it to. You can use an expression to represent either *base* or *exponent*. Therefore, to raise 2 to the third power, you write

> `pow(2.,3.);`

 TIP   **You should always include decimal points in any literal numeric** constants used within the `pow()` function. C expects any data provided to the `pow()` to be in floating-point form. To do this with a literal numeric constant, you must include the decimal point.

To raise the constant e to the power of `rate` times `time`, you write

```
pow(e, rate*time);
```

The `pow()` function itself is an expression. You can use it in an assignment statement or in any other place where it is valid to use an expression.

 TIP   **Before you can use the `pow()` function, you must include the** `math.h` header file in your program.

You can read more about mathematical functions like pow() *in chapter 25, "Make Your Work Easier with the C Function Library."*

Chapter 11, "The Functional Structure of C Programs," discusses functions in greater detail. However, the `pow()` function is introduced here because it is a commonly used mathematical function.

Syntax Error

Catch the bug

The following expression is used to subtract the variable B from the variable A and multiply the result by the variable C. Does it work?

```
Result = A - B * C;
```

Answer: *Actually, it doesn't, nor would you obtain the desired result if you enter the problem in just this way on a pocket calculator. Try it out, assuming A equals 4, B equals 2, and C equals 6. That gives*

```
Result = 4 - 2 * 6;
```

On my calculator, I get –8 as an answer, when I might have expected 12. I seem to be getting 4–12 rather than 2×6. This unexpected result is due to the way mathematical expressions are evaluated, in C and elsewhere. To get the right result, I have to add a step:

```
Intermediate = A - B;
Result = Intermediate * C;
```

However, there's an easier way to make sure the expression yields the correct answer, as you'll see in the next section.

Yes, there is order in math

The preceding "Catch the bug" points out an important fact regarding the way that mathematical expressions are evaluated in C (or in regular algebra, for that matter; it's the same in both cases). An expression is not evaluated strictly in left to right order. Instead, certain operations are said to have precedence over others, meaning they are performed first. The way this precedence is determined and carried out is referred to as the **order of operations**. This is an important concept with respect to formulating mathematical expressions.

It's not always left to right

Although mathematical expressions are generally evaluated from left to right—in the same way you read—this process is really done in stages, with certain operations being performed before others. In C, as in algebra, the order of operations is

1 Increment or decrement

2 Multiplication or division (includes modulus)

3 Addition or subtraction

You can now understand what went wrong in the last "Catch the bug." Recall that the expression was

```
4 - 2 * 6
```

According to the order of operations, multiplication comes before subtraction. Therefore, 2 is multiplied by 6, and the result is then subtracted from 4. The answer (–8) is probably the one given by the calculator.

Is there any way to alter the order of operations, or is it written in stone? Actually, there is something you can add to any expression to obtain the result exactly as you want—parentheses.

Tell C the order with parentheses

In C, as in algebra, you use parentheses to indicate operations that take precedence, perhaps altering the standard order of operations. The rule is, any operations within parentheses are performed first, before anything else.

Also, you can include one set of parentheses within another. This is referred to as **nesting** the parentheses. In this case, the rule states that operations in the innermost parentheses are performed first. You work your way out to the outermost set before performing the remaining operations in the regular way. Any expressions entirely within parentheses follow the standard order of operations.

Therefore, to have the expression that you have been working with to yield the desired result, you write it as

```
Result = (4 - 2) * 6;
```

The parentheses call for the subtraction operation to be done first.

You should now be able to make sense of all those parentheses in the following formula to find compound interest. It is given as

```
balance * (pow(2.7183,(rate/100)*years))
```

This expression is evaluated in this way:

1 Parentheses are present. Therefore, the expression is evaluated first from the innermost set of parentheses to the outermost. The innermost set of parentheses contains the expression `rate/100`; therefore, first the contents of `rate` are divided by `100`.

2 The next set of parentheses encloses the values to be given to the `pow()` function. Therefore, the expressions representing these values must be evaluated. The base is a constant—`2.7183`. The exponent becomes the result from step 1 times the contents of the variable `years`.

3 The outermost set of parentheses encloses the `pow()` function. That function is evaluated according to the values supplied to it in step 2.

4 All the parentheses have now been worked through. There is only one operation outside them—a multiplication. The value found by the function `pow()` is multiplied by the contents of the variable `balance`.

How can I use this in the real world?

One of the more complicated mathematical expressions encountered is finding the answers to a quadratic equation in standard form. For those who don't recall (or prefer not to recall) their high school algebra, a quadratic equation in standard form is

$$ax^2 + bx + c = 0$$

What is x equal to? It represents the answer to the equation, also known as the root. A quadratic equation actually has two roots, given by the formula:

$$x = \frac{-b \quad b2 - 4ac}{2a}$$

How do you go about translating this bit of algebrese into C? The answer is given in the following program fragment:

```
Root1 = (-b + pow((b*b - 4.*a*c),0.5))/(2. * a);
Root2 = (-b - pow((b*b - 4.*a*c),0.5))/(2. * a);
```

It is critical to know how to use the pow() function in this instance to find squares and other roots. In general, the *n*th root of a number is that number raised to the power 1/*n* (the reciprocal of *n*). Therefore, the square or second root of a number is that number raised to the 1/2 (or 0.5) power. The decimal point after the 4 is also critical; the pow() function doesn't like integers.

The following is a program that gives you the two roots of a quadratic equation, whose coefficients a, b, and c are entered by the user.

```
/*A program to find the roots to a quadratic equation*/
#include <stdio.h>
#include <math.h>
/*Declare Variables*/
float Root1,Root2;
int a,b,c;
main()
{
puts("\nThis program find the roots of a quadratic equation.\n");
puts("The standard form is ax2 + bx + c = 0\n");
puts ("Input a, b, and c in that order, separated by spaces\n\n");
/*Input a, b, c*/
scanf("%d %d %d", &a,&b,&c);
```

```
/*Calculate roots*/
Root1 = (-b + pow((b*b - 4.*a*c),0.5))/(2. * a);
Root2 = (-b - pow((b*b - 4.*a*c),0.5))/(2. * a);
/*Print results*/
printf("The equation is %dx2 + %dx + %d",a,b,c);
printf("\nThe roots are %f and %f", Root1,Root2);
/*Pause for the user to press Enter before Quitting*/
puts("\n\nEnter any number to quit");
scanf("%f",&a);
}
```

You should know that running this program with certain combinations of a, b, and c result in an error; this occurs when $4 \times a \times c$ is greater than b^2. The figure below shows the results of running this program with the values 1, −5, and 6.

This program has found both roots of the quadratic equation $x^2 - 5x + 6 = 0$.

```
This program finds the roots of a quadratic equation.
The standard form is ax2 + bx + c = 0
Input a, b, and c in that order, separated by spaces
1 -5 6
The equation is 1x2 + -5x + 6
The roots are 3.000000 and 2.000000

Enter any number to quit
```

You can easily verify with your calculator that the expression $x^2 - 5x + 6$ is equal to zero, when x is equal to 2 and x is equal to 3.

Summary

At the beginning of this chapter, you reviewed the concept of mathematical expressions. You then learned how to perform basic arithmetic using C, including addition, subtraction, multiplication, and division. As part of this, you saw how to use C's unique increment and decrement operators. After considering the pow() function, which is used for exponentiation, you learned how to use parentheses to make sure expressions are evaluated the way you want them to be.

Review questions

1 What does it mean to *evaluate an expression*?

2 Describe the difference between unary operators and binary operators.

3 What difference does it make if you place a unary operator after a variable, as opposed to before it?

4 What is meant by the phrase *order of operations*?

5 What is meant by the term *modulus*? What symbol represents the modulus operator?

Exercises

1 Write two lines of C code to find the number of hours in a given number of minutes and the number of minutes left over.

2 Write a C program to find the average of five numbers input by the user on one line. Recall that to compute the average of a set of numbers you first add all of them. Then you divided this sum by how many numbers there are.

3 Using the formula for the payment on a loan, write a C program to calculate and display the payment based on the loan amount, rate of interest, and length of term entered by the user. Have the term entered in months. The formula is

$$\text{payment} = (\text{rate} \times \text{amount} \times e^{\text{rate} * \text{time}})/(e^{\text{rate} * \text{time}} - 1)$$

Recall that e is approximately equal to 2.7183.

Finding the Truth of Expressions

● **In this chapter:**

- **To find the truth in C, use logical expressions**

- **Operators for finding the truth**

- **How to construct logical expressions**

Remember true/false quizzes from school? Well that experience is about to help you because all queries in C are phrased and answered in just that way . . . . ▷

Computers are nothing if not orderly. That is how their human designers wanted them to be. These same designers drew on principles of thought dating back to Aristotle in determining how a computer should behave. These principles of logic underlie everything from the architecture of computer hardware to the ways that computer programs determine what needs to be done next. Therefore, a good grasp of computer logic not only gives you insight into what computers are and how they're made, but also gives you the tools to add powerful decision-making capabilities to your own programs.

In this chapter, you learn how to set up tests for pieces of data. You create tests to determine when a variable's contents are less than zero, when one variable is larger than another, even tests to determine when both cases are simultaneously true. You learn about the logical operators available to you in C that let you pose Yes or No questions to your computer, which then uses the rules of logic to determine the answers.

Finding the truth in C depends on how you express it

The kind of logic you must be concerned with here is determining whether certain assertions are true or false. For example, consider the assertion "The value in the variable named Balance is greater than 0." Whether this assertion is true or false depends on what is in Balance at the time the assertion is evaluated. If Balance holds –135, the assertion is false.

You have seen the word *evaluated*, in the preceding paragraph and in this book before. I first talked about it when I introduced the concept of the expression. You phrase logical assertions in C using expressions.

Logical expressions are the logical choice for finding the truth

Chapter 6, "Expressing Yourself with C Statements," introduced you to logical expressions, although not in detail. A **logical expression** is one defining certain relationships among data items, and whose ultimate value is either 1 or 0. It is conventional to think of 1 as representing True and 0 as representing False. However, these values could be any of several other pairs of opposites. Yes and No would be the most common alternative. The main point is that a logical expression in C evaluates to one of the two integer values, 1 or 0. What goes into a logical expression? And how do you deal with those values 1 and 0? You learn these concepts in the following discussions.

TIP **Much of the formal work in logical notation was worked out by a** mathematician named George Boole, about 100 years ago. Mr. Boole lent his name to one aspect of the field of mathematical logic, now called Boolean algebra in his honor. The *American Heritage Dictionary*, Third Edition defines this sort of logic as "Of or relating to a logical combinatorial system treating variables, such as propositions and computer logic elements, through the operators AND, OR, NOT, IF, THEN, and EXCEPT." We'll learn more about some of these operators, as they relate to logic in C, later in the chapter.

What are the parts of a logical expression?

Like the mathematical expressions you looked at in chapter 8, "Performing Mathematical Calculations in C," logical expressions in C are composed of literal constants or variable names joined by operators. The symbols used for operators are different from those representing the operations of arithmetic, although they still ought to be familiar to you from your days in math class. The logical expression representing the question "Is the value in the variable Balance greater than 0?" for example, is

```
Balance > 0
```

This expression has the variable Balance, an operation symbol >, and a literal numeric constant 0.

You can form some rather complicated logical expressions in C, just as you can create complicated mathematical expressions. You use parentheses to isolate the parts of such a complicated expression and make certain it's evaluated the way you want. For example,

```
((Balance > 0) AND (Option = 1)) OR ((Balance = 0) AND (Option = 2))
```

is an example of a complicated logical expression. Notice in particular the operators AND and OR; there's nothing quite like these in arithmetic. You learn what they're for later in the chapter; for now, you need to know that they are used to combine the results of separate expressions in particular ways. This expression evaluates to 1 in two cases: if the value in Balance is greater than zero and the value in Option is exactly equal to 1 at the same time, or if the value in Balance is exactly equal to 0, and the value in Option is exactly equal to 2 at the same time. In all other cases, the expression evaluates to 0.

Clearing up logical expressions

There are probably some people who can clearly remember what those 1s and 0s represent in terms of logical results; others more than likely prefer to think of True and False as representing logical results. The latter is probably much more readable and easier to explain to others.

Usually, the actual results of a logical calculation are never the literal strings "True" and "False." Most of the time the result is expressed in a single bit of data, turned on if the result is True and turned off if the result is False. The compiler in question associates the literal constant True with *on* and the literal constant False with *off*.

Although C doesn't do this for you, you can do it for yourself using symbolic constants. Recall from chapter 5, "Paying Constant Attention to Data," that you define symbolic constants using the const keyword. The following two lines of C code define symbolic constants for the values 1 and 0:

```
const int True = 1;
const int False = 0;
```

With these lines at the beginning of a program, you can use the words True and False wherever you'd use 1 or 0.

Keep in mind when using these symbolic constants that whether a letter is capitalized or not makes a difference in C; therefore, the word true is not the same as the word True. Because capitalizing all the time can be a bit of a pain, you might want to define your symbolic constants for 1 and 0 as

```
const int true = 1;
const int false = 0;
```

You could, of course, define both, as you can have as many constants representing a single value as you like. Programming code that's written that way, however, tends to look sloppy. You can write your programs so that there's very little need for the actual results True and False in the code, making the way you define symbolic constants for the results less important.

What can I do with logical expressions?

You can move the results of a logical expression into a variable with an assignment statement, just as you might do with a mathematical expression. Therefore,

```
IsPositive = Balance > 0;
```

moves the value of the expression `Balance > 0` into the variable named `IsPositive`. For example, if the value in `Balance` is 500, the value in `IsPositive` becomes 1. If the value in `Balance` is –500, the value in `IsPositive` becomes 0.

The real power of logical expressions is in controlling how your programs run. Suppose, for example, that the variable `Balance` actually represents the opening balance of a savings account. In a program that calculates compound interest, it makes no sense to do the calculations on `Balance` if it is equal to 0. What's worse, the calculations as you've been using them return a wrong result if you calculated with a negative balance—there's no such thing as negative interest.

Now you know that it's possible to test the value in `Balance` to see if it's greater than zero. You can think of a logical expression as a question; the expression

```
Balance > 0
```

is similar to asking, "Is the value in `Balance` greater than 0?" There are statements in C that can take the results of just such a question and determine what the program should do next, based on those results. Any logical expression can have one of two results (1 or 0); a C statement that uses these results to make a decision can have the program do one of two things. In the case of computing compound interest on the contents of the variable `Balance`, the program could test `Balance` to see if it's positive, using a logical expression. Then the program could perform the interest calculation if `Balance` is positive, or ignore the calculation and print a message (`Non-Positive Balance, No Interest`) if `Balance` isn't positive.

Even more involved and powerful examples exist of using the results of a logical expression to determine what to do next. Chapter 10, "Control the Way a Program Runs," discusses this subject in detail. Next, you learn how to phrase various logical expressions using the different logical operators available in C.

Relational operators deal with relationships

The **relational operators** in C define, as you might expect, relationships between two data items. Again, these can be the contents of variables, literal constants, symbolic constants, or combinations of these and mathematical operators.

What are the relational operators?

C has six relational operators, which are in the following table. The six can be grouped into pairs where each member of a pair is the opposite of the other.

Operator	Meaning
==	Is equal to
!=	Is not equal to
>	Is greater than
<	Is less than
>=	Is greater than or equal to
<=	Is less than or equal to

Speaking of relational operators

A simple logical expression using a relational operator takes the following form:

```
expression1 symbol expression2
```

expression1 and *expression2* are both valid mathematical expressions. *symbol* is one of the C relational operator symbols. The value of a logical expression is either 1 or 0. For example,

```
(Balance + 1) > 1000
```

joins the expression Balance + 1 to the literal numeric constant 1000 using the relational operation symbol >. Presuming Balance is an integer variable, the expression evaluates to 1 if the value in Balance is 1000 or greater; otherwise, the expression evaluates to 0.

Again, keep in mind that a logical expression using any of these relational operators can be thought of as asking the question, "Is this relationship true?" With that in mind, let's look at the different relational operators in turn.

Equals and not equals

Perhaps the simplest relational concepts are equals and not equals, although each of these uses two symbols in C, rather than one. An expression using == evaluates to 1 if the two expressions on either side are exactly equal to each other; otherwise, the expression evaluates to 0. In the case of !=, the expression evaluates to 1 if the two expressions on either side don't have the same value; if they evaluate to exactly the same value, the expression takes the value 0.

For example, suppose the value in Balance is equal to 0 when a program encounters the two expressions

```
Balance == 0
Balance != 0
```

In this case, the first expression evaluates to 1 and the second to 0. If you put these two expressions back into question form, you end up with

Is the value in Balance equal to 0?

Is the value in Balance not equal to 0?

Greater than and less than

The second pair of relational operators evaluates the relative magnitude of two expressions that most likely don't have the same value. An expression using > (greater than) evaluates to 1 if the expression on the left is larger than the value on the right. If the two expressions have the same value, or if the one to the right is larger, then the expression takes the value 0.

With < (less than), the opposite if true. An expression using < evaluates to 1 if the value on the left is smaller than the value on the right. If the two expressions have the same value, or if the one to the right is smaller, then the expression takes on the value 0.

Again, suppose the integer variable Balance contains 500 when a program encounters the following two expressions:

```
Balance > 500

Balance < 501
```

In this case, the first expression evaluates to 0 because two expressions joined by the > symbol are equal; Balance in fact is *not* greater than 500. The second expression evaluates to 0; the value in Balance is indeed less than 501. Again, in question form, these two expressions read as

Is the value in Balance greater than 500?

Is the value in Balance less than 501?

Greater than or equal to and less than or equal to

The last pair of relational operators seem to combine the other four. An expression using the operator >= (is greater than or equal to) evaluates to 1 if the value on the left is larger than or exactly equal to the value on the right. An expression using the operator <= (is less than or equal to) evaluates to 1 if the value on the left is smaller than or exactly equal to the value on the right. Again, suppose that the integer variable Balance has the value 500 when the program encounters the following two expressions:

```
Balance >= 500
Balance <= 500
```

In this case, both expressions evaluate to 1 because the value in Balance is equal to 500 in both cases. Again, in question form, these two expressions read as

Is the value in Balance greater than or equal to 500?

Is the value in Balance less than or equal to 500?

How to use relational operators

Again, logical expressions that use relational operators are most useful to statements that control the way a program runs. As previously discussed, however, you can use such a logical expression in an assignment statement. This lets you perform a certain test once and then preserve the result to be used in one or more subsequent statements in your program. Therefore, the statement

```
= Balance >= NoFee 500;
```

compares the value in the variable Balance with 500; if the two are the same, or if the value in Balance is larger than 500, the expression evaluates to 1. Then that result is stored in NoFee. If the value in Balance is actually less than 500, the expression evaluates to 0. Then 0 is stored in NoFee. After this statement is executed, NoFee stores the results of the test. Subsequent parts of the program can check the value of NoFee to determine whether or not to perform certain actions—whether to deduct a service fee from a checking account balance, for instance.

Catch the bug

A problem exists with each of the following three statements that use relational operators. Can you determine what the problems are?

```
IsNegative = Balance =< 0;
IsZero = Balance = 0;
IsPositive = Balance <= 0;
```

Answer: *In the first statement, the two parts of the operator are in the wrong order. The second statement uses the wrong operator: = instead of ==. As written, it is actually a compound assignment statement that puts the value 0 into both Balance and IsPositive, effectively wiping out the contents of Balance. The last statement, although not wrong from a syntax point of view, is actually misphrased if you really want to determine whether the value in Balance is positive. The following are the corrected statements:*

```
IsNegative = Balance <= 0;
IsZero = Balance == 0;
IsPositive = Balance >= 0;
```

Compare the truth of two logical expressions with logical operators

Frequently it's quite useful to combine the results of two or more logical tests. Doing this lets you create complex conditions that certain actions are performed under. C provides three logical operators with which you can combine relational expressions.

What are the logical operators?

The following table shows the logical operators in C.

Operator	C symbol
AND	&&
OR	||
NOT	!

The first two of these operators join two expressions, as do the relational operators. The NOT operator applies to a single expression. Any expression using &&, | |, and ! evaluates to either 1 or 0.

AND and OR

The AND and OR operators join the results of two expressions. An expression using && evaluates to 1 only when both expressions it joins also evaluate to 1. An expression using | | evaluates to 1 if either (or both) of the expressions it joins evaluates to 1; if both expressions evaluate to 0, the expression as a whole evaluates to 0.

Speaking of logical operators

A simple logical expression using a logical operator takes the following form:

```
expression1 symbol expression2
```

expression1 and expression2 are both valid logical expressions. symbol is one of C's logical operator symbols. The value of a logical expression is either 1 or 0. For example,

```
(Balance > 0) && (Option == 1)
```

joins the expression Balance > 0 to the expression Option == 1 using the logical operation symbol &&.

One way to express the results of a logical operation like OR or AND is through the use of a **truth table**. A truth table sets out, in columnar form, the different results obtained from a logical operation given the possible combinations of input values. (Conventionally, two input values are represented by "p" and "q.") Truth tables for AND and OR appear as follows:

p	AND	q
True	True	True
True	False	False
False	False	True
False	False	False

p	OR	q
True	True	True
True	True	False
False	True	False
False	False	False

Suppose you have two variables, `Balance` and `Option`. At this time, `Balance` contains 500, and `Option` contains 1. Consider then the following two expressions:

```
(Balance >= 500) && (Option == 1)
```

The expression as a whole evaluates to 1, because both of the relational expressions joined by && evaluate to 1. The following expression also evaluates to 1:

```
(Balance >= 500) || (Option == 2)
```

Although (`Option == 2`) evaluates to 0, the expression as a whole evaluates to 1 because the first part, `Balance >= 500`, evaluates to 1.

Note the use of parentheses to isolate parts of the expression.

NOT

The NOT operator is used to change a logical result to its opposite: 1 becomes 0, and 0 becomes 1. You prefix the ! operator to the beginning of an expression that you want to negate. Therefore,

```
!(Balance == 500)
```

is the same as writing

```
(Balance != 500)
```

With the appropriate combinations of &&, ||, and !, and the relational operators, you can create any sort of logical test on your data.

How to use logical operators

Again, you use the logical operators to link the results obtained from other logical expressions, most especially those involving the relational operators. The expressions thereby formed can range from quite simple to relatively complex. The results of any of these expressions can be stored into a variable in an assignment statement and are also useful for program control statements like those that the next chapter discusses.

Some simple logical expressions

In their most basic form, the logical operators join two simple expressions. These might be variables, constants, or simple relational expressions. Therefore,

```
(IsPositive) && (Option == 1)
```

joins the value in the variable IsPositive with the expression Option==1. This expression only evaluates to 1 if the value in IsPositive is 1, and if the value in the variable Option is exactly equal to 0.

 TIP **Variables that contain values other than 0 and 1 can actually be** used in logical expressions; any non-zero value is treated as if it were 1. Therefore, if the value stored in IsPositive in the previous example were 100, the expression as a whole would still evaluate to 1.

Finding the truth depends on the order

As with mathematical expressions, logical expressions are not evaluated all at once. They are evaluated from left to right, with certain operators taking precedence over others. The order of precedence for operators within logical expressions is as follows:

How can I use this in the real world?

The following exercise is for those who have programmed in other languages. You might have noticed that C doesn't have an operator for the XOR (exclusive-or) operation. As a reminder for you, an expression using XOR is true if one or the other of the expressions it joins are true. However, it is false if both are true or both are false. Can you design an expression in C that mimics the result of XOR?

This is a tricky one to work out. It helps to list all the possible results; again, an arrangement of the results in column form is referred to as a truth table. The following shows all the possibilities for the two expressions (A and B are the expressions) joined by XOR and for XOR itself.

A	B	XOR
1	1	0
1	0	1
0	1	1
0	0	0

It turns out, the expression (A||B)&&(!(A&&B)) yields the same results as XOR. The following is a truth table for this expression.

(A	||	B)	&&	(!	(A	&&	B))
1	1	1	0	0	1	1	1
1	1	0	1	1	1	0	0
0	1	1	1	1	0	0	1
0	0	0	0	1	0	0	0

1 !

2 >, >=, <, <=

3 !=, ==

4 &&, ||

Therefore, NOT takes place before any other operation, while AND and OR are the last operations to be evaluated. Any relational operations are satisfied first. As with mathematical expressions, however, you can alter the order that logical expressions are evaluated in by using parentheses. Note however, that the ! operator associates right to left, whereas the other operators associate left to right. Strictly speaking, && is always performed before ||.

Some complex logical expressions

Use parentheses to enclose the parts of a logical expression that you want to have evaluated first. Consider the following expression:

```
!IsPositive && Option==1
```

According to the rules of precedence, the NOT (!) operation is performed first, followed by == and then &&. If what you want is merely the opposite of IsPositive && Option==1, the previous expression doesn't work. To get the ! operation to apply to the rest of the expression as a whole, you enclose the expression in parentheses:

```
!(IsPositive && Option==1)
```

You can form expressions with as many parentheses as you like, nesting parentheses within each other as you do with mathematical expressions.

Catch the bug

Can you spot the problem in the following logical expression?

(A || B) && (! (A && B))) || (!A && !B)

Answer: *The open and close parentheses don't match up; there is a close parenthesis with no partner just before the last || symbol. The corrected expression reads in this way:*

((A || B) && (! (A && B))) || (!A && !B)

One more operator

C has one other interesting operator. The **conditional operator** (?) combines the functions of the assignment operator (=) with the results of a logical expression; one of two values is assigned to the variable in question, depending on the results of the expression.

Speaking of conditional statements

The general form of a conditional assignment statement is as follows:

```
variable = testexpression ? expression1 : expression2;
```

testexpression is evaluated; if it evaluates to 1, the value of expression1 is put into variable; if testexpression evaluates to 0, the value of expression2 is put into variable. For example, consider the following statement:

```
Interest = (Balance>0) ? (Balance*1.05) : (0);
```

This statement reads the product of Balance times 1.05 into the variable named Interest if the value in Balance is greater than 0; if the value is equal to or less than 0, the value 0 is read into Interest.

Summary

In this chapter, you considered logical expressions, which are expressions that use the rules of orderly thought to obtain one of two results: 1 or 0. These results are conventionally expressed as True and False. It is possible to define symbolic constants to represent 1 and 0 as True and False, respectively. C has relational operators to define the relationship between data items. There are six such operators. C also has logical operators, representing the operations AND, OR, and NOT. These operators are used to combine logical results. C also has a conditional operator for determining which of two values to assign to a variable based on the results of a logical test.

How can I use this in the real world?

You would think that anyone would know that you really can't enter negative values for most financial calculations. For example, it makes no sense to try to calculate interest on a negative bank balance; perhaps this is why I never seem to earn any.

Using the conditional operator, however, you can solve this kind of problem. Use it to test the value in the variable that might be negative, the variable Balance, for instance. If the variable comes out to be less than zero, simply set the result equal to zero. If it's greater than zero, perform the calculation. The line shown previously,

```
Interest = (Balance>0) ? (Balance*1.05) : (0);
```

does just this. You can also use the conditional operator to "zero" out a variable with improper contents. A line setting Balance to 0 if it's initially negative (and leaving it alone if it isn't) looks like

```
Balance = (Balance < 0) ? (0): (Balance);
```

Review questions

1 What two results does a logical expression always evaluate to?

2 What is the relational operator that expresses the concept "is less than or equal to"?

3 Which operation is performed first: ! or > ?

4 When is an expression involving the && (AND) logical operation equal to 1? What about an expression with I I (OR)?

5 How would you use the conditional operator to change a negative value in a variable to 0, but leave the value alone if the variable's contents are positive or equal to 0?

Exercises

1 Write a relational expression that asks the question, "Are the contents of the variable AccountBalance greater than or equal to an amount that's 10 times the contents of the variable BadChecks?"

2 Combine the expression from Exercise 1 with a second expression that tests whether the value in the variable BadChecks is greater than 0. Create a logical expression from these two that evaluates to 1 (True) only if both expressions are true.

3 Modify the program to find the payment on a loan that you created in the final exercise of the last chapter. Have the modified program print 0 for the payment if a negative loan amount is entered.

10

Control the Way a Program Runs

● **In this chapter:**

- **You can control which code statements are skipped or run**

- **Repeating blocks of statements**

- **Putting statement blocks within statement blocks**

A straight road doesn't really get you anywhere...it definitely doesn't let you take some sidetrips to see other sights or escape a heavy rainstorm. Similarly, a program that just plows along, doesn't really let you do a lot of things. If only you could have options in a program. Well, you do . . . . ➤

I f a computer program always performs the same sequence of operations—the same manipulations no matter what the data is, it can be a pretty useful program, but not nearly as useful as it could be. The program might even end up being wrong. Data, you see, comes in different forms, and the one-size-fits-all approach is not adequate in all cases. For example, think of numbers: some are positive, some are negative, some are relatively small, and some are very large. A program might not be able to handle every number that a user puts into it. Large numbers calculate into a number that exceeds the program's capacity; negative numbers could produce a nonsensical result.

Fortunately, C includes a number of statements that allow you to alter the way a program runs based on what's going on at the time. You can think of these statements as signposts, pointing out the way your program should go, given current road conditions. For the most part, each such signpost marks a kind of fork in the program road. Your program can either take one path or the other, usually depending on some test performed on data.

Program roads taken and not taken

Using the conditional operator (discussed in the preceding chapter), you can formulate a C statement that performs a calculation only if a certain condition is met. In effect, a program using such a statement comes to a fork in its road. When the statement is encountered, the program might test the value of, say, a variable called `Balance` to see if it's nonzero. If it is, the program takes the first fork, perhaps calculating interest according to a formula. If, on the other hand, the balance is zero or less, the program takes the second fork, perhaps merely assigning the current value of `Balance` to the variable that holds the future, compounded sum.

To be sure, all of this action occurs in a single statement. C has other signposts you can put into a program that allow each alternative road to be as long as you like. Additionally, in these new roads you can use signposts for other roads. It's in using such signpost statements that you tap the true power of computer programming. The rest of this chapter considers such signposts. First, though, you ought to consider the straight and narrow way that programs without signposts take.

How a program runs, and how you can change that

As a rule, your computer executes a program one step at a time, taking each statement in sequence. We say that your computer **executes** a program; this doesn't mean the poor thing faces the firing squad each time you run it. You might just as well say your computer dispatches a program, although the term *execution* has passed firmly into the computer lexicon and just has to be dealt with. A statement that your computer can execute is called, appropriately enough, an **executable statement**. In C, all executable statements end with a semicolon. There are nonexecutable statements as well, such as comments and #include statements.

The following code to find the number of feet and inches in a given number of inches is an example to demonstrate step-by-step execution:

```
/*A program to find feet and inches
in an integral number of inches*/
#include <stdio.h>
/*Declare variables*/
int inches, feet;
main()
{
 puts("A program to find feet and inches
in an integral number of inches\n");
/*Have the user input the number of inches*/
 printf("\nEnter the number of inches: ");
scanf("%d",&inches);
 /*Calculate and Print the results*/
feet = inches/12;
 printf("\n%d inches represent %d feet and
%d inches",inches,feet, inches % 12);
/*Pause for the user to press Enter before Quitting*/
puts("\n\nPress the Enter key to quit");
scanf("%f",&inches);
}
```

 Here's how this program executes:

1 The first three lines are **nonexecutable**, which means that, when the program runs, these statements have no effect. The comments are left entirely out of the executable program by the compiler; the compiler itself takes care of the #include statement in the second line, which makes certain that the correct information is included in the executable version of the program.

2 The first executable statement is on the fourth line; this statement creates two integer variables.

3 The next two lines are nonexecutable; they merely set up the program's `main()` function and mark a block of executable statements.

4 The seventh line is executable; it writes a sentence onto the screen.

5 The next line is a comment and is nonexecutable.

6 The ninth and tenth lines are executable; the first writes a prompt onto the screen, asking the user to input the number of inches. The second reads the number input by the user into the variable named inches.

7 The next line is nonexecutable; it's another comment.

8 The two lines following are executable; the twelfth line calculates the integer number of feet in the given number of inches. The next line prints the number of inches input by the user, along with the number of feet found in the preceding line. It also calculates and prints the number of inches left over after the feet are accounted for.

9 The following line is a comment and nonexecutable.

10 The fifteenth and sixteenth lines are executable; the first prints a message on the screen. The second pauses for input until the user presses the Enter key. Anything typed by the user is input into a variable, although this is of no consequence; the value input is never used.

11 The last statement marks the end of the block of statements introduced in the sixth line. Like that statement, it is nonexecutable.

You can see that program execution proceeds from left to right and top to bottom. Executable statements are all executed as they're encountered; nonexecutable statements are, in effect, ignored. That's how it goes. Can you make a program deviate from this sequence? If so, why would you want to? Read on and find out.

Why put the fork in the road?

I've hinted at reasons to change the way a program executes already. One important reason is that some of the calculations in a program may produce nonsensical results if they're performed on certain data—for example, compound interest on a negative balance. In this case, it's helpful to include an alternative group of statements to handle the bad data. These statements execute if the data is bad or simply skip those statements if the data is good. This kind of statement handling is named conditional execution.

 Plain English, please!

Statements that are **conditionally executed** are either run or skipped, depending on the results of a test. This test is usually carried out with a logical expression of some kind. This test defines the condition that the statement or statements are executed under. **"**

Another time to alter the typical execution sequence is to repeat a group of statements. At the simplest, you might want to give the user the opportunity to repeat an entire program's calculations without having to quit and rerun it. There are also times when it's handy to perform the same calculation a set or even an unknown number of times. Rather than actually repeating the relevant statements in the code (lots of tedious typing), you can include statements that repeat the relevant calculations, a repetition named process looping. You can use process looping to find the average of a group of numbers input by the user.

 Plain English, please!

Process looping refers to the repetition of a statement or group of statements. A loop is executed statement-by-statement from top to bottom. At the bottom, a test is performed. Based on the results of the test, the loop either exits or begins execution again with the first statement in the loop. **"**

Both conditional execution and process looping are managed by the same kind of statements, introduced in chapter 6, "Expressing Yourself with C Statements." Such statements are named program control statements.

Program control statements are the roadsigns

A **program control statement** tells C how to execute the statements that follow. Again, you can think of these statements as signposts that tell a C program something about the road ahead. At the time the program executes, the value of the data the program's working on determines the exact path. Program control statements fall into three broad categories: those that define groups of statements, those that define conditionally executed statements, and those that define loops.

How to put several statements on the same road

C treats a block of statements more or less as a single executable statement. If any statement in a block executes, then all are, presuming there are no program control statements embedded within the block. A block of statements is marked by braces, each appearing on a line by itself. The one statement block within the feet and inches program previously shown follows:

```
{
 puts("A program to find feet and inches
➥in an integral number of inches\n");
 /*Have the user input the number of inches*/
 printf("\nEnter the number of inches: ");
 scanf("%d",&inches);
 /*Calculate and Print the results*/
 feet = inches/12;
 printf("\n%d inches represent %d feet and
➥%d inches",inches,feet, inches % 12);
 /*Pause for the user to press Enter before Quitting*/
 puts("\n\nPress the Enter key to quit");
 scanf("%f",&inches);
 }
```

The braces appear on the sixth and seventeenth lines. You can think of the braces as statements that mark the beginning and end of the block.

All C programs have at least one block of statements. An example like the previous one doesn't really show the power of blocks, though; it just shows that all C programs are required to have at least one statement block. Where blocks become important is in conjunction with other program control statements. You use blocks to set up entire groups of statements that are conditionally executed.

Which road do I take? Try testing a road

Earlier in the chapter I talked about one example of conditional execution; the conditional operator (?). You can use this statement to determine what value to put into a variable, based on the results of a test. For example, the following statement multiplies the contents of Balance by 1.5 if the variable is positive or leaves it alone otherwise:

```
Balance = (Balance>0)? (Balance*1.5),Balance;;
```

C has another statement to define conditional execution, one that is considerably more powerful. Using the `if` statement, you can define the conditions that a block of statements either executes or does not execute under. Some version or other of the `if` statement appears in pretty much about every high-level computer language you can name; if you've programmed before outside of C, you're probably quite familiar with `if`. Just a little later in this chapter you'll look at using `if` to entirely reject bad data in an interest program.

Process loop `for` a `while`

C has two statements that you define loops with; one sets up a loop to be executed a set number of times, the other sets up a loop that executes until a certain condition is met. The former are set up with the `for` statement; the latter are created with `while`. If you've programmed in other computer languages, you're probably familiar with both these statements; they're used in pretty much the same way in the latest versions of BASIC, for instance. Later in this chapter, as you look at looping in detail, you'll see how to use the `while` statement to allow the user to repeat a program without quitting. First, however, turn your attention back to `if`.

Use `if` to test the conditions

For more information about logical expressions, see chapter 9, "Finding the Truth of Expressions."

The `if` statement is the first program signpost you'll consider. An `if` statement marks a fork in the program's road. Which fork the program takes depends on the results of a test. The test is phrased in the form of a logical expression.

You might say that this form of `if` leaps over an entire section of the program's road. Suppose, however, you want to conditionally execute more than one statement. Do you have to repeat the `if` for each such statement? No, there's an alternative form of `if` you can use.

If I could block with `if`...

If you combine `if` with a block of statements, marked with braces, you can conditionally execute the entire block. This lets your program execute a group of statements or skip the entire group based on the results of a test.

Again, you might think of this form of if statement as one that skips an entire section of the program's road; that part marked by the braces. The statements following the block are always executed. Suppose, however, that you want to provide an alternative route, one that is itself skipped if the first block executes. How might you do that? Add an else clause to your if statement.

You can combine if statements with else

An if block supports the use of an additional clause, one introduced by the keyword else. In this form of if, the statement or statements following if execute if the condition evaluates to 1; the statements following else are

Speaking of if

The general form of an if statement is

```
if (logical_expression)
    statement;
```

If the logical_expression evaluates to 1, then *statement* executes; if the logical_expression evaluates to 0, then *statement* is skipped entirely. Note that the line containing if is not marked with a semicolon; the if statement itself is not executable as such. Consider this example:

```
if (Balance<0)
puts("You entered a negative balance.");
```

At the time the program's run, if the value in Balance is less than 0, the puts() statement following if executes, writing a message to the screen. If, on the other hand, the value in Balance is 0 or greater, the puts() statement is skipped, and no message appears.

TIP **Remember that C treats any nonzero value as True. Thus, you** can put a mathematical expression into an if statement, although the statement following is only skipped if the value of the mathematical expression is zero.

skipped. If the condition evaluates to 0, the statements following `if` are ignored and the statements following `else` execute.

Q&A ***What if I only want to have one statement execute after either `if` or `else`. Do I have to enclose that one statement in braces?***

No, you don't. In fact, you can even include the statement you want to execute on the same line with `if`. The following three lines of code are perfectly legal:

```
if (Balance<0) puts("You entered a bad balance");
else
puts("The balance is ok");
```

Speaking of combining `if` with a statement block

The general form of an `if` statement combined with a statement block is

```
if (logical_expression)
{
    statements;
}
```

If the `logical_expression` evaluates to 1, then the `statements` enclosed in braces execute; if the `logical_expression` evaluates to 0, the `statements` enclosed in braces are skipped entirely. Consider the following example:

```
if (Balance<0)
{
puts("You entered a negative balance.");
Balance = 0;
}
```

At the time the program's run, if the value in `Balance` is less than 0, then the `puts()` statement following `if` executes, writing a message to the screen. Then the assignment statement executes, changing the value in `Balance` to 0. If, on the other hand, the value in `Balance` is 0 or greater, the `puts()` statement and the assignment statement are skipped; no message appears, and the value in `Balance` is left unchanged.

How to use `if`

The exact form of `if` statement you use at a given point in a program depends on how much you need to make conditional. An important thing to keep in mind in this regard is that any and all statements following an `if` block always execute. You should make certain that these statements don't undo the work you're doing with the `if` statement in the first place. If they do, then the offending statements likely should be enclosed in braces and made part of an `else` block.

Speaking of `if...else`

The general form of an `if...else` block is

```
if (logical_expression)
{
    statements;
}
else
{
    statements;
}
```

Here's an example:

```
if (Balance<0)
{
puts("You entered a negative balance.");
Balance = 0;
}
else
{
Balance = Balance*1.05;
printf("The new balance is %d",Balance);
}
```

At the time the program's run, if the value in `Balance` is less than 0, then the `puts()` statement following `if` executes, writing a message to the screen. Then the assignment statement executes, changing the value in `Balance` to 0. If, on the other hand, the value in `Balance` is 0 or greater, the `puts()` statement and the assignment statement are skipped; instead, the value in `Balance` is replaced by the product of `Balance` times 1.05, and the new value appears on the screen along with a message.

Catch the bug

The following if...else block has three problems. Can you spot them?

```
if (test>=0);
puts("The test value is positive");
result = test * 10;
else
{
puts("The test value is negative");
test = 0;
}
result = 0;
```

Answer: First, the if statement has a semicolon following the test condition. While you can immediately follow the test condition with a statement to execute, C interprets the preceding example to mean that you want to do nothing at all if the test condition is met. Second, the two statements following if constitute a block prior to else, but aren't enclosed in braces, and they should be. Third, the statement result=0 following the else block automatically destroys the results obtained in the if block; likely this statement was meant to be part of the else block. The corrected code is

```
if (test>=0)
{
puts("The test value is positive");
result = test * 10;
}
else
{
puts("The test value is negative");
test = 0;
result = 0;
}
```

Listing 10.1 uses if statements to control execution. The program refuses to run at all if the user enters a negative balance, interest rate, or term. In this case, it displays an error message.

Listing 10.1   Use `if` statements to control which road to take

```
/*A program to find compound interest*/

#include <stdio.h>
#include <math.h>
/*Declare variables*/

float balance, rate, years, future;
main()
{

puts("A program to find compound interest");
/*Have the user input the values desired for
the present balance, the rate, and the time */

printf("\nEnter the opening balance: ");
scanf("%f",&balance);
printf("\nEnter the interest rate in percent per year:  ");
scanf("%f",&rate);
printf("\nEnter the number of years the balance is held: ");
scanf("%f",&years);

/*Verify amounts entered, skip calculation if any negative*/
if ((balance<=0)||(rate<=0)||(years<=0))
    puts("Invalid data entered");
else
{
    /*Calculate the future balance using
    the formula, reject non-positive balance*/
    future = (balance>0)? (balance
    * (pow(2.7183,(rate/100)*years))):balance;
    /*Print the results*/
    printf("\nThe future balance is %f\n", future);
}
/*Pause for the user to press Enter before Quitting*/
puts("\nPress the Enter key to quit");
scanf("%f",&rate);
}
```

code   This program relies on an `if...else` block to test input values. If any one or all of the values for `balance`, `rate`, or `years` is entered as 0 or less, the program prints an error message and skips the subsequent calculations and printing. Only if all the values are positive does the program go on to perform its calculations and print the results. I indented the blocks in the `if...else` construction for clarity's sake; C doesn't require such indentations. Figure 10.1 shows the new program in action.

Fig. 10.1
Entering a negative interest rate, even with the other values positive, causes the program to write an error message and decline to calculate further.

```
A program to find compound interest
Enter the opening balance: 1000

Enter the interest rate in percent per year: -5

Enter the number of years the balance is held: 10

Invalid data entered
Press the Enter key to quit
```

All the details about process loops you need to know

Some statements you want to skip at times; you do this using `if` blocks. On the other hand, there are actually times when you want to repeat one statement or a block of statements. Doing so can give your program added flexibility by enclosing a whole set of actions in a loop and letting the user run them as many times as desired. It can also make your code tighter by letting you rerun certain parts of it. As I said earlier in the chapter, C has

Speaking of for

The general form of a `for` statement is

```
for (initialize; test_condition; increment)
    statement;
```

`initialize` sets the initial value for the counter variable, which must have been previously declared in the program. The `test_condition` specifies what value of the variable results in termination of the loop. The `increment` is a mathematical expression specifying how to modify the counter variable on each pass through the loop.

```
for (counter = 1; counter<=10; counter++)
    sum = sum + counter;
```

In this example, the `for` statement first set the variable counter equal to 1. As long as counter is less than or equal to 10, the `for` loop executes. The variable counter is incremented by 1 each time through the loop.

two statements to create loops with: `for` and `while`. Either of these statements serves as a road sign that says, for instance, "Keep circling the block until you find a parking space."

Use `for`

You use the `for` statement to execute one statement or a block of statements for a given number of times. There's a similar statement in the BASIC programming language. Essentially, `for` maintains a **counter variable**; this variable is set equal to an initial value and increments by a set amount each time through the loop, until it reaches a specified final value. The statement following `for` executes each time through the loop.

You can also have the `for` statement execute a block of statements. You enclose the relevant statements in braces, as you do in an `if` block.

How can I use this in the real world?

Consider a harried school teacher, with 30 second-graders whose first semester grades are due. There have been a total of ten tests in each of five subjects. All these tests must now be averaged to compute each student's semester grade in each subject. Sounds like the old pocket calculator is about to get worn out, isn't it?

Not if the educator in question knows how to harness the power of `for` loops in C. It's quite easy to construct a program that lets the user input ten numbers, displays the average of those numbers, and then goes back to the beginning to accept another set of numbers. A `for` loop to average ten numbers might look like this:

```
for (counter = 1; counter <=10; counter++)
{
    puts("Enter a number to average:  ");
    scanf("%f",&input);
    sum = sum + input;
}
```

A program using this loop saves several calculator keystrokes on each set of grades to be averaged, which really adds up across 30 students and five subjects. If you think a program based on such a loop is only useful for educators, consider that you, as a parent, can always use it to check your own kids' teachers.

Use `while`

The `while` statement sets up an alternative form of loop, one perhaps slightly easier to understand than `for`. A `while` loop repeats until the specified test condition becomes `False`.

How to use process loops

As you can see from the preceding examples, you can formulate a `while` statement that is exactly equivalent to a `for` statement. Which of the two you use in such a case is a matter of taste. There are occasions, however, where only a `while` loop will do. For example, you might have a loop

Speaking of `while`

The general form of a `while` statement is

```
while (logical_expression )
    statements;
```

The *logical_expression* is tested; if it evaluates to 1, the statements following execute; if it evaluates to 0, the statements are skipped and the loop terminates. The following example is equivalent to the `for` loop shown in the previous "Speaking C" segment.

```
counter = 1;
while (counter<=10)
{
    sum = sum + counter;
    counter++;
}
```

In this example, the first statement sets the variable counter equal to 1. As long as counter is less than or equal to 10, the `while` loop executes. The variable counter is incremented by 1 each time through the loop.

CAUTION   **It is vitally important that the `while` loop itself does something** to change the value of the test condition. If the test condition isn't changed and continues to remain `True`, the `while` loop executes forever! (In chapter 20, "Control a Program—Where It Goes, What It Does...," you'll see another way to get out of such a loop, using Break.)

function until a user enters a specific value; in that case, you must use a `while` loop that executes as long as the input variable isn't equal to the specified value.

Now you're in position to modify the INTEREST program in listing 10.2 so that the user can run it multiple times without exiting. At the end of each pass through the program, you have it display a new message, asking the user to press a specific key (such as **y**) to rerun the program. The trick is to enclose the entire executable part of the program within a `while` loop. You have the `while` loop execute as long as the test variable is equal to the value of the key the user should press. To make certain the loop executes at least once, you have to make sure to initialize the input variable to the correct value before starting the loop.

Catch the bug

There's one error in the following `while` loop, although your C compiler would never spot it. Can you?

```
while (Sum >= 0)
{
    puts("Input a number: ");
    scanf("%f",&input);
}
```

Answer: *The body of the loop does nothing to change the value of the variable Sum, which is the only variable in the test condition. Thus, if the loop executes at all (because Sum is 0 or greater at the start), it executes forever. Likely this loop was phrased incorrectly. A corrected version follows.*

```
while (input >= 0)
{
    puts("Input a positive number; a negative number to
    ➦terminate: ");
    scanf("%f",&input);
    sum = sum + input;
}
```

Listing 10.2 The modified program for finding compound interest

```c
/*A program to find compound interest*/

#include <stdio.h>
#include <math.h>
/*Declare variables*/
char recycle;
float balance, rate, years, future;
main()
{
recycle = 1;
puts("A program to find compound interest");

while (recycle == 1)
    {
    /*Have the user input the values desired
    ⇒for the present balance, the rate, and the time */

    printf("\nEnter the opening balance: ");
    scanf("%f",&balance);
    printf("\nEnter the interest rate in percent per year:
    ⇒");
    scanf("%f",&rate);
    printf("\nEnter the number of years the balance is
    ⇒held: ");
    scanf("%f",&years);

    /*Verify amounts entered, skip calculation if any
    ⇒negative*/
    if ((balance<=0)||(rate<=0)||(years<=0))
        puts("Invalid data entered");
    else
        {
        /*Calculate the future balance using the formula,
        ⇒reject non-positive balance*/
        future = (balance>0)? (balance *
        ⇒(pow(2.7183,(rate/100)*years)))):balance;
        /*Print the results*/
        printf("\nThe future balance is %f\n", future);
    }
    /*Pause for the user to enter 1 to repeat program*/
    puts("\nEnter \"1\" to repeat the program ");
    recycle=0;
    scanf("%d", &recycle);
    }
}
```

Note that the entire program is enclosed with a `while` loop. At the end of this loop, the user is prompted to enter the number **1** to repeat the program. Because the program uses `scanf()`, nothing happens if the user just presses Enter. On the other hand, entering any value other than 1 causes the program to quit. Otherwise, the program is just the same as the last version in listing 10.1.

Figure 10.2 shows the results of two runs through the newly modified compound interest program

CAUTION   **By the way, one of the easiest mistakes for a programmer to make** is to substitute the assignment operator (=) for the equals-to comparison operator (==). It can take several minutes to locate this mistake.

Take a right at the fork; take another right at the stop sign; then take a left

As I said at the chapter's beginning, you can set up complicated paths for your program if you want to. To do so, you embed program control statements within each other. This process is called **nesting**. You can nest both `if` blocks and loops.

If I could only use more `if`s—well, you can

To nest one `if` statement within another, include that `if` statement as a block in the first one. For example,

```
if (InchesHigh > 60)
    if (InchesHigh<72)
        puts("The individual is of medium height");
    else
        puts("The individual is tall");
else
    puts("The individual is short");
```

Fig. 10.2

The user can now repeat the INTEREST program as many times as desired.

```
A program to find compound interest
Enter the opening balance: 1000

Enter the interest rate in percent per year: -5

Enter the number of years the balance is held: 10

Invalid data entered
Enter "1" to repeat the program
Enter the opening balance: 1000

Enter the interest rate in percent per year: 5

Enter the number of years the balance is held: 10

The future balance is 1648.726807
Enter "1" to repeat the program
```

You can see that nesting `if` statements lets you set up complicated conditions. The preceding example can handle data in one of three ranges: less than 60, from 60 to 72, and greater than 72.

There's another way to nest loops, using the construction `else if`. This sets up another `if` as part of the `else` clause. Here's the preceding example rewritten to take advantage of `else if`.

```
if (InchesHigh < 60)
    puts("The individual is short");
    else if (InchesHigh>72)
        puts("The individual is tall");
    else
        puts("The individual is of medium height");
```

If only I could have loops within loops— again, you can

You can also nest loops within each other. The most common use for such a construction is when you're working with multidimensional arrays. For now, a simple example of a nested loop suffices.

You learn more about multidimensional arrays in chapter 14, "Call Several Variables by the Same Name."

```
for (counter = 1; counter <= 10; counter++)
    {
    puts("\n");
    for (counter2 = 1; counter2 <= 3; counter2++)
        printf("\t%d",counter*counter2);
    }
```

The inner loop executes as many times as it's told—in this case, three times—for every single time the outer loop is executed. Can you tell what the results of running a program with this bit of code in it might be? The actual result is shown in figure 10.3.

Fig. 10.3

Nested loops in operation.

```
1    2    3
2    4    6
3    6    9
4    8    12
5    10   15
6    12   18
7    14   21
8    16   24
9    18   27
10   20   25
```

Summary

This chapter covered program control statements. You saw how a program typically runs—from left to right and top to bottom, taking each executable statement in turn. You learned about statement blocks. This chapter discussed using the `if` statement to execute certain blocks of statements conditionally. You also looked at how to repeat groups of statements, using the `for` and `while` statements. Finally, you saw how to place blocks of decision-making statements within each other, a process known as nesting.

Review questions

1 What does the term *conditional execution* refer to?

2 What is a loop? Is it possible to create a loop that never terminates?

3 What keyword is used to introduce an alternative block of statements after an `if` block?

4 Distinguish between `for` and `while`.

5 Define the term *nesting*.

Exercises

1 Write an `if` block that tests the value of a variable called `Age`, and prints the following messages under the given conditions:

If `Age` is less than 18, print `Child`.

If `Age` is between 18 and 44, print `Adult`.

If `Age` is between 45 and 65, print `Middle-Aged`.

If `Age` is greater than 65, print `Senior`.

Try to accomplish this task in as few statements as possible.

2 Write a loop that sums an input value into a variable called `Sum`, until the value in `Sum` exceeds 1000. Count the number of times the loop is executed and have a statement after the loop print this result.

3 Using `while` statements, modify the INTEREST program so that, if the user enters a nonpositive value for any of the variables in the program, the program displays a message indicating the value isn't appropriate and then gives the user the chance to re-enter it.

11

The Functional Structure of C Programs

● **In this chapter:**

- **Top-down design—how you build C programs**

- **Splitting programs into parts using functions**

- **How to use your own functions or existing library functions**

C Programs are built with blocks, like a child's set of interlocking blocks, that can be built into complex programs . . . . . ➤

magine a really grand program: a complete money manager. This money manager keeps track of your checking account balance; calculates loans, annuities, and returns on investments; and even keeps track of other account balances. Such a program is quite useful, but it is also certainly long and involved.

Writing the entire program as one long block of statements is possible. Definitely, the money manager uses plenty of program control statements, but everything is still found within the main() function of the program. If you had submitted such a program to my computer science instructor back in college, he'd have given you and your program an F. Why? It works, doesn't it?

Whether such a program works isn't the point. A long, involved, intricately structured program like the one imagined here performs certain calculations several times, with perhaps only the data varying. Having several sections perform the same calculation is unnecessarily repetitive; it's far better to define the calculation once and give separate parts of the program access to it. For another thing, understanding a long series of statements within a program, even with comments, can be very difficult. Although a program like this may work well enough, it becomes increasingly difficult to **maintain**—adding new features and improving existing ones. Also, locating an error that's keeping the program from running can be burdensome; in a long program, looking for an error is like trying to find a needle in a haystack.

To avoid these difficulties, breaking up programs into smaller units—ones that are even reusable—seems the best solution. Programs in small blocks are easier to manage and are more likely to be useful in other contexts. Naturally, this is just how C programs are meant to be structured.

How are C programs put together?

The fact is, C programs are built like a child's set of wooden blocks; they can be constructed into complex programs and reused and reconfigured in other programs. A function, such as the main() function, is one such building block. The process of taking a programming task, such as subtracting the month's income and the month's mortgage payment, and resolving it into its logical building blocks is called top-down design.

Small tasks are easier than large ones

Top-down design is all about taking large tasks and turning them into small ones. At a certain point, you reach the bottom, with a group of tasks that can't be resolved any further. These tasks are the functions within your program.

 Plain English, please!

A **function** is a discrete, named section of C programming code that performs a specific, discrete task. In its own right, a function is very much a C program. Rather than being run, programmers say that a function is **called**. The function can receive data from the part of the overall program that calls it and may return data to the same. **99**

Programming from the top down in C

C programs demand a certain amount of structure. A typical C program is composed of at least one function and may contain more. Some functions are defined by you, others are predefined and are made available through the use of #include statements. However, the overall structure of any C function is the same.

The main( ) function

Each C program requires a main() function. The following shows a very simple main() function:

```
main()
{
scanf("%d",&InchesHigh);
for (counter = 1; counter <= 10; counter++)
    {
    puts("\n");
    for (counter2 = 1; counter2 <= 3; counter2++)
        printf("\t%d",counter*counter2);
    }
scanf("%d",&InchesHigh);
}
```

The statements in the main() function follow main(). Note that the statements—the actual working part of the program—are enclosed in braces.

In a more advanced program, it's the task of the main() function to call the individual functions that do the program's actual work. A main() function structured in this way is referred to as a **driver program** because it does nothing else but call other functions; it drives the program. The driver was supposed to do nothing but call other functions. Although this is the epitome of structured programming and top-down design, it may be overkill for certain tasks. That's up to you to decide for each program.

A function for each task

In addition to the `main()` function, a C program may include code to define additional functions. Each accomplishes a specific task and, as a rule, returns a single data value. It's up to you to define which tasks are handled by functions, what data these functions receive, when they're called by the `main()` function, and what (if any) data value they return.

The code for a function just sits there until it is called by some other function—either the `main()` function or a function that the `main()` function has called. You can actually get pretty deep into function calls, with functions calling functions calling functions. How deep you can go depends on how much memory your computer has; each function call requires a good bit of extra RAM. When a function is called, it goes to work. When the function is finished executing, control in the program returns to the statement immediately following the one that called the function.

That's what functions are and what they do. Before you can use functions of your own, you need to know more about how they're put together. Not that this has necessarily stopped you before now. You've actually used a couple of functions within the `main()` function for most of the programs in this book.

Two kinds of functions

Functions fall into two broad types: those you write yourself and those that are already available as part of your C compiler package. The former are **user-defined functions**, and the latter are **library functions**. For the most part, library functions started life as user-defined functions. As such, the fundamental structure of any function—and how it's called within a program—is the same.

User-defined functions

A typical function—aside from the `main()` function—has three pieces:

- The **function prototype** tells your C compiler that a function definition occurs later in the program. All function prototypes should appear prior to the beginning of the `main()` function.

- The **function definition** appears after the conclusion of the `main()` function. The function definition is a single statement that gives the name of the function, the type of data the function expects to receive when it's called, and the type of data the function returns to the calling function.

- The third part of a function is the **function body**. This is where the function's real work takes place. As with the `main()` function, the user-defined function body is enclosed in braces. The function body follows the function definition.

Library functions

You use library functions the same way you use user-defined functions. Getting their definitions into your programs, however, is much easier. All the code necessary to make available a library function is included in a header file, such as the `stdio.h` and `math.h` header files I first talked about in chapter 3, "A Sample C Program."

 Plain English, please!

> A **header file** is a text file that contains function prototypes and variable and constant declarations. Putting a header file into a program with the `#include` statement makes the functions defined in that file available to that program.

Some examples of library functions are `puts()`, `scanf()`, and `printf()`, which are defined in the header file `stdio.h`. The `pow()` function, which performs exponentiation, is defined in `math.h`. These functions are not the only ones defined in their respective libraries; including either of these header files makes a number of other library functions available.

Creating functions

A function has three parts: prototype, definition, and body. Each part has its particular place. The prototype appears at the beginning of your C code, prior to the `main()` function. The definition occurs after the last statement in the `main()` function. The function body follows the definition. Taken together, these parts constitute a program building block; C programs as a whole are composed of these building blocks.

Function prototype

The function prototype serves as an alert to your C compiler. The prototype tells the compiler that a function definition occurs later in the program, defining a function with a certain name that expects certain data. Your compiler uses the prototype to ensure that statements within the `main()` function or other functions that refer to the function specified in the prototype supply the correct data and use the correct name. Otherwise, an error message is generated.

Speaking of a C function prototype

A C function prototype looks like

```
return_dtype func_name (arg_dtype1
➥arg_name1,...,arg_dtype_last arg_last);
```

return_dtype is the type of data—integer, floating point, character—expected by the calling function. The *func_name* is a valid C name, just like one for a variable (function names follow the same rules as variable names). The *arg_dtypes* and *arg_names* refer to the data that the calling function hands off to the function when it's called. (Arguments are discussed a little later.)

The following line sets up a prototype for a function called `AverageOf`; the function returns a floating-point value and expects to be supplied with two variables, both of integer type:

```
float AverageOf (int Sum, int HowMany);
```

Function definition and body

A function definition looks very much like a function prototype. In fact, you can make the definition exactly the same, and it's probably a good idea to do so. The only difference is that you omit the semicolon. Note that the argument and return value data types must be the same, however, and the prototype and definition must have the same number of arguments.

The function body consists of C statements that do the calculations and other work expected of the function. Again, the statements in the body immediately follow the definition and are enclosed in braces. A body for the `AverageOf` function might look like this:

```
{
return (Sum/HowMany);
}
```

This function has but a single executable statement, one that calculates the average and then passes it back to the `main()` function (or whatever called `AverageOf`). If you want a function to return a value, you must include a `return` statement as shown.

Speaking of a C function definition

A C function definition looks like

```
return_dtype func_name (arg_dtype1
➥arg_name1,...,arg_dtype_last arg_last)
```

return_dtype is the type of data—integer, floating point, character—the calling function expects back. The *func_name* is a valid C name, just like one for a variable (function names follow the same rules as variable names). The *arg_dtypes* and *arg_names* refer to the data that the calling function hands off to the function when it's called.

The following line sets up a definition for a function called `AverageOf`; it returns a floating-point value and expects to be supplied with two variables, both of type integer:

```
float AverageOf (int Sum, int HowMany)
```

Any variable names that appear in the function definition are available for use within the function; it's just as if the variables had been declared within the function. You can also declare variables within a function, for use strictly in that function. Other variables, especially those declared for the main() function, are not necessarily available. I'll have more to say on both subjects in chapter 13, "Some Optional Ways To Store Data." Before I say anything more, though, I want to take a closer look at variable names that appear in the function definition and what they're for.

How functions get data: arguments

The variables' names that appear in the function prototype and the function definition are very important; they provide the means whereby data is handed off to a function for the function to work on. These variables are named arguments.

Speaking of return

A return statement within a function has the following form:

```
return (expression);
```

When this statement is encountered in the function, the expression within parentheses is evaluated, and its value is passed back to the calling function. Thus,

```
return (x);
```

sends the value in the variable x back to the program that called the function in the first place. Other statements in the function, preceeding the return statement, have most likely modified x based on the arguments passed to the function. The return statement is merely used to explicitly tell the function to pass back a specific value and stop executing. Execution resumes in the calling function.

It's possible to have more than one return statement in the body of a function, although only the first such statement encountered will be executed. Such multiple return statements might occur in different parts of an if...else block, for instance, returning different values based on what path the function took.

Catch the bug

The following function finds the cube root of a number, and the function prototype is included. There are three errors in the function as it's defined. What are they?

```
int CubeRt (float Number);
    statements in main program
float CubeRt (float number);
    {
    return (pow(Number, 1./3.));
    }
```

Answer: First, the return variable type given in the prototype is wrong; it should be `float`, *not* `int`. *Second, the function definition line ends in a semicolon; it shouldn't. Third, the argument variable* `Number` *is capitalized everywhere but in the function definition; it must be capitalized there as well.*

 Plain English, please!

An **argument** is a variable of a given type used to pass data to a function. The exact name does not have to appear in the statement that calls the function, but the data type must be the same. Think of an argument as a placeholder for data.

The arguments to a function appear in the argument list—that's the part enclosed in parentheses—for example,

```
float AverageOf (int Sum, int HowMany)
```

In this example, the variables `Sum` and `HowMany` are arguments, both of `int` type.

The variable type associated with an argument is, as I've said, one of the standard C variable types: `int`, `long`, `float`, `double`, and `char`. Additionally, there's another type of data that functions support—`void`. You use `void` for functions that don't accept arguments or return values. The following are two such function definitions:

```
void PrintIt (char Arg1)
int RandomNumber (void)
```

Calling functions

Calling a function is really easy; in fact, you've already done it numerous times in this book. You've made several calls to library functions, like

```
puts("A Program to find Compound Interest");
```

To call a function, you simply put down its name at the appropriate place, and provide it with arguments. The arguments in a statement calling a function are called **parameters**. The parameters are enclosed in parentheses following the function name, just as arguments are.

The important thing to remember about parameters is that they don't have to have the same name as the arguments in the function definition. In fact, parameters don't have to be variables at all. They can be any kind of valid C expression, just as long as there are enough of them and each matches the data type of the associated argument.

Q&A *I'm a little confused. What's the difference between an argument and a parameter?*

If you think of an argument as a placeholder, a parameter is what the place is being held for. An argument is like an empty box, reserving space for data. When a function is called, a parameter takes the place of the argument. Unlike an argument, a parameter actually contains data.

Q&A   ***You say I can use expressions as parameters. Why would I want to do so?***

Suppose you want to pass the result of an interim calculation to a function. For example, you might want to find the square root of the sum of three numbers. Rather than placing the sum of the three numbers into a variable and passing that variable as a parameter to a square-root function, you could pass the entire expression that finds the sum, as in

```
value = sqrt(number1 + number2 + number3);
```

Compare this with

```
sum = number1 + number2 + number3;
value = sqrt(sum);
```

Both do exactly the same thing, but the former saves a variable (to hold the sum) and a step.

A call to a function doesn't necessarily have to appear on a line by itself, as the call to the previous puts() function does. If the function returns a value, then it is also a valid C expression and can appear anywhere an expression may appear. For example, you can employ this method of calling a function when using the pow() function to find the base e raised to a power, as part of an expression to find compound interest:

```
future = (balance>0)? (balance * (pow(2.7183,(rate/100)
➥*years))):balance;
```

Can you spot the parameters provided to the pow() function in the previous line of code? They're 2.7183 and (rate/100)*years.

Catch the bug

What's wrong with the following section of C programming code?

```
float MyFunction(int x, int y);
main()
{
variable1=Myfunction(a*b + c/d);
```

Answer: The last statement contains a call to the function MyFunction; *however, it only passes one parameter. According to the argument list in the function prototype,* MyFunction *requires two parameters.*

How to use functions in a real program

Okay, it's time to get serious. Suppose you try combining a compound interest program and a loan payment program into one, using functions. The specifications for this program are

1 Because both calculations require a principal amount, an interest rate, and a term, the main() function calls for user input and prints the answer.

2 After input, the user is given a choice of which calculation to perform. The user may also choose to quit. This is done with an if block nested within a while loop.

3 The compound interest and loan payment statements are isolated in separate functions called Compound and Payment.

Given these specifications, I developed the program in listing 11.1.

Listing 11.1   A C program that demonstrates the use of functions

```
/*A program to do certain financial calculations*/
 #include <stdio.h>
 #include <math.h>
 /*Declare variables*/
 char recycle;
 float balance, rate, months, future;
/*Function Prototypes*/
```

```
float Compound(float balance1, float rate1, float months1);
float Payment(float balance2, float rate2, float months2);
 main()
 {
 recycle = 1;
 puts("A program to find either compound
 ➥interest or a loan payment");

 while (recycle != 3)
     {
     /*Have the user input the values desired
     ➥for the present balance, the rate, and the time */

     printf("\nEnter the principal: ");
     scanf("%f",&balance);
     printf("\nEnter the interest rate in percent per year:  ");
     scanf("%f",&rate);
     printf("\nEnter the number of months: ");
     scanf("%f",&months);

     /*Verify amounts entered, skip calculation if any negative*/
     if ((balance<=0)¦¦(rate<=0)¦¦(months<=0))
         puts("Invalid data entered");
     else
     {
         /*Have the user choose the desired calculation*/
         puts("Enter 1 to calculate compound
         ➥interest, 2 to calculate loan payment, 3 to quit");
         scanf("%d", &recycle);
         if (recycle == 1)
             {
             puts("\nCalculating compound interest");
             future = Compound(balance, rate, months);
             printf("\nThe result is %f\n", future);
             }
         if (recycle ==2)
             {
             puts("\nCalculating loan payment");
             future = Payment(balance, rate, months);
             printf("\nThe result is %f\n", future);
             }
     }
 }
 }
 float Compound(float balance, float rate, float months)
 {
         return (balance * (pow(2.7183,(rate/1200.)*months)));
 }
 float Payment(float balance, float rate, float months)
```

continues

Listing 11.1   Continued

```
{
            return (((rate/1200)*months)*balance *
(pow(2.7183,(rate/1200)*months))/(pow(2.7183,(rate/1200)
➡*months))-1);
}
```

Figure 11.1 shows the results of running this combined version of the interest/loan payment program.

Fig. 11.1
A run through the
FINANCE program.

```
A program to find either compound interest or a loan payment
Enter the principal: 1000
Enter the interest rate in percent per year: 5
Enter the number of months: 60
Enter 1 to calculate compound interest, 2 to calculate loan
payment, 3 to quit
Calculating compound interest
The result is 1284.027588
```

Summary

In this chapter you saw how C programs are built. I explained top-down design and how it applies to C programming. You considered how to split programs into functions and then you learned how to use your own functions or existing library functions.

Review questions

1 Define the term *top-down design*. What relationship does this concept have to structured programming?

2 What function does every C program have?

3 What are the parts of a function?

4 What is an *argument*? What is a *parameter*?

5 What are library functions? What must you do to make a library function available within one of your own C programs?

Exercises

1 Write a function to find the cube of a number; don't use the pow( ) library function.

2 Incorporate the function you wrote in exercise 1 into a short program that asks for a number from the user and then finds the cube of the number and the cube of half the number, printing each result on a separate line with appropriate text accompanying the result.

3 A close look at the output from the new FINANCE program shown in figure 11.1 reveals that this program doesn't exit as elegantly as it should; it forces the user to go through entering the balance, rate, and number of months again before allowing the user to quit. Rewrite the program so that the user is given the opportunity to quit immediately after results are displayed.

4 Further rewrite the FINANCE program so that the input tasks are handled by a separate function.

12

About Data Streams

● **In this chapter:**

- **How do I deal with text entered by the user and results produced by my program on different computer systems?**

- **C works with data so that the same functions can be used on different kinds of computers**

- **What are the C stream input and output functions?**

- **Change the source or destination of data within your computer's operating system**

Getting data in and getting results back out—two of the most important tasks your programs must handle. One of the beauties of C is that it features built-in functions that make this task easy and also gives you the capability to run the same program on any computer system that has a C compiler. . . ➤

When you, as a programmer or a user, work with a computer program, all you see are the characters on-screen that represent the program's input, output, or source code. Whether such a program exists on a PC, a UNIX mainframe, or a Macintosh laptop is of no concern to you at all. When you're limited to using data in character form, as you are in this book, all programs look and act pretty much the same in any computing environment.

From your program's point of view, however, things are quite different. In order to read input and write output, a program must be provided with specific information about the innards of the computer that it's running on. This is the sort of information that gets folded into a program when its object code, having been compiled, is linked prior to running. The linker, by making available code from the appropriate function libraries, gives a program the ability to interface correctly with the hardware that it will be running on.

The manner that input data is provided in and output data is expected in varies from computer to computer. Because C is a portable language, these differences must be hidden from the source code, including any I/O instructions specific to a certain computer—such instructions prevent the program from running on other computers. What's needed is some way to interface the C programming language with the character-based I/O capabilities of different computing systems. C accomplishes this by using data streams.

Data streaming along

In this chapter, through the medium of data streams, you explore the concept of device-independent I/O. Naturally, I'll offer a technical definition of what constitutes a data stream. For now, think of data streams as sections of a garden hose; they can be coupled to a number of standard C files whose internal workings aren't important to your program.

 Plain English, please!

Device-independent I/O refers to getting data into and out of a computer program without regard to the specific hardware that's being used. Details regarding the keyboard and the monitor, for instance, are of no importance to a program using device-independent I/O.

What's a data stream?

For more information about disk operations, see chapter 24, "What You Need To Know about Disks and Their Files."

All I/O operations in C are done using data streams. There are other C operations, such as working with disk files, that also use streams. Since data streams are so important to C, what exactly are they?

 Plain English, please!

> A **data stream** is a sequence of characters flowing either into (input) or out of (output) a program. Each character in a stream is represented by a single byte, which is eight binary digits. Numerically, a byte can represent any integer from 0 to 255. By convention, each possible value of a byte is associated with a single character or with a control action. The standard used most often is called ASCII. **99**

Where and how C uses data streams

C uses data streams every place where data flows from or to a program. Sources for such data include the keyboard and disk files, while destinations include the monitor, printer, and disk files. In fact, there's a special file associated with each data stream. Different streams can also be distinguished from each other by the exact nature of the data they're carrying, as you'll see.

There are five predefined streams

A C program has immediate access to five predefined data streams, each associated with a specific stream file. When I say file, I'm talking about something slightly different than a text file such as the source code for a C program. Like disk files, these standard stream files serve as destinations for data. Unlike disk files, however, you don't have to do anything to make the stream files available. They're set up and enabled automatically every time a C program is run.

The names, descriptions, and associated devices of the five standard C data streams are listed in the following table.

Name	Description	Device
stdin	Standard input	Keyboard
stdout	Standard output	Screen

continues

Name	Description	Device
stderr	Standard error messages	Screen
stdprn	Standard printer	Printer (such as LPT1 in DOS)
stdaux	Standard auxiliary	Serial communications port (such as COM1 in DOS)

Each of these stream files is connected, like your home's plumbing, to the appropriate device. Establishing or maintaining the connection requires nothing from you. All you need to concern yourself with is how to interact with the streams themselves; a task you accomplish using the appropriate library functions. How to use these functions is the subject of the greater part of this chapter.

Two different types of data streams

Before moving to the C library functions that work with streams, you need to consider one other fact about C data streams. Data streams differ from each other in the way that data flows through them. It's not that the data are of a different nature—like a hose carrying water versus one carrying compressed air. Rather, the difference is in how the data is sent through—like a hose carrying a continuous stream of water versus one carrying water in pulses or bursts. Smoothly flowing data applies to binary data streams; pulsed data applies to text data streams.

A **binary data stream** is a continuous flow of 1s and 0s. Depending on the computer system, this flow may be interpreted as coming in words, which are equal-length groups of bits. A byte (eight bits) is one example of a word of a certain length, but systems use other word lengths; 16-, 32-, and 64-bit words are common these days. However the computer sees it, a binary data stream is still just a continuous flow. The data in it can be interpreted in any way conceivable; it's up to the device receiving the binary data stream to attach the correct interpretation to the data it's receiving.

A **text data stream**, on the other hand, has a very specific interpretation. The data in such a stream is organized very definitely into bytes, each byte representing a text character. These characters are further organized into **lines**; a line is really just a string of characters. The end of each line is marked by a special ASCII character called the **new-line character**; this is one of the special control characters mentioned earlier in this chapter. The new-line character has a decimal value of 10 (binary 00001010). A line of characters in a text data stream can have up to 255 characters in C, although it's the presence of a new-line character and not the actual line length that separates one line from the next.

Binary streams in C are used principally with disk files; as such, they're a subject for a later chapter. The remainder of this chapter devotes itself to the library functions, which is intended for use with text streams. All these functions are concerned with I/O; some of them you've learned about already—though not yet in detail. You'll look at the functions available, what stream each is associated with, when and how streams can be changed or specified, and how to use the more common I/O functions.

How do I use I/O stream functions?

C divides the I/O stream functions into two groups: those dealing with input and those intended for output. The former are associated entirely with the standard input stream `stdin`, which is the stream connected to the keyboard. The latter group of I/O functions is usually associated with the standard output stream, `stdout`, which is the stream associated with the monitor. Some of these functions, however, also work with the other output streams (`stderr`, `stdprn`, `stdaux`).

For the most part, the prototypes for the standard I/O stream functions are found in the header file `stdio.h`. Some of the functions require other header files, such as `stdlib.h`, `stdargs.h`, and `conio.h`. Table 12.1 lists the stream I/O functions available in ANSI Standard C. You'll note that the functions tend to come in pairs; one member of a pair is associated with a specific stream, and the other must be connected to an appropriate stream using that stream's name as a parameter. Both members of a pair of functions accomplish much the same task, however.

Table 12.1 Library functions for stream input and output

Specific stream	Specify stream	Action performed
Output functions		
`printf()`	`fprintf()`	Formatted output
`vprintf()`	`vfprintf()`	Formatted output; variable argument list

continues

Table 12.1 Continued

Specific stream	Specify stream	Action performed
Output functions		
puts()	fputs()	String output
putchar()	putc(), fputc()	Character output
Input functions		
scanf()	fscanf()	Formatted input
gets()	fgets()	String input
getchar()	getc(), fgetc()	Character input
perror()	None	Output error string

In the remainder of the chapter I cover the more important functions listed in table 12.1. Before you're done, you apply what you've learned to sprucing up the input and output of any of your existing C programs. Now, because no program can function without data to work on, let's start by looking at stream input functions.

Getting input from the keyboard

Although some of the C input functions require you to specify what stream to use, the kind of input you're concerned with in this chapter always comes from the keyboard. C input functions can work with single characters, entire lines of data, and with input that's formatted to certain specifications.

Functions for character input

The character input functions retrieve a single character at a time from the specified input stream; generally stdin. If there are no more characters remaining in the stream, the function returns the code for end of file (EOF). In the header file stdio.h, EOF is a symbolic constant with the value -1.

 Plain English, please!

The code for **end of file** (**EOF**) is a single, ASCII character that tells a program that there's no more data in the file currently being looked at. This character has the binary value 11111111. **99**

Whenever a C program encounters a character input function, it pauses and waits for user input. A function may wait for the user to press the Enter key before proceeding. Such a function is said to use **buffered input** because all the keys pressed by the user prior to Enter are stored in memory in the **keyboard buffer**. If a function retrieves a character immediately from stdin without waiting for Enter to be pressed, that function is said to be **unbuffered**.

In addition to buffering, another key difference between character input functions is whether they display typed characters on the screen. A function that sends the character typed to stdout **echoes** the character. Because stdout is the data stream associated with the monitor, such an input function displays every character typed by the user. Functions that don't send characters typed to stdout are said to be **non-echoing**.

With these facts established, let's look at some of the character input functions available in C.

getchar()

The getchar() function uses the buffer and echoes input back to stdout. It retrieves a single character from stdin, the input stream that the function is automatically and unalterably associated with.

Speaking of getchar()

The function prototype for getchar() is provided in the header file stdio.h. The prototype for this function is

```
int getchar(void);
```

The keyword void in the prototype indicates that the getchar() function doesn't accept any parameters, which is typical for the input functions that are already associated with an input stream. The function returns an integer value; this is an integer from 0 to 255 representing the ASCII code for the character typed by the user. (Refer to appendix B, "ASCII Characters," for what numbers are associated with each character or control code.)

To call the getchar() function, you place it on a line by itself, or include it in an assignment statement, as in

```
CharacterTyped = getchar();
```

The following short program uses the getchar() function to retrieve characters typed from the keyboard. It prints the characters using the putchar() function, the output counterpart to getchar().

```
#include <stdio.h>
int CharacterTyped;
main()
{
while (CharacterTyped != '\n')
        {
        CharacterTyped = getchar();
        putchar(CharacterTyped);
        }
}
```

The integer value obtained for each character typed is stored in the variable CharacterTyped. The while loop in this program compares each character with the new-line character (that's what \n means). The getchar() function waits until the user presses Enter; then each character entered is read, one at a time, into CharacterTyped. The character is compared with the new-line character. If it isn't a new-line character, the character is sent to the screen by the putchar() function, and the next character is read in. In effect, this program echoes back to the screen whatever the user enters.

Some more functions for character input

The getch() function is an unbuffered, non-echoing version of the getchar() function described in the previous section. When you use this function, the character typed by the user is immediately retrieved by the function, without the user having to press the Enter key first. This function also does not echo its output to stdout, meaning characters typed don't appear on the screen unless you put them there with some sort of output statement. The getche() function is similar to getch(), except it echoes input to the screen.

The only problem with these two functions is that they are not part of ANSI Standard C. Your compiler might have them; then again, it might not.

Function keys are special

Before going on to consider line input, there's a special group of keys for PC users to consider: the function keys. When a user presses one of these keys, two character values are generated and fed to stdin. The first is the **null character**, 0; that's how a program recognizes that a function key has been pressed. The second character returned is an integer value indicating the actual key. These keys are called **extended keys** because the values returned when they're pressed extend beyond one byte—they're two bytes.

A program that handles input from the function keys needs to be on the lookout for the null character. If a getchar() function returns the null character, the program needs to immediately check the value of the next character to determine exactly what function key was pressed. It can then go on to do whatever task is associated with that key—for example, quitting the program altogether if the user pressed the F1 key. You look at handling function keys in chapter 20, "Control a Program—Where It Goes, What It Does...." For now, knowing that the second character in the code for the F1 key is 59, you ought to be able to make sense of the following brief example:

```
#include <stdio.h>
#include <conio.h>
int CharacterTyped;
main()
{
CharacterTyped = 1;
while (CharacterTyped != 0)
        {
        CharacterTyped = getch();
        }
CharacterTyped = getch();
if (CharacterTyped==59)
    puts("User pressed F1");
}
```

How can I use this in the real world?

How many times within a program have you been asked to "Enter y to continue; enter n to quit," or something of that sort? Ever wondered how to do it? It's easy using the getch() function. All you need to do is have getch() read a character typed by the user into a variable, then compare that character using if. A simple routine to do so might look like this:

```
puts("\nEnter y to to continue, anything else to quit");
CharacterTyped = getch();
if (CharacterTyped == 'y')
    {
    "YES" STATEMENTS
    }
else
    {
    "NO" STATEMENTS
    }
```

code The preceding code first sets an integer variable named CharacterTyped equal to 1 to initialize it. It then enters a while loop that executes as long as CharacterTyped isn't 0. (That's the reason for setting the variable equal to 1, so the loop executes at least once.) Within the loop, the program uses the getch() function to get input from the user. If the user presses any key other than a function key, nothing happens. The loop continues.

If the user presses a function key, however, two bytes are entered into the input buffer, represented by the stream file stdin. The first byte is equal to 0; thus, the program exits the while loop. Using getch() again, the program immediately retrieves the next byte from stdin. If this byte is equal to 59, the user pressed the F1 key. The if statement's test expression evaluates to True in this case, and the message "User pressed F1" is printed to the screen. Otherwise, nothing is printed, and the program quits.

Functions for line input

The C line input functions include gets() and fgets(). Each of these functions reads everything in the input stream up to the next new-line character. From here it gets complicated. First of all, these two functions work with strings; a topic you haven't yet learned about. Secondly, they both take and return pointers as their arguments and results. This is another subject yet to be talked about. Chapter 15, "String Variables as Places for Characters," discusses strings. Pointers are first discussed in chapter 17, "How to Indirectly Access Data Storage with Pointers." For these reasons, discussion of gets() and fgets() is deferred until chapter 19, "Get Strings To Do What You Want." Having punted line input out of the way, you now take a look at the last type of input: formatted input.

Functions for formatted input

The scanf() function reads an entire line of input from studin, interprets that input according to a format string, and then assigns the interpreted input to one or more variables.

The following is a list of a number of conversion specifiers to use with scanf():

Specifier	Meaning
d	Decimal integer
i	Integer in octal, decimal, or hexadecimal form
o	Integer in octal notation
u	Unsigned decimal integer
x	Hexadecimal integer
c	Character
s	Character string
e	Floating-point number
f	Floating-point number
g	Floating-point number
[characters]	A string of characters; only those listed in brackets are acceptable
[^characters]	A string of characters; only those not listed in brackets are acceptable

Speaking of scanf()

The general form of the scanf() function is

```
scanf("format_string", &variable1[,...&variablelast]);
```

The *format_string* is very important; it tells C how to interpret the characters entered by the user. The *format_string* must contain one conversion specifier for each *variable* that data is read into. Conversion specifiers are groups of characters introduced by the percent sign. A conversion specifier has the form

```
%[*][field_width][precision_modifier]type_specifier
```

The asterisk is optional, telling C to perform the required conversion to the data, but avoiding assigning it to a variable. The optional *field_width* specifier tells C how many characters to read into the variable. The *precision_modifier*, also optional, indicates how much RAM should be assigned to the result. Only the *type_specifier* is required; it indicates how the data should actually be converted.

Thus, to read four characters into an integer variable called MyVariable, interpreting the characters as an unsigned decimal, you use

```
scanf("%4u", &MyVariable);
```

One extra thing about the scanf() function: When a program runs, scanf() only takes as much data from stdin as it requires to meet the conversion specifiers in the format string. If the user types extra data, that data is left in the input buffer—ready and willing to be input the next time an input function is called. Because the extra data more than likely will be garbage (it's extra data not asked for or accommodated by the program), the program produces bad results.

What to do? You need some way to flush the input buffer (that is, remove the data that's there) every time scanf() is called. One way to do this is to use the gets() function immediately after calling scanf(). The gets() discussion is delayed until chapter 19; flushing the input buffer is discussed there as well. For now, keep in mind that if you enter bad data in any of your practice programs, you might get some very strange results.

Creating screen output

There's a companion output function for each of the input functions you've seen so far. As with input functions, the C stream output functions can be

---

Catch the bug

What's wrong with the scanf() statement in the following code?

```
int inputvar;
main()
{
scanf("%5f",&inputvar);
```

Answer: *This* scanf() *statement uses* f *as a type specifier in the format string. This specifies a floating-point number. The variable being read into, however, is an integer. Even if the user enters nothing but decimal digits, the result is garbage. The solution is to either make* inputvar *a floating-point variable or change the type specifier to an integer type (such as* u *or* d*).*

divided into those that deal with characters, those that work with lines, and those that return formatted output. The output functions tend to come in pairs that accomplish the same task, one function being devoted exclusively to the stream stdout, and the other being available for use with other output streams.

Creating character output

The putchar() function, first introduced in conjunction with getchar() earlier in the chapter, outputs a single ASCII character to the screen. The function takes a single integer or character argument. The result is sent to stdout.

The function fputc() is similar to putchar(), except that it allows you to specify what output stream to use; putchar() itself is permanently connected to stdout. The prototype for fputc() is

```
int fputc(int c, FILE file_pointer);
```

The argument *file_pointer* represents a pointer to the output file. Again, pointers are covered starting with chapter 17. However, the name of one of the standard output streams suffices. Thus, you can send a single character to the system printer using

```
fputc(CharacterToPrint, stdprn);
```

Speaking of putchar()

The prototype for putchar() is found in the header file stdio.h. It is

```
int putchar(int c);
```

The value c is an expression that evaluates to either an integer or character. Integers must be in the range from 0 to 255. As for character results, the contents of a char type variable suffice. (Recall that a variable of type char is just a one-byte integer.) Although it might seem superfluous, the function returns an integer value that corresponds to the character sent to stdout. Of course, your program can entirely ignore this returned result. The following call to putchar() sends a single character a to the screen:

```
putchar(97);
```

Producing line output

The input functions `gets()` and `fgets()` have their counterparts in the output functions `puts()` and `fputs()`. Each of these functions takes a string as an argument and sends the string to the relevant output stream. The `puts()` function is permanently connected to `stdout`. To use `fputs()`, you must specify what stream to send the output to.

Up until now in this book, you've only used literal string constants with the `puts()` function. Keep in mind that this function also accepts a string variable as an argument. Because strings are covered in chapter 15, the string output functions are discussed there.

Creating formatted output

These functions are `printf()`, which sends output to `stdout`, and `fprintf()`, whose output stream you must specify as a parameter.

Speaking of `printf()`

The standard form of a call to `printf()` is

```
printf("format_string",variable1[,...variablelast]);
```

The *format_string* is similar to the format string used for the formatted input function `scanf()`, except that any literal text that appears in the string is sent to `stdout`, rather than ignored as in `scanf()`. Embedded within the *format_string* are conversion specifiers similar to those used for `scanf()`, which tell C how to output the *variables* or expressions that follow the *format_string*. A conversion specifier is necessary for each expression if you want output. Conversion specifiers take the following form:

```
%[flag][field_width][.precision][l]conversion_type
```

The *flag*, an optional part of the specifier, indicates certain formatting options:

- The - flag causes output to be left-justified

- The + flag precedes signed numbers with + or -

- A space means positive numbers are preceded by a space.

continues

The *field_width* indicates how many characters to display. *precision*, intro-duced by a decimal point, is important: it indicates how many characters to the right of the decimal to display. The l character is used to modify the results of other specifiers. Only the *conversion_type* character is required. Conversion types follow:

Type character	Meaning
d or i	Signed decimal integer
u	Unsigned decimal integer
o	Unsigned octal integer
x or X	Unsigned hexadecimal integer
c	ASCII character
e or E	Floating-point number in scientific notation
f	Floating-point number in decimal notation
g or G	Engineering notation; converts to scientific for certain exponent values
n	Suppress corresponding variable and display nothing
s	String
%	Display the % character

Of all the aspects of a conversion specifier, the part indicating precision may be of the most use to you immediately. Up until now, floating-point calculations have displayed results with six decimals to the right of the point. But many of your calculations have involved dollars and cents, for which only two decimals are needed. To suppress the extra decimals, you can use an expression like

```
printf("The result is %.2f ", amount);
```

%...f indicates that the contents in the floating-point variable amount should be printed in floating-point decimal notation, and .2 indicates that only two digits to the right of the decimal point should be shown.

Sending your input or output someplace else

I've said several times in this chapter that certain stream I/O functions in C are permanently connected to a given stream (`stdin` or `stdout`), and that there's nothing you can do to change this. As it turns out, depending on what computer system you're using, this may not be strictly true. While from C's point of view the given I/O stream may be fixed, from the point of view of the operating system you might be able to change it, particularly within DOS and UNIX, with a process named I/O redirection.

 Plain English, please!

I/O redirection is the process of taking information destined for one source and changing its direction to another. It's like taking the garden hose off your lawn sprinkler and putting it into a child's wading pool. You accomplish the process by issuing a command to your computer's operating system, telling it the new source or new destination for its input or output. **99**

Catch the bug

There are a few problems with the call to `printf()` in the following short section of code. What are they?

```
int x,y;
float z;
main()
{
scanf("%d %d %f", &x, &y, &z);
printf("The values entered are %f and %f.2",x,z,y);
```

Answer: First, there are three variables listed in the call to `printf()` *but only two conversion specifiers. The first conversion specifier pairs up with the variable x; however, this variable is an integer. Attempting to display it in floating-point form yields strange results. The second conversion specifier appears to be trying to display only two decimals to the right of the point; the* `.2` *part should be before the* `f`. *A correct call to* `printf()` *follows:*

```
printf("The values entered are %d, %d and %.2f",x,y,z);
```

You redirect I/O to outside your C programs from within the operating system that the program is running on. The exact way you do it depends on the operating system. In DOS, you include extra instructions on the command line when you enter a program's name to be run. For example,

```
finance >foutput.txt
```

redirects the output from a program called FINANCE to a text file named `foutput.txt`. You can also redirect the output to a printer with

```
finance >prn
```

Again, the details depend on the operating system. Reversing the redirection character (at least in DOS), you can redirect input:

```
finance <testval.txt
```

The preceding line causes the FINANCE program to take its input not from the keyboard but from a text file named `testval.txt`. You can use this sort of redirection to automate testing of your programs, for instance. If the text file is properly formatted, with each entry on a separate line and coming in the correct order, you can use input redirection to run modified versions of your program with the same input, without having to rekey the input each time.

Summary

In this chapter you learned more about character-based I/O. You saw that C uses input and output data streams to handle I/O. Data streams are dedicated files that data is sent to or gotten from. You looked at both stream input functions and stream output functions. Finally, you considered redirecting I/O within your computer's operating system.

Review questions

1 What is meant by *device independence*? How is this related to C streams?

2 Define *echoing* and *buffering*.

3 What is the name of the standard input stream? Of the stream connected to the system printer?

4 Name a function for character input and another for formatted output.

5 Define *I/O redirection*. Can you do it from within a C program?

Exercises

1 Write a short program that reads a single character from the keyboard and writes it immediately back to the screen on a separate line, until the user enters a capital **Q**.

2 Write a `printf()` statement to output four variables: the first two unsigned integers and the last two floating point. Separate the variables with tabs. Have eight characters print for each variable, with three digits to the right of the decimal for the floating-point variables. Use a, b, c, and d for the variable names.

3 Write a short program that produces some sort of numerical result (calculating compound interest will do) while drawing boxes around the results using asterisks. Allow the user to repeat the program, pressing **n** to quit. Use output field widths of nine characters, and include a box around the program's title.

13

Some Optional Ways To Store Data

● **In this chapter:**

- **Functions can refer to variables in different ways**

- **Use the same variable name for different variables!**

- **The real differences between variables**

Like a good waiter, you want variables to be there the moment you need them and invisible when you don't need them. Scope helps you keep variables in all the right places at all the right times . . . . ▶

'll admit, coming up with new names for variables all the time can strain one's creativity, especially when you're developing variables for different parts of a program that store much the same data. If, for example, you were working with an account balance within `main()` and several of its constituent functions, you might be tempted to give the value the name `Balance` everywhere, to save having to come up with several different but intelligible names. Unfortunately, creating such a variable in the way you've done so far will certainly cause problems.

Unless you find some way to restrict its field of action, the same name refers to the same variable in all parts of a program. If the program is always working with the same data under this name, you won't encounter problems. However, if you want to preserve the variable's contents in one place while performing a manipulation on it in another, you'll run into trouble. Any assignment statement that reads data into the problem variable in one place will wipe out its old contents in another. Again, you can just create multiple variables, giving each a distinct name, but this adds unnecessary lines to your program and makes your code hard to read and understand. What you need is some way to let you reuse the same variable name in different contexts, which is actually something that C makes easy.

A variable's field of action

C, along with most other computer languages, allows you to restrict any variable's field of action. You can, for instance, restrict a variable to use only within a certain function. Even if you have a variable with the exact same name in another function, the two have no relationship to each other. They act like two separate variables with two separate names. You can think of such variables as "on-duty" and "off-duty," with the same storage space in the computer possibly occupied by "shifts" of variables, with each shift accomplishing much the same work without interfering with other variables of the same name, and with, presumably, the same job to do.

Scoping out places for variables

Depending on where and how a variable is declared, it ends up with a certain specific field of action: that is, a function or a group of functions within which it may be used. This field of action is usually called the variable's scope.

Plain English, please!

Scope refers to the extent to which different functions within a program can access the contents of a variable. A variable that a given function can access is said to be **visible** to that function. Scope also refers to how long a variable persists in the computer's memory: When it's created, and when it and its contents are destroyed.

As an example, consider the following two short programs. At first glance, each seems to do the same thing, but the results of running each are quite different.

```c
#include <stdio.h>
int MyVariable;
void MyFunction(void);
main()
{
MyVariable=100;
printf("%d\n",MyVariable);
MyVariable=99;
MyFunction();
}

void MyFunction(void)
{
printf("%d\n",MyVariable);
}
```

Running this program produces the results shown in figure 13.1.

Fig. 13.1

Results of running a program with one variable whose scope makes it available to every function in the program.

```
100
 99
```

Now, compare the preceding program with the following:

```c
#include <stdio.h>
void MyFunction(void);
main()
{
int MyVariable;
```

```
MyVariable=100;
printf("%d\n",MyVariable);
MyVariable=99;
MyFunction();
}

void MyFunction(void)
{
int MyVariable;
printf("%d\n",MyVariable);
}
```

If you compare the second example with the first, you'll see that the line that declares MyVariable has been moved to within the main() function. Also, the line has been copied and inserted into the MyFunction function. Otherwise, nothing changed. Compare the results in figure 13.2, though.

Fig. 13.2
Results of running a program with one variable, whose scope makes it available only to the function within which it is declared.

```
100
71
```

The first time through, the MyVariable variable retains the value of 99 that it was assigned in the main() function. This value is printed by the MyFunction function, even though the variable wasn't passed to the function in a formal parameter list. In the revised version of the program, however, printing MyVariable produces a seemingly random result. The main() function still assigns 99 to MyVariable, but MyFunction doesn't seem to be aware of this assignment.

There's a good reason for this result. In the second program, MyVariable actually represents two different variables that have nothing to do with each other. The second MyVariable is created when MyFunction runs. As the variable wasn't assigned a value, accessing it with the printf() function returns whatever old data was left in RAM. (Recall from chapter 4, "Places To Store Data," the importance of initializing variables so as to avoid picking up garbage data like this.) In the first example, MyVariable refers to the same variable in both functions; either one can access or modify its contents.

What good is scope?

Perhaps the most important use of scope is to keep data in a procedure isolated from meddling by other procedures. As you might glean from the preceding examples, a variable declared within a function is only accessible within that function. We say that the variable is local to the function that created it. Returning to our shift analogy, the variable is only on duty as long as the function that created it is running. When that function stops executing and returns a value to the function that called it, the variable goes off duty. Its contents are inaccessible to other procedures.

This process works the other way, and that may be more important yet. If the variables within the main() function are declared to be local to main(), functions called by main() can't change these variables' contents. The following short program (a modified version of the example shown previously) demonstrates this fact:

```
#include <stdio.h>

void MyFunction(void);
main()
{
int MyVariable;
MyVariable=100;
printf("%d\n",MyVariable);
MyVariable=99;
MyFunction();
printf("%d\n",MyVariable);
}

void MyFunction(void)
{
int MyVariable;
printf("%d\n",MyVariable);
MyVariable=125;
}
```

MyFunction appears to change MyVariable's value to 125 before returning to main(). Look at figure 13.3 for what happens when you run the program, though:

Fig. 13.3
The value of
MyVariable within
main() remains 99,
even though
MyFunction appears
to have changed it to
125.

```
100
 87
 99
```

The contents of MyVariable within the function MyFunction varies from computer to computer, depending on what leftover garbage happens to be in RAM.

Variables declared outside of functions

The example in the preceding section shows the danger of using variables that are declared outside of any function. Up until now, this is the way you've always declared variables. You were creating what are called external variables, even if you didn't know it. External variables can be useful if treated carefully, but they can also cause a lot of trouble.

 Plain English, please!

An **external variable** is one created outside of all the functions in a program. The declaration for such a variable precedes that of the main() function, as in the following example, which creates an external integer variable called x:

```
int x;
main()
{
```

External variables and scope

An external variable is available to all functions within a program. You might say it's on call, ready to divulge its contents to any function that asks. As I've said, up until this chapter, every variable you've created has been an external variable.

Another word for an external variable is **global variable**. Just as global warming refers to increased heat the world over, global variables are

For more information on source code files, see chapter 29, "Use Code That You or Somebody Else Has Already Written."

useable throughout a program. It turns out, though, that I need to define what I mean by "program." In this context, the word refers to all the code within a single source code file. You see, you can create a program that uses more than one source code file. External variables behave differently in such instances.

For now, though, all our programs have been contained within a single file, and so external variables apply to every part of them. You declare them once

Catch the bug

The following short program uses a function to return the cube of a number. It then takes the value returned and adds it to another number, printing the result. As written, though, the program won't obtain the correct result. Why not?

```
#include <stdio.h>
float x,y,z;
float FindCube(float x);
main()
{
x=10;
z=9;
printf("%f\t%f\n",x,z);
y=FindCube(x);
y=y+z;
printf("%f\n",y);
scanf("%f",&x);
}

float FindCube(float x)
{
z=x*x*x;
return z;
}
```

Answer: *The number to be added to the cube of* x *is maintained in the variable* z. *Unfortunately,* FindCube() *uses* z *to return the cube of* x. *In the process,* FindCube() *destroys the old contents of* z. *The easiest way to correct this is to eliminate the reference to* z *within the function* FindCube *and have it return the expression* (x*x*x) *directly.*

and use them everywhere. If, however, external variables can be dangerous, when should you use them if at all?

What do I need external variables for?

One of the most important principles of top-down design and structured programming is that functions should be kept as isolated from each other as possible. A function should make no assumptions about other functions in a program, including what variables those functions may use. A function accepts its data by means of its formal argument list and returns data through the return statement. Anything it does in the meantime is personal and private.

The advantage to this way of programming is that you can reuse such a function in another context without having to modify it. At the very least, you can copy the function's source code and insert it into a new program, confident that the function will continue to work in its new setting just as it did in the old one.

Programming in this way requires you to use local variables. This is the only way to keep the data in each function isolated from all the others. Times may occur, however, when you need external variables. If, for example, most of the functions in a program need access to a particular item of data and it does not matter if the function changes that item, then it's not just okay but probably recommended that you use an external variable.

How can I use this in the real world?

Among the most important uses for external variables are the symbolic constants you use in your program. Constants, after all, can't be changed, so no danger exists of a function disturbing a constant's contents. Passing a constant's value as a parameter also makes little sense. So does redefining it within a function, when you can define it once for the entire program. If you choose to define True as 1 as False as 0, for instance, you can define them as external symbolic constants, and use them throughout every function in your program.

To reconcile using external variables with good structured programming techniques, you ought to make your use of such variables explicit within each function that uses them. You do so using the keyword extern, which explicitly declares that the function that it appears in is using an external variable. As a programmer, you may find such information useful at a later time, when trying to incorporate the function into a new project.

Although you can explicitly declare external symbolic constants in this manner, this is probably overkill.

So is there an internal variable?

No, but the opposite of an external variable does exist; it is a **local variable**. If an external variable is on call, a local variable works a shift. It is only active while the function that created it is running. Unless you specify otherwise, its contents disappear when the function itself terminates. Whether the variable's data disappears, it's never accessible to any function other than the one that created it.

Speaking of external variable declaration statements

An external variable declaration statement takes the form

```
function_name()
{
extern type name;
```

type refers to a C variable type, and *name* is the name of the variable. To declare the external floating-point variable Balance, you'd include the line

```
extern float Balance;
```

in the function, immediately after the opening brace.

To use local variables, declare them in the function

Again, to declare a local variable, include its definition after the name of the function that it's declared in, right after the opening brace that marks the function's statement block. The following example shows such a declaration:

```
int z;
main()
{
int x,y;
```

In this example, the variable z is external; variables x and y are local to the main() function.

Variables declared as part of a function's argument list are considered local to that function: you don't declare them again. In effect, the function definition itself declares the variables and makes them local. Consider this example:

```
float MyFunction(int x, int y)
{
int z;
```

These lines actually declare three variables: the argument variables x and y and the integer variable z. All three are local to the MyFunction() function. Remember that the variables themselves are not passed when one function calls another, but the variables' contents are.

Local variables in blocks are specific to that block

You can actually make variables so local that they aren't even available to all parts of a procedure. If you declare a variable within a statement block, that variable is local to the block only: other blocks within the procedure don't have access to it. Again, you declare these local variables immediately after the opening brace that marks the beginning of the block.

A good use for such local variables is as counters in for loops. You could use the same variable name for each counter of this type without having to worry that leftover data will interfere. The following code shows two variables called Counter, each local to a particular block:

```
#include <stdio.h>
main()
{
    {
    int Counter;
    for (Counter =0; Counter<=10; Counter++)
        {
            {
            int Counter;
            for (Counter =5; Counter<=7; Counter++)
            printf("%d",Counter);
            }
            printf("%d",Counter);
        }
    }
}
```

In this way, you can use the same name for the counter variable, even though one block appears entirely within the other. The variable named Counter in the inner for loop has no effect on the variable named Counter in the outer loop.

How can I use this in the real world?

Of all the probems solved by scoped variables, the eternal need to come up with different variable names is, to me, among the most important. This is especially true of temporary, work-a-day variables like loop counters. By making loop counters and such entirely local to the statement blocks in which they're used, you avoid having to come up with a different name for counter variables, thus relieving you of a considerable intellectual strain.

Using local variables wherever possible also makes it easier to spot and correct program errors. A lot of errors are caused by statements in one function doing naughty things to variables in another. This is only possible if the variables are available in both. Making variables local shields them from other, naughty functions.

Local and external aren't the only types of variables

Earlier in the chapter, I said that a local variable's contents are destroyed when the function or block that it's declared in exits, *unless you specify otherwise*. Now it's time to explain what I meant. It turns out, you can have a function preserve the contents of one or more of its variables if you want. Such variables are called static variables.

 Plain English, please!

A **static variable** is one whose contents remain in memory in-between executions of the function that created it. After it is created the first time, a static variable remains in existence, preserving its contents at all times, until the entire program finishes executing. A static local variable is still only available within the function that created it. The opposite of a static variable is an **automatic variable**, one that is created each time it's declared and destroyed each time the function or block that created it exits.

What is the difference between static and automatic variables?

By default, all local variables are automatic. They're created when needed and destroyed when no longer needed. Static variables persist in memory, even when the function that created them isn't active. You don't need to do anything special to make a variable automatic, but you need to include the keyword `static` in the definition of a static variable.

To see the difference between static and automatic variables, consider the following two examples:

```
#include <stdio.h>
int Increment(void);
main()
{
int counter, x;
for (counter = 1; counter <=10; counter++)
    {
```

```
            x = Increment();
            printf("%d\n",x);
        }
}
int Increment(void)
{
int x = 0;
x++;
return x;
}
```

The preceding simply prints the value 1 on ten separate lines. Now, alter the code by adding the keyword static.

```
#include <stdio.h>
int Increment(void);
main()
{
int counter, x;
for (counter = 1; counter <=10; counter++)
    {
        x = Increment();
        printf("%d\n",x);
    }
}
int Increment(void)
{
static int x = 0;
x++;
return x;
}
```

Now the program prints a new value each time.

Speaking of static local variables

To declare a static local variable, use the form:

    static *type name*;

type is a valid C variable type, and *name* is the variable's name. The following creates a static variable named Persist within the main() function:

    main()
    {
    static int Persist;

Catch the bug

What's wrong with the following program?

```
#include <stdio.h>
int Increment(void);
main()
{
int y, x;
for (y = 1; y <=10; y++)
    {
        x = Increment();
    }
        printf("The function was called %d times\n",x);
}
int Increment(void)
{
int Counter = 0;
Counter++;
return Counter;
}
```

Answer: *The function has no idea how many times it was called. You need to make the* Counter *variable within it static.*

Q&A *Okay, in the preceding example, why isn't the variable* x *reset to 0 every time* Increment() *is called? It seems like the line* static int x = 0; *ought to do just that.*

The x = 0 part on the line declaring the variable x only works when the variable is first created; on subsequent calls to Increment(), the entire line declaring x is ignored. That's because the variable has already been created and is being kept in place because the keyword static was used. In practical terms, this means you can initialize any static variable without worrying that its former contents will be destroyed when you re-call the procedure that the variable was created in.

When do I use static variables?

Obviously, you should use static variables when you want to preserve the contents of a local variable between successive uses of the function that created it. You can't be much more precise than that because circumstances vary so much. However, if a function must know that it's been called before, you need to have at least one static variable within it. This might just be an integer variable that's set to 1 if the function has been called and is set to 0 initially when it hasn't yet been called.

Summary

In this chapter, you learned that the scope of a variable is its field of action. You then considered external, local, static, and automatic variables.

Review questions

1 Contrast an external variable with a local one. Where do you declare each?

2 What part of a function declaration also declares variables? What scope do these variables have?

3 What is an *automatic variable*? a *static variable*?

4 Would it make sense to have a static variable local to the `main()` function? For what reason?

5 Name a good use for external variables.

Exercises

1 Write declaration statements for a static integer variable named `Memory` and an automatic floating-point variable named `Answer`, making both local to a function named `Doodle` that accepts a single floating-point argument and returns a floating-point answer.

2 Write a short program that prints the sum of all the positive integers between zero and that number, for the integers 1 though 100. Use a nested `for` loop, with the same name for the variable counter within each loop.

3 Write a function to find the fourth power of a number. Have the function check to see if it's just been called with the same value. If so, have it return the answer immediately without recalculating it.

14

Call Several Variables by the Same Name

● **In this chapter:**

- **I have a whole bunch of variables and they're making my code difficult to read**

- **Grouping variables into something manageable**

- **Okay, I've got a group of variables, but how do I get information into or out of them**

- **Arrays sound like they were made to order for use in loops; am I right?**

Looking for a way to call several variables by the same name and allow your programs to specify which to use at any given time? C makes it easy using array variables . . . . ❯

Up to this point, you've considered variables that hold one value, although that value can be a character, an integer, or a floating-point number. You can have as many variables as you want, even several with similar names that store similar data: your closing bank balance at the end of each month is one example. In some cases, though, you can more conveniently group several such values under a single heading, referring to them by their position number or numbers within the group.

Real life is full of things that look and act like variables with multiple values. Think of a chess board, for instance. You can specify any square on the board by indicating the row and column. In this way, you can uniquely identify each square on the board without individually naming one. An old-fashioned desk with cubbyholes is another example: each cubbyhole was meant to hold letters from correspondents whose last name began with a particular letter. Even a modern spreadsheet is an example of a multivalue variable: each cell holds a unique value that you can specify using its row and column number. The good news is that C makes it easy to create variables that work in much the same way as cubbyholes and spreadsheets.

All these variables are related; is there any easier way to work with them?

Think of the structure of a cubbyhole desk. You could mimic it with 26 separate variables, but handling that many variables in code is cumbersome. A single, multivalue variable is much easier to manage. As in most programming languages, you create multiple-value variables in C using arrays.

 Plain English, please!

An **array** is a collection of variables, and each member of an array has the same name and the same data type. Individual members are referred to using a **subscript**, which is an integer expression enclosed in brackets, specifying one member of the array. For example, `MyArray[2]` refers to the third variable in an array (C starts numbering with 0).

You create arrays at the same time and in the same manner as you create other variables: with variable declaration statements. The only difference between a statement that creates an array and one that creates an ordinary variable is that for an array you must specify how many members it is to have. I'll show you exactly how to do this, later in the chapter.

There are limits when using arrays

You need to be aware that some limits exist on creating and using arrays. Arrays must have a definite size when you first create them. I mention this because a little later you will notice that you want to set the size of an array when a program runs, depending on the exact amount of data a program needs to hold. You can't really do this with standard arrays.

Faced with this restriction, you'll be tempted to make all your arrays quite large and ignore the unused space. That's fine, except you may run into a problem with RAM. Arrays have a way of consuming lots of memory. Exactly how much depends on the kind of data they're meant to hold. An array with 1,000 members of type `double`, for instance, occupies 8,000 bytes. This may not seem like much on an 8M computer, but not all of that vast RAM space is available to your C programs.

You see, your C compiler dictates the exact amount of memory available to you. In the process of compiling and linking a program, the maximum amount of RAM the program has access to is predetermined. If a program runs out of memory in this RAM space, even if there are acres and acres of RAM available outside it, the program crashes.

How can I use this in the real world?

Arrays are particularly useful for holding several values that you want to perform the same operation on. With an interest-bearing checking account, for instance, you can calculate the interest due on the account balance at the end of each month and add the interest to that balance, all using a single array and a loop rather than 12 separate variables and 12 separate pieces of code.

Arrays are also handy for keeping together data that is somehow related. The contents of a teacher's gradebook come to mind. An array for grades can hold the results of every test and exercise grade made by a given student. In fact, you could even combine the grade arrays for each student in a class into a single master array, much like a spreadsheet. The "columns" correspond to the test grades, while the "rows" refer to individual students. You then process such an array with nested loops.

Depending on the compiler, you may be dealing with as little as 64K of RAM at this point. In chapter 26, "Make Memory Work for You," you'll look at the different memory models your compiler might have and how to change them to give your programs more RAM. For now, though, just be aware of how much RAM arrays can eat, how limited your C program RAM may be, and how to design your arrays accordingly. After all, a good programming practice is not to consume computer resources indiscriminately, even if they seem to be there for the taking.

Create an array like you create a variable— sort of

Having dispensed with these preliminaries, you can now go on to creating and using these little sets of cubbyholes that C calls arrays. You need to examine when and where you create arrays, how to create arrays that look like a grid or spreadsheet in addition to those that look like a line of cubbyholes, and how to access the individual elements in an array. You'll start with how to create simple arrays and move on from there.

Speaking of creating an array variable

The general form of a statement to create an array variable is

    type array_name[#members];

type is a valid C data type, and *array_name* is a valid C variable name. The expression in square brackets defines how many array elements there are. Note that C begins numbering the elements in an array with 0. (Some compilers begin numbering with 1 as an option. You'll need to check out your particular case. For the remainder of this chapter, I'll assume your compiler numbers starting with 0.) The following statement creates a floating-point array called Balances with 12 members:

    float Balances[12];

Declaring an array is no different than declaring a variable

To repeat, you create arrays at the same time and place you create other variables, with a particular form of variable declaration statement.

Interpreting how many elements are in an array

The number in brackets following an array's name is important—important enough to merit its own name. In this book, I'll call this number the array's **index**. (Some writers call it a subscript.) When you declare an array, the index specifies how many members the array has. Later on, though, in the body of your program, you use the index to refer to a specific member of an array. For instance,

```
Balance[3]
```

refers to the fourth member of the array `Balance`. (Remember, you start counting with 0.)

Now here's the fun part. Within a program, you don't have to use a literal number or even a numeric expression in an array's index. You can actually use a variable or an expression containing a variable. In this case, the exact value referred to depends on the contents of the variable. For example,

```
Index = 2
Balance[Index]
```

In this case, the third member of `Balance` is referred to on the second line of the example. In effect, the computer replaces `Index` with its value and proceeds from there.

Enter another dimension— multidimensional arrays

Indices are so important, why not have lots of them? I've already hinted that arrays can have multiple indices, when I referred to arrays that resemble spreadsheets. For such an array, you seem to need two indices: one to specify the rows, the other the columns. Such an array is called a **multi-dimensional array**. You create multidimensional arrays the same way you create one-dimensional ones, but you tack on the extra index or indices. For example,

```
int Grades[10][30];
```

creates a two-dimensional array with 10 columns and 30 rows (or vice versa because C doesn't care about the conceptual relationship between the two dimensions). The expression

```
Grades[2][27]
```

refers to the twenty-eighth element in the third column.

Q&A ***Is there a limit to the number of indices I can give an array and thus to the number of dimensions it can have?***

Formally speaking, no. Practically speaking, yes. The limit has to do, again, with how much memory you have. Suppose you want to create an array to hold the grades on all exams for every student in a large school district. Suppose there are 10 exams, 10 students in a class (yeah, right), 10 classes in a school, 10 schools in an area, and 10 areas in the district. An appropriate array seems to need five indices and is specified with

```
float DistrictGrades[10][10][10][10][10];
```

I made it a floating-point array because teachers like to assign grades like 77.5 and 98.6. So far, so good. But how much memory does this array need? Multiply 10×10×10×10×10×4 bytes (for each floating-point value) to get 400,000 bytes (roughly 400K). Yet earlier, I said that your compiler might not let you have more than 64K! This array is going to bust that limit all to pieces and then some. Adding another dimension to this array, to let it track 10 districts, takes the RAM needed to 4,000,000 bytes.

So you see, multidimensional arrays grow very rapidly. You need to be aware of how much storage such an array needs before you blithely attempt to create it. Multiply the values of all the indices together, and multiply by the number of bytes needed for each member. If the value is much more than 10,000 (for now), consider splitting the array into smaller arrays.

Catch the bug

The following statement is meant to declare an integer array with a total of 60 members. What's wrong with it?

```
int LastFiveYears[4][11];
```

Answer: The array actually has 44 members. Although you access arrays beginning with 0 and not with 1, that isn't how you declare them. Thus, as it is, this array declaration creates an array with four columns and eleven rows, for a total of 44 members. The corrected declaration reads

```
int LastFiveYears[5][12];
```

I assume that arrays have to be initialized?

As with ordinary variables, arrays when first created contain whatever leftover garbage happens to be in RAM at the place assigned to them. Like ordinary variables, you can initialize arrays in the same statement you use to create them. You merely enclose the initial values in braces, separated by commas.

You can also initialize multidimensional arrays. Of course, you need to know how C does this. C starts with the last dimension, holding the earlier

Speaking of initializing an array

The general form of a statement to create and initialize an array is

```
type array_name[index] = {value1, value2[,...value_last]};
```

You must provide a value for each element in the array. If you don't provide enough values, elements later in the array will still contain garbage. If you provide too many values, you'll receive an error message from your compiler.

The following statement creates a five-element array and initializes each value to zero:

```
int MyArray[5] = {0, 0, 0, 0, 0};
```

dimensions at 0 while it fills the last dimension. Then it moves to the next to last dimension and so on until it fills the first dimension. As an example, consider this statement meant to initialize an eight-member, three-dimensional array:

```
int MyArray[2][2][2] = {1,2,3,4,5,6,7,8};
```

The array starts filling at the end, so the values 1 and 2 go into MyArray[0][0][0] and MyArray[0][0][1], respectively. The procedure goes on from there, with 7 going into MyArray[1][1][0] and 8 going into MyArray[1][1][1].

You can, if you want, make your source code easier to read by adding extra braces to the initialization part of the statement: one level of braces for each dimension in the array. The following line of code shows MyArray with these extra braces:

```
int MyArray[1][1][1] = {{{1,2},{3,4}},{{5,6},{7,8}}};
```

Using these braces emphasizes to the program reader, at least, how the array is filled. They show that the array is filled first starting with the first four values and out of these with the first two. You should note that your compiler really doesn't care how you group the variables, as long as you provide the correct number of braces.

I've got an array...but how do I use it?

So you've created and initialized an array. What next? Obviously, you'd like to use the thing and in such a way as to make your programming life easier.

Catch the bug

The following statement creates and initializes an array. Can you detect a problem?

```
int ExampleArray[2][5] = {1970, 1971, 1972, 1973, 1974,
  1975, 1976, 1977, 1978, 1979, 1980};
```

Answer: The initialization part of this statement provides 11 values, but there are only 10 elements available in the array. The last value should be taken out (it doesn't belong in the '70s anyway).

To use arrays properly, you need to know something about moving data into and out of array elements and how to work with arrays within loops.

Getting information into and out of arrays

To access data in an array, you must specify—using the array's indices—which element you want. Otherwise, you work with an array in the same manner as you do with an ordinary variable. The following statement moves the value 125 into the fourth element of the array `Balance`:

```
Balance[3]=125;
```

You can also move the contents of a specific array element into another variable, as in

```
Holder = Balance[3];
```

The preceding moves the value in the fourth element of `Balance` into an ordinary variable called `Holder`.

Again, you aren't limited to numbers and numerical expressions when specifying an array index. You can use variables as well. Consider the following statements:

```
IndexArray[3]= 4;
Balance[IndexArray[3]] = 5;
```

The second statement moves the value 5 into the fifth element of the `Balance` array. The exact index value is specified by the array variable `IndexArray`, whose fourth member is 4. Counting from 0, this yields the fifth element in `Balance`.

Loops and arrays will make your life easier

For more information on loops, see chapter 10, "Control the Way a Program Runs."

Probably the most useful instance of having a variable serve as an array's index is when you use arrays with loops. Loops allow just a few statements to do the work of many. For example, the following five statements solicit number input from the program user; each value is stored in an element of `MyArray`:

```
scanf("%d",&MyArray[0]);
scanf("%d",&MyArray[1]);
```

```
scanf("%d",&MyArray[2]);
scanf("%d",&MyArray[3]);
scanf("%d",&MyArray[4]);
```

Now, look at the same task accomplished with a loop:

```
For (counter = 0; counter <= 4; counter++)
    scanf("%d",&MyArray[counter]);
```

These two statements do the same work as the preceding five. Each time through the loop, the value of the variable counter is incremented. Because the variable serves as the array's index, the exact element referred to in the scanf() statement increases each time as well. The elements 0 through 4 of MyArray are each filled in order, based on what the user enters.

Summary

This chapter covered array variables, which are collections of variables sharing the same name. You saw how to declare and initialize array variables and how to use array indices to access individual members of an array. You also saw how to create multidimensional arrays. Finally, you looked at using arrays with loops.

Review questions

1 Define *array*. What is meant by initializing an array?

2 What is an array's index?

3 What can go into an array's index when the array is being declared? When it's being used within a program?

4 What are the limits on how many dimensions an array can have?

5 Of what use is the counter variable within a loop when working with an array?

Exercises

1 Write a declaration statement to create a three-dimensional array to hold an integer value for each day in each month of five consecutive years. Name the array Days.

2 Write a short loop to print the values in a ten-member array named Items, printing each member in Items one to a line.

3 Matrices are constructs from mathematics that represent orderly collections of numbers. A three-by-three matrix of numbers looks like

```
 1      2      3
10     -6      7
18      0     12
```

Develop a C program that lets the user input two three-by-three matrices and adds the two matrices together to produce a third matrix. To add two matrices, you add the corresponding elements, so

```
 1     2     3       1    1    1         2    3    4
10    -6     7  +    2    2    2    =    12   -4    9
18     0    12       3    3    3        21    3   15
```

Have your program print out both input matrices, and print the matrix resulting from their addition.

15

String Variables as Places for Characters

- ● **In this chapter:**

- ● **More on char-type variables**

- ● **You've heard about strings; now it's time to play**

- ● **How to make string variables**

- ● **Are string variables like regular variables?**

A string variable is one capable of holding a sequence of characters, like beads on a string or the lines of characters produced by the tape-dispensing label makers . . . .

Prior to this chapter you worked with strings quite a bit, generally printing them out to dress up our program output. All of these strings have been in the form of literal string constants. What you haven't considered very much are string variables, which are places to store and work with strings. Now that you've had a chance to look over arrays in chapter 14, "Call Several Variables by the Same Name," you can now consider string variables.

What are strings and string variables?

Strings are sequences of characters. A character is anything that can appear on your computer's screen. Each individual character is stored in your computer's memory in the form of an integer from 0 to 255. A convention or code called ASCII defines which integers go with which characters. You can see these number-character associations in appendix B, "ASCII Characters."

So a **string variable** is a variable capable of holding a sequence of characters, like the lines of characters produced by tape-dispensing label makers. A string variable requires a separate place for each character in the different strings the variable might hold. What's also needed is a way to mark the end of a string, since strings can be of different lengths: compare your full name with your street address, for instance. In this chapter I'll show you how to create string variables, how to initialize them, and how to get data into and out of them.

What can I use a string variable for?

You can use a string variable anywhere you can use a literal string constant. This opens up quite a realm of possibilities. By using a variable in a `puts()` statement, rather than a literal string, you can have that statement print different messages depending on what has happened in the program, without resorting to multiple `puts()` statements as done in earlier chapters of this book. The exact message printed depends on the contents of the variable.

For more information on format strings, see chapter 12, "About Data Streams."

You can even have your programs tailor your strings to match conditions. You might find this very useful, for example, when putting together the format string for a `printf()` statement; that's right, you can use a string variable there as well. Using some of C's string manipulating functions, you can put together new strings out of pieces of old ones, storing the results in a string variable. In this manner, your programs can assemble their own format strings. At a minimum, this lets you center a message on the screen.

The limitations of C strings

Although even these brief examples seem to indicate the power you have in C when working with string variables, the fact is that C isn't as string-friendly as many other computer languages. BASIC in particular—especially newer flavors of BASIC, such as Quick BASIC and Visual Basic—makes working with strings much easier. Where C requires you to use functions, BASIC and other languages have simple operators, much like those used for arithmetic.

In fact, you must use functions to do just about every string manipulation in the book, except declaring a string variable. Even assigning data to a string variable, a task accomplished in a simple assignment statement in BASIC, requires you to use a function in C. Compare

```
MyString = "This is assigning a literal to a string in BASIC"
```

with

```
strcpy(MyString, "This is assigning a literal to a string in
➥C");
```

Although neither statement is much shorter or longer than the other, the former is more straightforward to read than the latter. This is something you'll just have to get used to. The rest of this chapter shows you other things you need to get used to regarding strings in C and demonstrates some ways to make this learning easier on you. You start by taking a closer look at the type of data that strings are made out of.

Strings are made of char data

Back in chapter 4, "Places To Store Data," char variables are described as storing single ASCII characters. A single character isn't much. Friends of James Bond like Q and M get by on one character, but the rest of us seem to need more. Still, you have to crawl before you can walk, and you have to know all about working with char-type data before you move on to full-fledged strings.

How C stores characters

Within your computer's memory, a single character looks exactly like any other data; it's just a series of bits, each turned on or off. On most systems there are eight such bits per character. Because each bit can represent two possibilities, it should be clear that eight bits can represent $2 \times 2 \times 2 \times 2 \times 2 \times 2 \times 2 \times 2 = 256$ possibilities. Sometimes eight bits (commonly called a byte) represent a number from –127 through 128, sometimes a number between 0 and 255. And sometimes a character.

The computer program itself interprets what's stored in RAM; your computer really couldn't care less. Part of setting aside a place in RAM to store an item of data—declaring a variable, in other words—is telling C what kind of data to expect when it looks into that storage spot. So the char keyword, used in a char variable declaration statement, tells C that it should find a single ASCII character when it looks into the relevant place in RAM.

Working with the char data type

In a way, a char variable is just a special kind of numeric variable; an unsigned one restricted to a single byte. This makes it very much like an integer variable. In fact, in many cases in C you can use integer variables to

Speaking of char-type variables

To create a char-type variable, include a statement like

        char *variable_name*;

in the variable declaration part of your program. Thus,

        char character;

creates a char-type variable named, appropriately enough, character.

You can also initialize char-type variables at the time you create them. Include an equal sign and a value for the character; enclose the value in single quotes. Thus,

        char character = 'q';

creates the variable named character and places the ASCII value of the letter q into it.

hold character values. The functions `getchar()` and `putchar()` in particular take and return integer values that they associate ASCII characters with.

Still, there are good reasons for using `char`-type variables rather than integers. Most importantly, an integer can hold data way outside the range that ASCII characters are defined for. If a large value is assigned to such a variable, which is then subsequently interpreted as a character, an error definitely results. By using `char`-type variables instead, you automatically restrict your programs to only using the correct values.

You can include a `char`-type variable in an assignment statement. Usually, the right part of the statement is a literal character. Again, you must enclose such a character in single quotes; that's how C recognizes a single character. If you enclose it in double quotes, C treats it as a string with a length of one, but more on that a little later.

Use arrays for creating string variables

For more information on arrays, see chapter 14, "Call Several Variables by the Same Name."

By now you should have it firmly drilled into you that strings are sequences of characters. Now C, unlike many other computer languages, doesn't have a separate data type for strings. Given that it does have one for characters and that strings are groups of characters, you handle strings in C with arrays. So to create a place in RAM to store string data, you create an array of `char`-type variables. The following sections show you how to create and use such arrays.

Catch the bug

The following short section of code is supposed to assign the value q to a `char`-type variable, and then print it out. Can you spot a problem?

```
{
char character = 'q';
printf("%d",character);
}
```

Answer: *This little block of code actually ends up printing the ASCII value of the letter* q, *which is 113. The fault lies in the* `printf()` *statement's format string. The code* %d *specifies a decimal integer; for a character, you need the conversion specifier* %c.

Creating a character array

You create a `char`-type array variable just as you do any other variable, using a standard variable definition statement and an index indicating how many members the array has. In C, the term **string variable** is just another way of referring to a `char`-type array variable. That's the term I'll use from here on.

Can I initialize strings like other variables?

Just as with `char`-type variables, you can set string variables to an initial value. You can do so in the same statement that created the string. In fact, you can even omit the string's length in such a case. The following three statements are exactly the same:

```
char Animal[4]={'c','a','t','\0'};
char Animal[4]="cat";
char Animal[]="cat";
```

Speaking of string variables

The general form of a statement to create a string variable is

```
char string_name[string_length];
```

string_name is a valid C variable name. *string_length* is the number of characters the string can hold *minus one*. That last bit is important; the last character in any C string is the null character, represented by the escape code \0. A string must have space for the null character. The following statement creates a string variable named MyName:

```
char MyName[12];
```

With most C compilers, this string variable holds 11 characters. There are 12 members to this array, minus one for the null character.

Catch the bug

What's wrong with the following string variable declaration statement?

```
char ThisString[5] = "Clinton";
```

Answer: *The string variable isn't long enough for the data being assigned to it. Merely removing the 5 results in a statement that creates a string of exactly the right length.*

Putting text in double quotes makes C treat it as a string, which means your compiler automatically adds a null character to the end of the string; in the first statement shown just preceding, the null character has to be added explicitly. If you omit the index for your string variable, C counts how many characters there are in the string you're assigning to it, adds one for the null character, and creates a string variable that exactly fits the text you're assigning to it.

Working with strings

Working with strings is not quite as straightforward as working with numerical data, but once you get the hang of it, you'll find there's much you can do. Just about everything you do with strings relies on C functions. To use these functions, you must include the appropriate header file—such as `string.h` and `stdio.h`—in your programs. You'll look at using the functions defined in each of these files in turn. A nice thing about all these functions is that you need only provide the names of the relevant string variables; you entirely omit the indexes.

Show me three simple string operations

What are the most common operations to perform with strings? Joining two strings is one such operation; the fancy name for this process is **concatenation**. Another common thing to do is to copy one string to another, especially copying a literal string into a string variable. And for I/O purposes, it's useful to know how long the current contents of a string variable are. Each of these processes relies on a function defined in `string.h`.

Q&A *You say I can omit the indexes when I use string variables with functions. Why don't I need to tell the function how big the string is?*

The C string functions rely on one important piece of information when determining where a string ends: the presence of a newline character (escape code \n). When a string function receives a string variable as a parameter, it starts at the place in memory where the string is stored, and then proceeds until it finds a newline character, which marks the end of the string.

This has important implications! When you build a string out of individual characters, you must be certain to include a newline character at the end. Otherwise, when you pass the string to a function, your program just searches through RAM until it finds a newline. Who knows where it will end up?

How do I join two strings?

To concatenate two strings is to take the second and tack it onto the end of the first, creating a new string that's the sum, so to speak, of the two old ones. In a sort of algebraic notation, you could write:

"Clint " + "Hicks" = "Clint Hicks"

In some computer languages (BASIC again), this is pretty much exactly the way you concatenate strings. C is not so simple. C requires that you use the strcat() function.

Speaking of strcat()

The prototype for the strcat() function is

```
char strcat(char string1, char string2);
```

This function takes the string contained in *string2* and appends it to the string contained in *string1*. For example,

```
strcat(FullName,LastName);
```

appends the contents of LastName to those of FullName.

The short block of code shown below demonstrates use of the strcat()
function. It appends one string to another, and prints the results. (Just to be
on the safe side, I made the first string bigger than it needs to be. The string
you're concatentating into must be large enough to accept the new data, or
you'll get an error.)

```
{
char FullName[15]="Clint ";
char LastName[]="Hicks";
strcat(FullName,LastName);
puts(FullName);
}
```

A thing to note about strcat() is that it changes the former contents of the
first parameter, which is the string being appended to. If you want to preserve this string's contents, you need to copy them first to another variable.
Doing so requires—you guessed it, another C function.

Replacing one string's contents with another

Copying data from a numerical expression into a variable is simple; you just
use the equal sign. The same thing works when you copy the contents of one
variable to another, *except* when those two variables happen to be strings. In
this case, you must use the strcpy() function.

Speaking of strcpy()

The prototype for the strcpy() function is

```
char strcpy(char destination_string, char source_string);
```

This function takes the string contained in *source_string* and copies it to
destination_string, obliterating that string variable's former contents. For
example,

```
strcpy(FullName,FirstName);
```

copies the contents of FirstName to FullName. The destination string must
be long enough to accept the contents of the source string. Otherwise, you'll
get an error.

The following short example improves on the one shown for concatenating two strings. It takes two strings and concatenates them into a third string variable, thus leaving both the original string variables undisturbed.

```
{
char FirstName[]="Clint ";
char LastName[]="Hicks";
char FullName[13];
strcpy(FullName,FirstName);
strcat(FullName,LastName);
puts(FullName);
}
```

Finding out how many characters are in a string

Another useful operation is finding the length of a string. A string variable can store strings of varying length; the null character marks a string's end. In order to find the exact length of a string variable's contents, a fact that is occasionally useful, you need a function: `strlen()`.

The example block of C code you've been using in the last couple of sections has been modified so that the full name given is printed at the center of the line.

```
{
char BlankBuffer[81];
int Length, Counter;
char FirstName[]="Clint ";
char LastName[]="Hicks";
char FullName[20];
strcpy(FullName,FirstName);
strcat(FullName,LastName);
Length=strlen(FullName);
```

Speaking of `strlen()`

The prototype for the `strlen()` function is

```
unsigned int strlen(char string_name);
```

This function returns an unsigned integer equal to the length of the string, minus the terminating null character. You use it in an assignment statement, such as

```
Length = strlen(FullName);
```

```
for (Counter = 0; Counter <= ((80-Length)/2); Counter++)
    BlankBuffer[Counter]=' ';
    BlankBuffer[Counter]='\0';

printf("%s%s", BlankBuffer,FullName);
}
```

This bit of code treats the BlankBuffer string variable just like the array it is. The for loop adds blanks to BlankBuffer, putting a blank at each position until a specific value is reached. That value happens to be the amount of space that should be included to the left of the name in order to center it. This value is found by taking the length of the name, subtracting it from 80 (the width of the screen in characters), and dividing the result in half. After the loop, the program makes sure to append a null character (\0) to BlankBuffer. The final printf() statement then prints two strings; the string full of blanks, and then the string containing the name.

I/O with strings

If you're going to start throwing strings around in printf() statements and such, you'd better take a brief look at inputting and outputting strings. This subject was introduced in chapter 12, "About Data Streams."

Use gets() for string input

You've seen how to input a single character at a time. But what about entire strings, such as a person's name? In chapter 12, you learned that the gets() function is meant to input strings. Now it's time to see how to use it.

How can I use this in the real world?

You'll find yourself working with string functions each time you want to work with text data. Suppose you want to assemble an address label out of text entered by the program user. If you had the user enter each part of her name individually, you'd need to use both strcpy() and strcat() to assemble a complete name. The same would hold true for city, state, and ZIP. Later, if you wanted to center the label on the longest line, you'd use the strlen() function to determine which line was longest.

Now you're in a position to modify this chapter's example so that the user inputs the name to be printed, rather than using mine.

```
{
char BlankBuffer[81];
int Length, Counter;
char FirstName[12];
char LastName[12];
char FullName[20];
puts("\nEnter your first name:  ");
gets(FirstName);
puts("\nEnter your last name:  ");
gets(LastName);
strcpy(FullName,FirstName);
strcat(FullName, " ");
strcat(FullName,LastName);
Length=strlen(FullName);
for (Counter = 0; Counter <= ((80-Length)/2); Counter++)
     BlankBuffer[Counter]=' ';
     BlankBuffer[Counter]='\0';

printf("%s%s", BlankBuffer,FullName);
}
```

The block now uses the `gets()` statement to record text entered by the user into the appropriate string variables.

TIP **Another use for the `gets()` function is to flush the input buffer** after you obtain formatted input. Sometimes there are characters left in the buffer; a subsequent input function may pick up those characters and produce erroneous results. Use statements like

```
char Trash[80];
gets(Trash);
```

SPEAKING C

Speaking of `gets()`

The `gets()` function has the prototype

```
char gets(char input_string);
```

The function inputs an entire line of text from the keyboard, and puts into the *input_string*, along with a terminating null character. The following line reads input from the keyboard into a string variable called `LastName`:

```
gets(LastName);
```

Use `puts()` and `printf()` for string output

Previous chapters, such as chapter 12, used the `puts()` and `printf()` statements to output literal strings, such as text prompts and labels for results. You can also use both of these functions to send the contents of string variables to the standard output stream, thereby printing them on the screen.

Working with `puts()` is simplicity itself; you merely include the name of the string you want to display, omitting, of course, the index. Thus,

```
puts(FullName);
```

prints the contents of the string variable `FullName` onto the screen.

For cases when you want to print more than one string on a line and perhaps want to add additional formatting, you need to use `printf()`. Chapter 12 reveals a lot about the `printf()` statement. The most important thing to know here is that to print a string with `printf()`, you need to use the correct conversion specifier. This happens to be `%s`. As with `puts()`, you include the name of the string variable whose contents you want to output, minus the index. So

```
printf("%s",FullName);
```

prints the contents of the string variable `FullName` to the standard output stream, `stdout`. This statement is pretty much the same as the preceding `puts()` example.

Summary

In this chapter, you looked at creating places to store string data. You learned more about the `char` data type, and how data is stored in a `char`-type variable. You know that strings are defined as arrays of `char`-type variables and how to initialize concatenate, copy, and find the length of strings. This chapter finished with a brief look at string input and output.

Review questions

1 Define *string*. What character marks the end of a string in C?

2 What is meant by the term *concatenation*?

3 How do you designate a literal character constant? A string constant?

4 What do you omit from a string's name when using the string as a parameter in most string functions?

5 Why is it important to flush the input buffer after obtaining formatted input?

Exercises

1 Write a statement to create a string variable capable of holding 80 characters. Name the variable `Line`.

2 Write a statement to create and initialize a string variable, setting it equal to your full name. Name the variable `FullName`.

3 Write a program to print an address entered with last name first, followed by a comma and then the first name. Allow the user to enter an organization, such as **XYZ Co.** or **Macmillan Computer Publishing** as an optional second line. Output all four lines, omitting the organization line if it was left blank.

16

Structure Storage To Meet Your Own Needs

● **In this chapter:**

● You want to store your variables in a group of some sort

● Ever hear of structures?

● How do I get data into and out of structures?

● Can I put arrays or even other structures into structures?

In your dream house, your rooms are for different things— master bedroom, bath, kitchen, etc. Why not do something similar with data in your C programs?. . . . . ●>

Y ou can use arrays to pull several items of data together under one heading. You can also use arrays to create places to store strings. Both these operations involve grouping like elements. Is it possible to group unlike elements, and if so, would such a grouping be useful?

Think about using a mailing address within a program. The address itself might comprise three lines, each of which has its own parts. Nothing keeps these parts together, so to speak, except for the way the programming code treats them. But aren't there times when having the entire address stored under one variable name would be very helpful?

Indeed there are. For one thing, putting the entire address under one variable name makes storing the address in a disk file much easier. Also, having such a variable makes it very easy to move a whole group of data from one variable to another—something that you've already seen is kind of complicated using strings. C lets you define constructs that greatly simplify the task of manipulating collections of data.

Grouping unlike variables for easy use

As no one variable definition can handle all the different ways you can put data together under one name (a name and address; a name and phone number; a name, social security number, and date of hire), what you need is some way to define collections of any sort of data. In doing so, you draw up the blueprints for a sort of custom-built house for your data where each room is devoted to a very particular item: a name or a social security number, for instance. With a blueprint in hand, you can create one or many copies of your data dream home. In C, you can do exactly this for your data, using the data constructs called structures.

What is a structure?

Structures are among the most important and flexible data storage types in C and indeed in any computer language. They allow you to precisely tailor your data storage needs to the kind of data that your program is working with.

Plain English, please!

> A **structure** is an assembly of variables—one or many—grouped under a single name. Each variable in the structure has its own name and definition. Further, each variable can hold different forms of data.

What can I use structures for?

If you think about an address, you can see that an address label is a perfect candidate for a structure. Each of the string variables you create to hold an address line can be a member of the structure. When referring to the structure as a whole, you merely use its name, instead of each individual variable name.

Because structures are flexible, there's really no limit to what you can do with them. Fundamentally, a structure is useful in any place where several variables need to be treated as a single entity. What's more, you aren't limited to simple structures of numeric or even string variables. Structures can contain other structures, and they can contain arrays. You can even fashion entire arrays of structures, allowing you to hold several address labels in memory at once, for instance, without having to create and manage a whole nest of separate variables for each label. In this chapter, I'll show you how to define and work with structures, from the simple to the elaborate.

Two steps for creating simple structures

Working with a structure requires two steps. First, you must define the structure, indicating what data it will store, under what names that data will be accessed. With a definition prepared, you can then actually create an individual structure that matches the definition. Perhaps most importantly, you can then go on to clone as many individual structures—each under a separate name—out of the original definition as you have memory to hold.

You declare a structure, and then you use it

Both the process of defining a structure and creating an individual instance of it involve the struct keyword. struct helps create a structure by defining what data the structure holds.

A structure definition like the preceding one should go where you normally declare variables. However, your work is not yet done. What you have at this point is a set of blueprints, not an actual house. You must now tell C to build at least one example, called an **instance**, of the structure.

Having defined and created an instance of a structure, the next thing to do is use it. Getting to the individual parts of a structure is not exactly like accessing other variables, as you'll see shortly.

Speaking of defining a structure

The general form of a statement to define a structure is

```
struct tag_name {
    variable_type variable_name;
    variable_type variable_name;
    ...
    variable_type variable_name;
};
```

The tag_name is how this definition is known to C. You use it later when creating an actual structure out of the definition. You can see that there's a separate line for each variable in the structure. The three dots on the fourth line merely indicate that you can have as many variable definitions as you wish. The following statements define a very simple structure containing three integer variables:

```
struct circle {
    int radius;
    int xcoord;
    int ycoord;
};
```

The three variables in this structure define the *radius* of a circle and the x and y coordinates (*xcoord* and *ycoord*) of its center.

Okay, I've got a structure; how do I get the information I need into or out of it?

You move data into and read it out of individual elements of a structure in much the same way you do with ordinary variables, using assignment statements. However, in the case of structure variables, a bit of extra information is required. You must identify the structure that the variable belongs to. You do this by means of the **dot operator**, a single period used to separate the parts of a structure's name.

Consider the following example:

```
struct circle {
     int radius;
     int xcoord;
     int ycoord;
} MyCircle;
MyCircle.radius = 15;
```

Speaking of instances

The general form of a statement to create an instance of a structure out of an existing definition is

```
struct tag_name instance_name;
```

This statement tells C to create an instance of the structure defined as *tag_name*, giving this instance the name *instance_name*. Remember, *tag_name* is the blueprint, and *instance_name* is the actual structure. The following creates an instance of *circle* as defined in the previous Speaking C example:

```
struct circle MyCircle;
```

The variable *MyCircle* is now an instance of the structure-type *circle*.

Alternatively, you can create an instance of a given structure immediately following its definition, just following the closing brace. The following code also creates an instance of the *circle* structure:

```
struct circle {
     int radius;
     int xcoord;
     int ycoord;
} MyCircle;
```

Catch the bug

What's wrong with the following structure definition?

```
struct square {
    int xtopcorner
    int ytopcorner
    int xbottomcorner
    int ybottomcorner
} ;
MySquare;
```

Answer: *The semicolon is missing on each of the lines declaring a variable within the structure. You should actually move the line declaring an instance to precede the semicolon following the structure definition's closing brace. The corrected definition reads*

```
struct square {
    int xtopcorner;
    int ytopcorner;
    int xbottomcorner;
    int ybottomcorner;
} MySquare;
```

It declares an instance, named `MyCircle`, of a structure with the tag name `circle`. The last statement assigns the value 15 to the `radius` variable contained within `MyCircle`.

Use one blueprint to create several structures

You may think that structures are limited in their usefulness at this point because they seem to involve some extra typing without apparent benefit. The power of structures lies in your use of the original blueprint for a structure to create additional structures as required.

Create several instances of a structure at one time

You can, if you need to, create several instances of a given structure at once, as in:

```
struct circle MyCircle, YourCircle, OurCircle;
```

This also works when you declare instances of a structure immediately following its definition:

```
struct circle {
    int radius;
    int xcoord;
    int ycoord;
} MyCircle, YourCircle, OurCircle;
```

With this done, you can then move the entire contents of one structure instance into another, as in

```
YourCircle = MyCircle;
```

An alternative to struct

An alternative to declaring and working with simple structures is using the typedef keyword, which saves you a little bit of typing. The following code lines are equivalent to the definition for the structure circle previously given:

```
typedef struct {
    int radius;
    int xcoord;
    int ycoord;
}circle;
```

This definition creates a blueprint for a structure, with the tag circle, just as before. To create an instance of this structure, though, you use a statement like

```
circle MyCircle;
```

The difference being, you get to omit the keyword struct. Otherwise, creating structure definitions using typedef is exactly the same.

You've got simple structures down... now it's time to move to complex structures

Structures can contain more than just simple numeric variables, as I claimed earlier in the chapter. For example, if you work with string variables in structures, you end up defining structures that contain arrays. The arrays, of course, represent string variables in that case, but they could just as easily be numerical arrays. In addition to arrays, structures can contain other structures, allowing additional levels of grouping and complexity. And, turning arrays and structures around on each other, you can create arrays of structures, perhaps the most useful construct of all.

Use a structure in another structure

Suppose you've previously defined a structure, you can then include its definition in that of a larger structure. Consider the following example:

```
struct circle {
      int radius;
      int xcoord;
      int ycoord;
};
struct colorcircle
{
      struct circle MyCircle;
      int color;
} AColorCircle;
```

This group of statements first creates a definition for the structure named circle. It then incorporates that definition into a new structure called colorcircle. Note that the circle part of colorcircle is referred to a specific name. You can think of it as an instance of circle, if you like. Finally, a new instance of colorcircle is created, and given the name AColorCircle.

To refer to structure elements within a structure, use the dot operator twice. To assign a value to the circle's radius in the previous example, you'd use

```
AColorCircle.MyCircle.radius = 25;
```

Structures can use arrays...

To include an array in a structure, you need only include the array definition as a regular part of the structures definition, as in the following example:

```
struct HasArray
{
int Months[11];
int Rate;
} ArrayInstance;
```

To access a particular member of an array within a structure, you include the index as you would normally. The following statement assigns the value 1,000 to the fourth member of Months within ArrayInstance:

```
ArrayInstance.Months[3]=1000;
```

...and arrays can use structures

Finally, you can create entire arrays of structures out of an existing definition. Here's where you begin to tap the real power of structures. The same blueprint, the structure definition, provides the instructions to create a host of places to store complicated data, such as an address. All you have to do to create an array of structures is to include an index when you create the instance. The following block of C code does just that:

```
struct circle {
    int radius;
    int xcoord;
    int ycoord;
};
struct colorcircle
{
    struct circle MyCircle;
    int color;
} SomeColorCircles[4];
```

These statements create an array of `colorcircle` structures under the name `SomeColorCircles`. To refer to a particular structure within the array, simply include the appropriate index value. The following statement, for instance, sets the second member of the array equal to the first:

```
SomeColorCircles[1] = SomeColorCircles[0];
```

How can I use this in the real world?

A handy use for an array of structures is for holding several names and addresses, much like a simple database program or a Rolodex file. A database, of course, is just a file where information is stored in a highly organized way. Databases are divided into records, and a record corresponds to a structure. Within a record are fields; the individual elements in a structure correspond to database fields. In fact,
if you come up with the correct structure definition, you can work with an existing database file, although you'll need to know the file-handling techniques discussed in chapter 24, "What You Need To Know about Disks and Their Files," as well as how the database file itself is laid out.

Summary

In this chapter, you looked at storing collections of variables as structures. You saw how to go about creating structure definitions and instances of structures. You then examined moving data into and out of structures. Finally, You looked at complex structures involving arrays and other structures, including arrays of structures.

Review questions

1 Define a *structure*. What is meant by the structure's *tag*?

2 What is the purpose of the dot operator?

3 What is the difference between using `struct` and `typedef` for defining a structure?

4 How do you reference a member of an array that is a structure element? a structure that is a member of an array?

5 What's required to incorporate a structure into a larger structure?

Exercises

1 Write a definition for a structure named `Collection` to hold an integer variable, `Count`, a floating-point array, `Values`, and a string variable (length 25), `Designation`. Create an instance of `Collection` named `MyCollection`.

2 Incorporate the structure `Collection` from exercise 1 into a new structure, which also includes an integer value, `Rate`, and a floating-point value, `Time`. Give the new structure the name `BigCollection`, and create an instance of it called `MyBigCollection`.

3 Rewrite the structure definition from exercise 2 using the `typedef` keyword. Create two instances of the structure named `MBC1` and `MBC2`.

4 Write a program to input ten collections of values consisting of a balance, an interest rate, and a term. Store the results in an array of structures. Compute compound interest according to the formula and print the results, along with the input values.

17

How To Indirectly Access Data Storage with Pointers

● **In this chapter:**

- **Work directly with your computer's memory in C**

- **How do I create and set up pointers?**

- **What's the indirection operator used for?**

- **Can pointers be used with arrays?**

You can think of a pointer as an address book entry; it shows the actual location of another specific variable . . . . ➤

By now, you think you've looked at just about every way to store data. If you thought so, you're pretty close to being correct. You've looked at variables to store numeric and character data, to store single items and arrays of items, to store character strings, and to store complex assemblages of all these items. Yet no matter what kind of data variables may hold, they share an underlying fundamental identity: any variable is simply a name that your C compiler associates with a particular address in your computer's memory. Thus, in addition to its name, a variable has an address and contents at that address.

Now, to a computer, everything in memory is just data, whether it's a variable's contents or its address. This means you should be able to treat a variable's address as if it were any other form of data: retrieving it, manipulating it, and storing the results. If you think about it, this is just what a program does when it works with a variable's contents. It seems like you should be able to do the same thing explicitly, eh? You can, using pointers.

Why pointers?

"But why?" you ask. You can do some very powerful things when working with the addresses of variables. To cite just one example: using code that relies on an address rather than a variable's name can generalize that code to work with any one of a number of variables, depending on circumstances. Of course, you need some place to store the address of the variable that you want to work with. C provides you with just such a type of variable. You can think of such a variable as an address book entry: it shows the actual location of another, specific variable. This variable is called a pointer, which is the subject of this chapter.

 Plain English, please!

A **pointer** is a variable that contains the address in memory of another variable. Programmers say that the pointer "points to" the other variable because a program can use the pointer's contents to find the other variable.

A computer memory refresher

Recall from chapter 4, "Places To Store Data," that your computer's working memory is a long sequence of individual bytes, each capable of representing a single character or a small number. In some cases, such as character strings and floating-point numbers, several bytes are taken together to represent a single value.

So that you can find things in memory, each byte has a unique number that identifies its location in memory: call this the byte's **address**. Given an address, your computer's processor can retrieve data from or write new data to a given byte.

Exactly how much RAM a C program has available and how it's addressed depends on your C compiler and on the computer operating system that you're writing for. The amount and structure of memory together constitute what is called a **memory model**. Generally you have several memory models available, some with small amounts of memory and some with large amounts. For purposes of this book, a small memory model is always sufficient. You may need a large memory model if, for instance, you're working with large multidimensional arrays. You can find out what memory models are available to you and how each is built by consulting the documentation accompanying your C compiler.

Pointers and their relationship to memory

A pointer is just another type of variable. It just so happens that a pointer's contents are the address of another variable in memory. Although a pointer has a certain awareness of the size of the variable that it's pointing to, the address contained by the pointer really specifies just the beginning, the first byte, of the variable in question.

A pointer can point to anything in RAM. What's more, you can perform arithmetic on a pointer's contents, making it point to another variable or to another part of, say, an array variable. This is a powerful feature of C, and one that's relied on to perform many important tasks, including interfacing with your computer's operating system.

CAUTION   **Using pointers has drawbacks for the inexperienced. You should**
note that more than just your program's data are stored in RAM. Some very
critical parts of your computer's operating system are stored there as well.
Depending on the memory model you're using, you might possibly, through
injudicious use of pointers, wreak temporary havoc with your operating
system, thereby crashing your computer. Just this sort of thing causes a
considerable percentage of computer crashes.

Although you can do damage with pointers, you can also do a great deal of
good. The rest of this chapter shows you how to avoid problems.

A few basics about pointers

A pointer is just a variable, so it stands to reason that you must declare a
pointer before you can use it. Initializing a pointer is another important
operation. In fact, properly initializing pointers is much more important than
initializing other variables. Both these operations rely on a couple of C
operators, one of which you've seen before.

Speaking of declaring a pointer

The general form of a statement to declare a pointer is

```
type_name *pointer_name;
```

The asterisk is important; it tells C you're creating a pointer and not a variable.
In C, the asterisk is referred to as the **indirection operator**. When you create a
pointer, you specify which type of variable that the pointer points to. This is
important because different variable types have different lengths (in bytes). The
following statement creates a pointer to a floating-point variable:

```
float *pMyPointer;
```

The p at the beginning of the pointer's name isn't necessary, but it's a good idea
to develop some way of distinguishing pointers from other variables because
they're used differently. The less confusion you allow within your code, the better
off you'll be later.

First, declare the pointer

A pointer has a name and a data type just like any other variable. The only difference in declaring a pointer and any other variable is the addition of a little operator that tells C you're creating a pointer.

Because the indirection operator creates a pointer, you can mix pointer declarations in with those declaring other variables. Thus,

```
float *pMyPointer, Balance;
```

creates two variables: `pMyPointer` is a pointer to a floating-point variable, and `Balance` is an ordinary floating-point variable.

Second, initialize the pointer

Before you can use a pointer, you must initialize it. This means giving it an initial value. Otherwise, the pointer points to byte number 0 or, worse yet, to some random value. Using pointers with random contents will surely lead to a crash. You initialize a pointer in an assignment statement, using the address-of operator (&).

Speaking of initializing a pointer

The general form of a statement to initialize a pointer is

```
pointer_name = &variable_name;
```

The ampersand is the address-of operator: it determines the address of the variable. This result is then stored in the pointer. After the statement executes, the pointer points to the variable's location. The following sets the `pMyPointer` pointer to point to the floating-point variable `Balance`.

```
pMyPointer = &Balance;
```

Note that the pointer and the variable should be of the same type.

Q&A *I'm not sure I get the difference between a pointer and a variable. Can you sum it up for me?*

It's worth stopping here to think about what pointers mean. The subject has tripped up several people, including yours truly, who was stopped dead cold by it in my first programming course at college. After executing a statement like the one preceding, we have two variables. One is a pointer to a floating-point variable, the other is a floating-point variable. The pointer contains the address, in memory, of the floating-point variable's contents. The contents themselves are not known, but you can access them easily, even using the pointer.

Catch the bug

There's a problem with the following block of statements. What is it?

```
int *pNumber;
float Number;
Number = 12000.15;
pNumber = &Number;
```

Answer: The pointer and the variable pointed to are of different data types. To point to a floating-point variable, the pNumber pointer should be given the type float. The following shows the corrected code.

```
float *pNumber;
float Number;
Number = 12000.15;
pNumber = &Number;
```

How do I use pointers?

What good is a pointer once you've created and initialized it? Well, you can now use it in place of the variable that it points to. You can also reinitialize, or reset, a pointer to point to another variable at any time. This means that pointers let you write code that can use the contents of any number of different variables, depending on the contents of the pointer used in the code.

You can use pointers in expressions

Within any expression that involves a variable name, you can use the name of a pointer. If it's the variable pointed to that you're really concerned with, you use the indirection operator again to specify that it's that variable and not the pointer's actual contents that you're referring to.

Let's clear this up with a couple of example code lines. Consider the following:

```
pMyPointer = 125;
*pMyPointer = 125;
```

These two statements are identical, except for the addition of the indirection operator to the second one. Now, the first statement merely stores the value 125 into the pMyPointer pointer. So now the pointer points to byte location 125 in memory—who knows what's there? The second statement, on the other hand, stores 125 in the variable pointed to by pMyPointer. Using the indirection operator with a pointer is the same as using the name of the variable. So in the following group of statements, the last two are identical: both store 100.10 in the variable Number.

```
float *pMyPointer, Number;
pMyPointer = &Number;
*pMyPointer = 100.10;
Number = 100.10.
```

Outside of a variable declaration statement, which is actually used to create a pointer, the indirection operator refers to the contents of the variable—not to the contents of the pointer itself. Remember, the pointer's actual contents are an address and not a piece of data. The actual data is contained in the variable with the address that the pointer stores.

Returning to our address-book analogy, a pointer might be a particular entry in the book: the first entry under the letter *D*, for instance. The contents of that entry are an address. At that address, you find the real person (the contents of the variable, if you will).

Some information on pointer and variable data types

For more on the void keyword, see chapter 22, "Cool Things To Do with Pointers."

Always keep in mind that pointers, unless declared with the keyword void, always point to a variable of a particular data type. So part of what an initialized pointer knows about a variable is how much memory it occupies. C uses this information to retrieve the correct amount of data when you use the indirection operator to retrieve the contents of the variable.

For this reason, mixing types is dangerous, like having an integer pointer point to a floating-point variable. Floating-point variables occupy more bytes than do integer variables. Using indirection on such an integer pointer results in only a part of the original variable being accessed. Therefore, any results using that data are wrong.

You can point to arrays

Arrays are among the most useful variables to point to because you can do operations on a pointer's contents to specify what element in an array you want to access. Working with pointers to arrays is a little different than working with pointers to regular variables, as you'll see.

How is an array name like a pointer?

You don't really need to create and initialize a pointer to array. Without knowing it, you've already done so when you first created the array. The array's name, with the index, is a pointer to the first element in the array. This kind of pointer is called a **pointer constant**. You can't change it the way you can a pointer variable, so in the following two statements, both using pointers, the first is invalid while the second is OK.

```
MyArray = &NewElement;
pPointer = &NewElement;
```

Here's an interesting use of pointers: recall that the scanf() function, used to read formatted input, takes a variable name along with the address-of operator. Well, a pointer can store the address of a variable. Therefore, instead of using a variable's name and the address-of operator, you can use a pointer to that variable. Because an array's name is a pointer to the array, you can use an array's name in `scanf()` as well. You can do just that to scan strings into string variables, which after all are just arrays of characters. Consider the following example:

```
char MyString[9];
scanf("%s", MyString);
```

Input from the keyboard is read into memory as a string, starting at the beginning of the character array (that is, string variable) named `MyString`.

Pointers have mathematical abilities

When working with pointers and arrays, you should keep in mind how C stores arrays in the first place. An array occupies a contiguous block of memory, starting with the first element in the array. This also happens to be the address of the array, as specified by the array's name: a pointer constant that points to the array's beginning. Each element in the array occupies the same number of bytes. The exact number depends on the data type. The elements are stored starting with the first and preceding in order to the last.

For single-dimensional arrays, the way they're stored in memory mirrors their structure pretty well: a long sequence of values. Multidimensional arrays are trickier to visualize. In memory, they too are stored as a long sequence; your computer's memory has only one dimension. Recall how multidimensional variables are initialized, however, with the last dimension changing first. That's how values are stored, with the last dimension changing first. The following shows how:

```
     Array initialization
Char MyArray [3][2] = {'a','b','c','d','e','f'};
     Array conceptually
a      b
c      d
e      f
     Array in memory
badcfe
```

Working with pointers and multidimensional arrays is quite difficult both conceptually and in practice. It's a subject best studied later in chapter 22, "Cool Things To Do with Pointers."

To access a particular item in an array with a pointer, you need, therefore, to know how far away from the beginning that item is. This value is sometimes called the **offset**. So using the indirection operator

```
*(MyArray + 2)
```

refers to the third element in the array; `*(MyArray)` refers to the first. Two is the offset in the preceding example; the offset of the first array element is, of course, zero.

Another way you can get to array elements is by using pointer arithmetic. You can perform both the increment and decrement operation on a pointer variable (not, however, on a pointer constant like an array name). When you increment or decrement a pointer, its value isn't just changed by one, it's changed by however many bytes are occupied by the type of variable pointed to by the pointer. That is, the pointer is changed by just enough to point to the next variable. In the following statements, the next-to-last statement sets a pointer variable to the first element in the array; the last sets the pointer to the second element.

```
char *pPointer, MyArray [3][2] = {'a','b','c','d','e','f'};
pPointer = MyArray;
pPointer++;
```

Can I see an example of pointer arithmetic?

I've written a program to find the average of ten numbers. The program uses an array and uses pointer arithmetic to access parts of the array. The program listing follows:

```
/*A program to print the average of ten numbers*/
/*The program demonstrates pointer arithmetic*/

#include <stdio.h>
float *pPointer, MyArray[10], sum = 0;
int counter;

main()
{
/*Input numbers using a loop*/
pPointer = MyArray;
for (counter = 0; counter <= 9; counter++)
{
puts("Input a number:  ");
scanf("%f", pPointer++);
}

/*Find the average of the numbers*/
pPointer = MyArray;
```

```
for (counter = 0; counter <= 10; counter++)
{
sum += *pPointer++;
}
sum = sum/10.0;

/*Print results*/
pPointer = MyArray;
puts("\n You entered: ");
for (counter = 0; counter <= 9; counter++)
printf("\n%f", *pPointer++);

printf("\nThe average is %f", sum);

}
```

The program produces the results shown in figure 17.1.

Fig. 17.1

Finding the average of ten values using an array and pointer arithmetic.

```
Input a number:
11
Input a number:
22
Input a number:
33
Input a number:
44
Input a number:
55
Input a number:
66
Input a number:
77
Input a number:
88
Input a number:
99
Input a number:
101
 You entered:
11.000000
22.000000
33.000000
44.000000
55.000000
66.000000
77.000000
88.000000
99.000000
101.000000
The average is 59.599998
```

Using pointers like this may not seem like much of an advantage, but in later chapters you'll begin to see the usefulness of this approach.

Something important to remember about strings

Most of the string functions take pointers as arguments. The pointer in question is, of course, a pointer to an array of characters. The last character in the array is expected to be the null character, \0. Because the name of an array is a pointer constant to the array's beginning, you need only supply the function with the name of a string variable.

You should know that all of these functions look for the null character in order to find the end of the string. They don't just look for the last element in the array. For this reason, if your character array (that is, string variable) doesn't have a null character, your program will not work correctly.

How can I use this in the real world?

String manipulations provide an important area of use for pointers, but if you delve very far into programming at all, you'll find yourself running into pointers all over. Interfacing with your computer's operating system, for instance, frequently requires use of pointers. If you want to send data to the operating system, you need to store it at a certain location in memory. You'd store this memory address in a pointer. Later, you'd use the pointer to make sure the data you wanted to send got to the right address for the operating system to pick it up. Even working strictly within your own programs, there are places where you must use pointers: to pass an array as a parameter to a function, for instance. You can learn more about such uses of pointers in chapter 22, "Cool Things To Do with Pointers."

Summary

In this chapter, you looked at working with pointers. You defined what pointers are, saw how to declare them, and looked at how they're initialized. You also saw how to use the indirection operator to retrieve the variable with the contents pointed to by the pointer. This chapter concluded with a brief look at pointers and arrays, including how to use pointer arithmetic to access array elements without using the array's index.

Review questions

1 What is a *pointer*? What data does a pointer contain?

2 What is the *indirection operator*? the *address-of operator*? How is each used?

3 Why is the data type of a pointer important?

4 What is a *pointer constant*? Give an example of one.

5 What arithmetic operations can be performed on a pointer variable? What use are these operations?

Exercises

1 Write a declaration statement to create a pointer to a string variable, and a string to which to point. Make the string 12 characters long.

2 Create a pointer to a floating-point variable, and initialize it to that variable's contents. Write all the code necessary to declare the pointer and the variable.

3 Modify the averaging program from this chapter to enter the values into the table in reverse order and print them out in forward order. (Hint: use the decrement operator, discussed in chapter 8, "Performing Mathematical Calculations in C.")

18

Turning One Data Type into Another

● **In this chapter:**

● **How does C store data?**

● **I've got an integer variable that I now need as a character variable; what do I do?**

● **You have a few different ways of converting data**

To understand Russian, most of us English speakers need a translation. Well, for C to understand some data correctly, you must tell it how the data should be interpreted. . . . . **>**

Ry now it should be quite clear to you that computer data comes in all shapes and sizes. There are characters, and there are numbers. Characters can be single or arrayed into strings. Numbers can be integers or have fractional parts. Floating-point numbers can have a few or many digits. Any of these data types can be linked together into arrays, structures, or both.

Usually data follows the rule that "birds of a feather flock together," meaning expressions are composed of like data types. Sometimes, however, expressions may contain mixed data types, especially when you're dealing with numeric data and mathematical functions. In fact, you've actually mixed a few types in this book. You may have gotten warnings from your C compiler when you compiled some of your programs that contain such expressions: `Warning! Mixed floating point types in expression.` Things like that.

Mostly such warnings are just a nuisance, but occasionally, they reveal a problem with a program—one that produces bad results. Underneath it all, data looks the same to your computer—just 1s and 0s. So your computer eagerly attempts to treat certain data as if it is in another form, just to suit the preferences of the expression it happens to be in. Depending on the context, this can change the data altogether, making any results meaningless.

At other times, you may want to deliberately take data in one form and change it to another. The most obvious example is converting numeric results into character strings. Why do that? So you can add commas and dollar signs in the right places, making the results look nice and professional. Once you mix in symbols like the dollar sign and commas, you've created a character string. Merely treating a number as if it were a group of characters is going to yield weird and incorrect results. So you need some way to turn your number results into the appropriate characters.

How to change one kind of data into another

Fortunately, C offers ways for you to convert data from one form into another, either implicitly or explicitly. Doing so implicitly, just by using the data in an expression with mixed types, can work if you understand how C goes about such conversions. For occasions when implicit conversion isn't the way to go, you can explicitly tell C to convert data. Either way, data conversions are like translating words from one language into another; without the translation, results are unintelligible.

The forms that data is stored in

All data, from single characters to complex structures, is stored as a sequence of bytes. Each fundamental C data type is stored in a fixed number of bytes. A character variable occupies one byte; an integer occupies two, a floating-point variable four, and so on. (Some of these values vary on different computer systems.) It's up to your C programs to interpret these bytes, based on some general rules.

For example, in conventional notation a floating-point number is represented by some decimal digits times a power of ten; for instance, 3.5×10^6, which is the same as 3,500,000. The digits are usually called the expression's mantissa, the particular power of ten used is called the exponent; ten itself is the base. In the previous example, the mantissa is 3.5 and the exponent is 6.

When C stores a floating-point value, some of the bytes set aside for it are used for the mantissa and its sign (positive or negative); the remainder of the bytes are used for the exponent and its sign. (Actually, the exponent occupies a fraction of a byte.) No matter what data is stored in the four particular bytes that C is expecting to find a floating-point value in, it interprets the data in just that way.

Other data is stored differently. You've seen how a character variable contains a single byte that is associated with a letter, numeral, or symbol by a code (ASCII). Integers are interpreted as binary numbers. Long integers and double-precision floating-point numbers are interpreted just like their smaller counterparts but have twice as many bytes.

Why you need to convert from data type to data type

At times, it's necessary to translate data from one form to another; say from "integerese" into "floating pointese." This may be necessary because you've mixed data types in an expression of your own. However, data conversions may be necessary through no fault of your own.

For example, the mathematical function pow(), which raises a number to a power (first discussed in chapter 8, "Performing Mathematical Calculations in C"), actually expects and returns values in double-precision floating-point form. The prototype for this function is

```
double pow(double base, double power);
```

If you provide this function with data that isn't in the correct form, which is a double-precision floating-point number, you won't get the results you expect. I wasted hours and hours on just this problem when I was first learning C. The trouble really comes if you supply an integer or an integer variable as the power to raise the base to, as in

```
pow(2.0, 3);
```

Since the function expects to find a double-precision floating-point value there, it looks for both a mantissa and exponent. Now, reading the bytes in such a variable from left to right, the mantissa is to the left, the exponent to the right. A small integer value, however, only occupies the rightmost part of its two bytes; the left part contains zeroes. If this number is then interpreted as a floating-point number, C sees something like $0.0000 \times 10^{integer}$.

No matter what the value of *integer* is, the expression is always 0. Depending on what base is being raised to a power—and the form it's in as well—the results returned by pow() in this case are going to be either 0 or 1. (Any number to the zeroeth power is one; zero to the zeroeth is zero.) Obviously this isn't correct.

One way to eliminate such a problem when you use this function is to include a decimal point in any number forming part of the expressions offered as arguments to pow(). This is one way of forcing a conversion to floating-point data, something that is clearly necessary. There are other ways to do this, as you'll see in the remainder of the chapter. Again, it may be that you don't have to do anything at all and can rely on C to convert for you. Then again, it may not.

C may automatically convert data types

If you mix data types in an expression, your C compiler may get upset at you, but it tries to make sense of what you've given it anyway. Exactly how it attempts to make sense of what you've given depends on the context.

Within an expression, C relies on **type promotion**; changing a data type to a more inclusive form. In assignment statements, C attempts to force the source data to conform to the target.

Promote a data type to another data type

When evaluating an expression with mixed data types, C looks for the most inclusive data type in the expression. It then converts—or promotes—the values of every other element in the expression to that type. You should note that variables aren't actually changed; an int-type variable remains an integer if its contents are promoted to floating-point data. The following table shows the C data types from most inclusive to least:

Rank	Type
1	double
2	float
3	long
4	int
5	char

If even one element in an expression is a double, then every other element is promoted to double. For example,

```
float x, y, Result;
int z;
scanf("%f %f %d", &x, &y, &z);
Result = x*y+z;
```

In the expression x*y+z, x and y are a floating-point number, and z is an integer. Thus, z is promoted to float, and the value obtained by evaluating the expression is a floating-point value.

There's a catch to promotions

Now, let's modify the preceding example. Suppose you change the data type of the variable Balance:

```
float x, y;
int z, Result;
scanf("%f %f %d", &x, &y, &z);
Result = x*y+z;
```

Result is now an integer variable. What happens within the assignment statement?

Result is not promoted to a float-type variable. Rather, the expression is forced into int-type variable and the results are stored in Result as an integer result. In this case, floating-point data has been demoted to integer form.

That's the way it works within an assignment statement; the data from the right side of the equal sign is converted into the form of the variable on the left. This is one way to force data into a desired format. There is another, as you'll see soon enough.

You should know that, in certain cases, forcing an integer value into floating-point form may yield results that are not exactly equal to the original number. This is because floating-point variables can't precisely represent every conceivable number; they're only as good as the number of digits the variable can store. The following short example demonstrates this phenomenon.

```
#include <stdio.h>
/*Show that converting a large integer to type float */
/*may yield imprecise results                         */
long First = 1234567890;
float Second;
main()
{
/*The following uses an assignment statement to force */
/*data into floating-point form                       */
Second = First;

/*Show the results                                     */
printf("The contents of Second are now %f", Second);
/*Pause before quitting*/
scanf("%d", First);
}
```

When you run this program, you get the result

```
1234567936.000000
```

You might have expected to get 1234567890.000000. Now, the two numbers are very close to the same, but they aren't exactly the same. The difference is only about ten parts per billion, but in some cases (concentrations of toxic chemicals, for example) that difference is a lot. (By the way, changing the variable Second to a double-type variable, which can support lots more digits, solves the problem.)

Catch the bug

The following block of code has a problem that causes it to produce incorrect results. Can you find the problem?

```
float x, y, z;
int Result;
scanf("%f %f %d", &x, &y, &z);
Result = x*y+z;
printf("\nThe result is %f", Result);
```

Answer: *It would appear from the* printf() *statement that a floating-point result is desired; after all, the input variables are all in that form, and the conversion specifier is* %f, *which gives a floating-point result. However, the variable* Result *is an integer variable, so attempting to print its contents with the* %f *conversion specifier yields bad results. The value obtained by the expression* x*y+z *is forced into integer form. If this is really desired, then the conversion specifier should be changed, as follows:*

```
float x, y, z;
int Result;
scanf("%f %f %d", &x, &y, &z);
Result = x*y+z;
printf("\nThe result is %d", Result);
```

If, on the other hand, the result really should be in floating-point form, then the Result's *type should be changed:*

```
float x, y, z, Result;
scanf("%f %f %d", &x, &y, &z);
Result = x*y+z;
printf("\nThe result is %f", Result);
```

Telling C what you want

While you can force data into a specific type using an assignment statement to a variable of that type, there's another, easier way to change data types. You can explicitly tell C to convert an item into a given form. You do so by means of **type casts**. These are modifiers affixed to a variable or expression that tell C to force the data in question into the specified form.

Typecast a variable in a certain role

A type cast is a C variable type enclosed in parentheses. Thus, there's a specific type cast for each C variable type. The casts are

Cast	Meaning
(double)	Double-precision floating point
(float)	Single-precision floating point
(long)	Long integer
(int)	Integer
(char)	Character

You put the desired type cast in front of the variable, constant, or expression whose form you want to change—for example

```
int x,y;
float z;
    ...statements to assign values to x and y
z = (float)x/y;
```

In this case, the type cast forces the value of x into floating-point form. The expression as a whole is therefore promoted to a float type, so the fractional part of x/y isn't lost; without the type cast, the expression yields an integer result.

Typecast an entire expression

If you want to convert an expression as a whole into a more inclusive data type than any of its elements, you need only cast one element to that type. The rules of type promotion take care of the rest. For example,

```
int x,y,z;
double Result;
     ...statements to assign values to x,y,z
Result = pow((double)x/y + z, (double)z);
```

The final line contains two expressions. You use the type cast (double) to force both to a double type. In the first, x/y + z, it's only necessary to affix the type cast to x; C automatically promotes the contents of y and z to double-type variables.

Catch the bug

What's wrong with the following block of statements?

```
int x,y, z;
     ...statements to assign values to x and y
(float)z = x/y;
printf("The result is %f",z);
```

Answer: The type cast is in the wrong place and won't have the desired effect anyway. Recall that no type of data conversion has any affect on a variable's data type; conversions merely change the contents into another form for use elsewhere. To force a floating-point value out of the expression x/y, and print it as such, the block has to be changed to

```
 int x,y;
float z;
     ...statements to assign values to x and y
z = (float)x/y;
printf("The result is %f",z);
```

Change character strings to numbers

Sometimes you may find yourself needing to change a value input as a string into a strict numeric value. You can't do so using assignment statements or type casts, but C does have three functions that take a string and return a numeric result. The prototypes for these functions are

```
int atoi(char *pointer);
long atol(char *pointer);
double atof(char *pointer);
```

Each of these functions takes a *pointer* to a char-type variable; for strings, this is just the name of the character array holding the string. Supposing MyString is a string variable with a length of six, the following statement converts its value to a number and stores it in a long integer named Long:

```
Long = atol(MyString);
```

For the ASCII chart, see appendix B "ASCII Characters."

What about converting data the other way, from a number into a string? Unfortunately, there's no single function to do this for you. You essentially have to compute the correct ASCII code for each digit, and assign it to a part of a string. The ASCII code for 0 is 48; for each subsequent digit, it's the digit plus 48. You have to rely on such a procedure, for example, to print a number with commas in it. The best way is by means of a loop.

How can I use this in the real world?

Think of the output from some sort of financial program. Would you rather see nothing but digits and a decimal point, like 1234.619999, or would you rather have a dollar sign, commas (if needed) and only two decimal digits for cents, like $1,234.62.

Clearly the latter is preferable. So how would you go about taking numerical results in C and getting them into this standard financial format?

The first part of the procedure is finding out how many digits the answer has. This indicates how many times through a processing loop you need. At each pass through the loop, the relevant digit is extracted from the answer, converted to a character, and put into the result string. At certain places, commas are added. A decimal point is also added just before the cents values are appended. A section of C code to accomplish this might look like the following:

```
/*Start with the dollar sign*/
Result[0]='$';
/*find the number of digits in the answer*/
digits = log10(future);
/*set the string position to the place after the $*/
strpos = 1;
/*loop for the number of digits, including two to the right
➥of the decimal*/
for (;digits>=-2; digits--)
```

```
{
/*Raise 10 to the power of the current digit*/
digitpower = pow((double) 10.0, (double)digits);
/*Isolate the current digit in the result, */
/*convert to character, store in the correct*/
/*place of the result string*/
Result[strpos] = ((int)(future/digitpower))+ (int)48;
strpos++;
/*strip the leading digit; it's been converted*/
future = future- (int)(future/digitpower) * digitpower;
/*put in a comma if we're at millions or thousands place*/
if ((digits==6)||(digits==3))
{
Result[strpos]=',';
strpos++;
}
/*put in a period if we're at ones place*/
if (digits==0)
{
Result[strpos]='.';
strpos++;
}
}
/*don't forget the null character at the string's end!*/

Result[strpos]='\0';
```

The really tricky part of the conversion procedure is to strip off the leading digit of the numeric result variable on each pass through the loop. If the result had been an integer value, you could have used the modulus operator (see chapter 8, "Performing Mathematical Calculations in C"); the modulus of the number by the power of that digit position would have been the remainder; that is, everything to the right of that digit. For example 65,125%10,000 is 5,125. Unfortunately, you've got those cents to the right of the decimal. This makes the result a floating-point number; you can't use the modulus operator with floating-point numbers.

Thus, you have to create a modulus operation of your own; one that works with floating-point numbers:

```
future- (int)(future/digitpower) * digitpower
```

This line strips the leading digit off future on each pass.

Summary

In this chapter you looked at converting data from one form to another. C automatically converts data using type promotion and assignment conversion. You learned how to explicitly convert data using type casts and then briefly touched on some string-to-number functions, to convert string data into numerical form.

Review questions

1   A long integer and a single-precision floating-point integer (types `long` and `float`) both occupy four bytes in memory. What's the difference (if any) in how values are stored in these variables?

2   What is meant by *type promotion* and *most inclusive type*? What are the most and least inclusive data type?

3   What happens when you assign a floating-point value to an integer variable?

4   What's a *type cast*?

5   What's the only difference in the three string-to-number functions?

Exercises

1   Write an expression to convert the result of dividing two floating-point numbers by each other into an integer value. There are actually two ways of doing this; see if you can find both.

2   Write a short block of statements that takes input from the keyboard in string form—use `gets()`—and then converts the result into an integer and prints it.

3   Write a short program that takes separate digits from an input number in floating-point form and prints each digit on a separate line.

19

Get Strings To Do
What You Want

● **In this chapter:**

- **What do I need to know about C string functions?**

- **You can copy and compare strings**

- **Search for one string inside another string**

You know that word processors have a search–and–replace capability. But did you know that many of C's string functions are like that search–and–replace capability? . . . . ▶

Handling strings isn't as easy in C as it is in many other programming languages. However, you're not completely hamstrung when working with strings in C. In fact, there are some fairly powerful manipulations available to you in this language; you merely have to know how to use them properly. C string manipulations require more thought and precision on your part as programmer, that's all.

What you need to know about string functions

Although using strings in C is an art, many of the things you can do with strings will seem quite familiar to you. All of these manipulations are handled by C's string functions. String functions appear to duplicate real-life operations. In fact, you'll find that many of the string functions are like the search-and-replace capability of a word processor, among other things. In this chapter you learn several more ANSI Standard C string functions (and a few that aren't but are very common). First, though, a little more about strings themselves.

What you need to know about strings

To repeat, a string in C is an array of variables with the type char. A char-type variable stores a single byte; each unique byte (there are 256 possibilities) is associated with a single alphanumeric character or symbol or with a control code. A string can be initialized when first declared; this sets it equal to a literal string constant. The following line of code creates a string variable and initializes it:

```
char MyString[12]="Your Name";
```

What does string length really mean?

The length of a string refers to how many characters it contains. A string actually has two lengths: a **maximum length** and a **current length**. The maximum length is the number of character variables in the array constituting the string. The preceding code line created MyString, which has a maximum length of 12 (not 13—you learn why in just a bit).

The current length of a string refers to how many characters are actually stored in it at a given time. In the case of `MyString`, which was initialized to `Your Name`, the string's current length is nine. That's how many characters there are (the blank space counts as one) in the literal string constant with which `MyString` was initialized.

Chapter 15, "String Variables as Places for Characters," introduced a handy function for determining the length of a string, `strlen()`. The function's prototype is

```
int strlen(char *pointer);
```

The function expects a *pointer* to a char-type variable. This, of course, is just the name of the string variable whose length you want to determine. The following line finds the current length of the string variable `MyString` and puts it into an integer variable named `Length`.

```
Length = strlen(MyString);
```

How strings are stored

For more information about pointers, see chapter 17, "How To Indirectly Access Data Storage with Pointers."

How is it that a function like `strlen()` "knows" how long a string is? It looks for the null character that terminates every string. The null character is represented by the escape code `\0`. The `strlen()` function starts at the beginning of the string and proceeds character by character through the string until it comes to the null character. The beginning of the string is passed to the function as an argument; it's a pointer. (Recall that a pointer contains the address of a variable's beginning.) In C, the name of an array constitutes a string constant pointing to the array's first element. As C strings are arrays of char-type variables, the name of a string constitutes a pointer to the string's beginning.

The null character is very important. If you write a program that assembles a string without including the null character at the string's end, you're going to be in for some grief. C does not care how many elements you gave to the array that constitutes the string (unless you try to directly access an element out of the initial range; then watch out!). What it looks for is the null character. C continues zipping through memory byte by byte until it finds a null character. You may end up with a lot of garbage data stored way past the end of your original string variable.

The basics of string functions

Most of the prototypes for the C string functions are included in the string.h header file. All the string functions expect at the very least a pointer to a string as an argument. Some expect pointers to additional strings. Some require integer values as well. While some functions return integer values, others return a pointer to a new string.

Again, the name of a string variable serves as a pointer to a string, so you can use a string's name anywhere you're required to supply a pointer. A literal string constant—text enclosed in double quotation marks—also serves anywhere you'd use a pointer to a string. However, don't use single quotes. An item enclosed in single quotes does not have the terminating null character that C string functions require.

Catch the bug

The following short program is supposed to find the length of a string input by the user. Can you spot what's wrong with it?

```
#include <stdio.h>
char inputstring[20]="";
int length;
main()
{
puts("\nEnter a string whose length you want to know");
gets(inputstring);
length = strlen(inputstring);
printf("\nThe string's length is %d characters", length);
}
```

Answer: *The prototype for the* strlen() *function is contained in the* string.h *header file. The preceding program listing omits an* #include *statement with this file. Consequently, your C compiler has no idea what you're talking about. The corrected line follows:*

```
#include <string.h>
```

You can copy strings with...

Perhaps one of the most common things to do with strings is to copy one into another. This is because C doesn't let you copy strings in an assignment statement. For example, the following statement copies the contents of the integer variable MyVariable to the integer variable YourVariable:

```
YourVariable = MyVariable;
```

However, trying to copy strings this way doesn't work. You can't have

```
YourString = MyString;
```

and expect the contents of MyString to be copied to YourString. You could write a loop to copy a string, proceeding character by character to copy the contents of each element in MyString to the corresponding element in YourString, until the null character is reached. You'd have to be sure to copy that one as well. However, it's much simpler to use the C string copying functions already provided. There are two: one to copy an entire string to another string and one to copy a specified number of characters.

...strcpy()...

You use the strcpy() function to copy one string to another (refer to chapter 15, "String Variables as Places for Characters," for an introduction to strcpy()). The prototype for the strcpy() function is

```
char *strcpy(char *destination_string, const char
➥*source_string);
```

This function copies all of the *source_string* to the *destination_string*, whose original contents are destroyed. The source can be a literal string constant. The function actually returns a value, a pointer to the *destination_string*. This value is seldom needed. The *destination_string* variable must be long enough, or you'll run into trouble.

The following copies a single dollar sign to the Result string variable:

```
strcpy(Result, "$");
```

...and `strncpy()`

You use the `strncpy()` function to copy a specified number of characters from a source string to a destination string, whose former original is destroyed. The prototype for this function is

```
char *strncpy(char *dest_string, const char *source_string,
    int num_to_cpy);
```

This function copies *num_to_copy* characters of the *source_string* to the *dest_string*. The parameter *num_to_copy* can be an expression. The source can be a literal string constant. The function actually returns a value, a pointer to the *dest_string*. This value is seldom needed. The *dest_string* variable must be long enough.

If *source_string* is shorter than the number of characters you specified it should copy, null characters pad out the result. The following short program illustrates use of the `strncpy()` function:

```
#include <stdio.h>
#include <string.h>
char source[25], dest[25]="";
int numchar;
main()
{
puts("\nEnter a string");
gets(source);
puts("Enter the number of characters to copy");
scanf("%d",&numchar);
strncpy(dest,source,numchar);
printf("The first %d characters of
    the string are\n%s\n",numchar,dest);
```

code The preceding short program prompts the user to enter a string, which is then read into the variable `source`. The user is next prompted to enter a number of characters to copy; this number is stored in `numchar`. The program then uses `strncpy()` to copy `numchar` number of characters from source into the string variable `dest`. Finally, it prints the contents of `dest` in a message indicating how many characters were copied.

You can compare strings

Another thing to do to two strings is to compare them. When you do this, you find out if the two strings are equal or unequal. If they're unequal, that means that one of them comes before the other in alphabetical order. So you can use the string comparison functions to sort a group of strings into order. There are three such functions. Unfortunately, they are not ANSI Standard C. However, many C compilers support them.

CAUTION **If you use a non-ANSI Standard C function that happens to be** supported by your compiler, you'll be comprising the portability of your program. If you don't want to try to run the program on another type of computer system, this isn't a problem. However, use of non-ANSI Standard C functions can make it difficult or impossible to port a program from one system to another—for example, from Windows 95 to UNIX.

Your basic string comparison with strcmp()

The strcmp() function compares two strings and, depending on how the two strings compare, returns an integer value. The prototype for this function is

```
int strcmp(const char *string1, const char *string2);
```

The value returned by strcmp() is less than zero if *string1* is less than *string2* (that is, if *string1* comes before *string2* in alphabetical order). The value is zero if the two strings are identical. The value is greater than zero if *string2* is less than *string1*. Note that strcmp() is case-sensitive, meaning "Hicks" is not the same as "hicks" as far as this function is concerned. (The former comes first because capital letters precede small letters in ASCII.)

The following short program demonstrates using strcmp() to find which of two strings input by the user should come first in alphabetical order.

```
#include <stdio.h>
#include <string.h>
char first[25], second[25];
int result;
main()
{
```

```
puts("\nEnter a string");
gets(first);
puts("\nEnter another string");
gets(second);
result = strcmp(first, second);
if (result > 0)
{
printf("\n%s\n%s",second, first);
}
else
printf("\n%s\n%s",first, second);
}
```

This program first prompts the user to enter two separate strings. It then uses strcmp() to compare the two. If the result returned from strcmp() is greater than zero, then the second string is earlier in the alphabet than the first; the two strings are printed in that order. Otherwise, the first string comes first and is printed that way.

If you don't want to worry about capitalization, use strcmpi()

The strcmp() function is case-sensitive; this means that capitalization counts. The string NAME is not the same as name in this scheme. Now, some C compilers include a string comparison function that ignores case; viewing strings such as NAME and name is done the same way.

The exact name of this function depends on the compiler you're using. So you'll need to check your documentation to see if the function is even available, and if so, what it's called. Usually it's something like strcmpi() or stricmp(). Again, this function is non-ANSI Standard C, so using it at all may compromise your program's portability.

If you only want to compare a part of two strings, use strncmp()

Just as you can copy a certain number of characters from one string to another, you can compare a portion of two strings. The function to do this is strncmp(). Its prototype is

```
int strncmp(const char *str1, const char *str2, int
➥num_of_char);
```

This function looks at the first *num_of_char* in each string and compares them. The results returned are the same as for the strcmp() function: greater than zero if *str2* is smaller than *str1*, zero if the two are equal, and less than zero if *str1* is smaller than *str2*.

Catch the bug

The following block of code is intended to compare an input string with a reference value to determine what message to print. Specifically, it scans a text string to see if the first three characters are equal to Mr. Can you spot a problem?

```
puts("Input your full name, title included:);
gets(FullName);
result = strncmp(FullName, "MR.", 3);
if (result==0)
{
strcpy(Salutation, "Sir");
}
else
strcpy(Salutation, "Madame");
```

Answer: *In the call to strncmp(), the reference value is given as MR. This value is entirely in uppercase. If the user enters Mr., the program is going to print a salutation of Madame. If available, a case-insensitive string com-parison function should be used. If not, then you must use strncmp() twice, searching for both MR. and Mr.*

You can search for a string inside another string with...

The last group of useful functions you'll consider in this chapter are those that look for one string within another. These are the functions that behave much like the find or search-and-replace capabilities of a word processor. You provide them with text to search and something to search for; they tell you where (or if) the search text occurs.

...strchr()...

The strchr() function returns the first location of a specific character within another string. Its prototype is

```
char *strchr(const char *search_string, int
➥character_to_find);
```

The strchr() function returns a pointer to the location of the *character_to_find* if found. A null value is returned if the character isn't found. To find the actual character position, you'll need to perform pointer arithmetic. Subtract from the value of this pointer the value of the pointer to the string's first character; the result is the character position as an integer.

For example, the following two lines of code use the strchr() function to return the position of the first space in the string MyString. The second line uses pointer arithmetic to convert the absolute position in memory of the first space into a relative position—relative, that is, to the first character in the string:

```
pLocation = strchr(MyString, ' ');
Position = pLocation - MyString;
```

...strrchr()...

The function strrchr() is identical to strchar(), except that it looks for the *last* occurrence of a specific character in a string. Otherwise, it behaves in precisely the same way.

...strcspn()...

The function strcspn() searches a string for the first occurrence of any of the characters in a second, reference string. Its prototype is

```
int strcspn(const char *search_string, const char
➥*char_string);
```

The function returns an integer equal to the position of the first character from *char_string* found in *search_string*. If no such character is found, then the value returned is equal to the length of *search_string*.

You can use this function to look for any of the characters that might logically break a string, say a name, into parts. In the case of a name, a space, comma, or period might divide the name. The function might also look for an operation symbol like *, +, -, or /. The following line of code uses strcspn() to search the string FullName for a space, period, or comma:

```
Result = strcspn(FullName, " .,");
```

...and strstr()

This is the function that searches a source string for the first occurrence of a target string. Its prototype is

```
char *strstr(const char *source_string, const char *
➥tar_string);
```

This function returns a pointer to the location of the first character in the first occurrence of *source_string* within *tar_string*. If nothing is found, the null value is returned.

Show me an example of using string functions

Now it's time to put all this stuff (or much of it, anyway) into a program.

You want a program that lets the user input ten names in ordinary form. That is, first name, middle initial, and then last name. The title (Mr., Mrs., etc.) is optional; the program won't blow up if it's entered. Now, after the names are entered, the program rearranges them into last-name-first order, that is, if the input is

```
Clint R. Hicks
```

the program outputs

```
Hicks, Clint R.
```

Finally, the program looks at all the names and alphabetizes the list. The alphabetized list, in last-name-first order, is what the program prints. Listing 19.1 shows the program.

Listing 19.1   An alphabetizing program

```
#include <stdio.h>
#include <string.h>

/*A program to put into inverse order,
➥and alphabetize a list of names*/

struct names
{
char FullName[40];
} NameList[10];

struct holder
{
char NameHolder[40];
} Hold;

int counter, counter2, counter3, position, result;
char *pLastPosition;


main()
{
puts("This program lets the user
➥input ten names, then reverse the order");
puts("of each, and prints the entire list in alphabetical
➥order");

 /*Have the user input ten names*/
 for (counter = 1; counter<= 10; counter++)
     {
     puts("Enter a name, first name first, title optional");
     gets(NameList[counter].FullName);
     }

 /*Reverse the order of each name; look for the last space*/

 for (counter = 1; counter <= 10; counter++)
     {
     pLastPosition =strrchr(NameList[counter].FullName,
     ➥' ');
     position = pLastPosition - NameList[counter].FullName;
     /*Copy the characters from the blank position + 1
     ➥forward*/
     counter3 = 0;
      for (counter2 = position+1; counter2<=strlen
      ➥(NameList[counter].FullName); counter2++)
          {
          Hold.NameHolder[counter3++]=NameList
          ➥[counter].FullName[counter2];
          }
```

```
                strcat (Hold.NameHolder, ", ");
                strncat(Hold.NameHolder, NameList
                ➥[counter].FullName, position);
                strcpy (NameList[counter].FullName , Hold.NameHolder);
                }

        /*Now alphabetize the list*/
        for (counter = 1; counter <=10; counter++)
            {
            for (counter2 = counter+1; counter2<=10; counter2++)
                {
                result = strcmp(NameList[counter].FullName,
                ➥NameList[counter2].FullName);
                if (result>0)
                    {
                    strcpy(Hold.NameHolder,NameList[counter].FullName);
                     strcpy(NameList[counter].FullName ,
                     ➥NameList[counter2].FullName);
                     strcpy(NameList[counter2].FullName ,
                     ➥Hold.NameHolder);
                     }
                }
            }
        /*print the results*/
        puts("");
         for (counter =1; counter <=10;        counter++)
         puts(NameList[counter].FullName);

        /*Pause for input*/
        scanf("%d",result);
    }
```

For clarity and relative ease of manipulation, the names are input into a
structure of string variables. You also need an "assembly" area for the newly
ordered names; this, too, is a structure. It's in this assembly area that the
reverse-order names are constructed, prior to being read back into place in
the original list. This assembly area also serves to hold values as they're
sorted.

The program relies on the strrchr() function to locate the last blank in a
name; this is assumed to be the one preceding the last name. This information is used to isolate that part of the name. The strcmp() function is used
to determine alphabetical order, using a form of loop referred to as a bubble
search; the lower values are said to "bubble" up to the top as the loop
proceeds.

The code starts with the first member of the array `NameList`. It compares this member with each subsequent member in turn. If a subsequent member is found to be less than the current member, then the two are swapped. Otherwise, nothing happens. After all the comparisons have been done on the first member of `NameList`, the sort proceeds to the second member and repeats the procedure. This continues to the next-to-last member. Names that are closer to first in an alphabetical listing are constantly being swapped up to higher positions; bubbling to the top as it were.

You should note that this sorting algorithm, although fine for small lists, is grossly inefficient for sorting large numbers of items.

Figure 19.1 shows the results of running this program.

Fig. 19.1

Reversing and sorting some names entered by the user.

```
Enter a name, first name first, title optional:
Angelina Ballerina
Enter a name, first name first, title optional:
Mr. Clinton R. Hicks
Enter a name, first name first, title optional:
Dr. Rosa Fernandez
Enter a name, first name first, title optional:
Ms. Rosanna Dill
Enter a name, first name first, title optional:
Master Gabriel Richard Allen Hicks
Enter a name, first name first, title optional:
F. Lee Aardvark
Enter a name, first name first, title optional:
Efram Zimbalist
Enter a name, first name first, title optional:
Angelina G. Hicks
Enter a name, first name first, title optional:
Lady Margaret Thatcher
Enter a name, first name first, title optional:
Elizabeth Tudor

Aardvark, F. Lee
Ballerina, Angelina
Dill, Ms. Rosanna
Fernandez, Dr. Rosa
Hicks, Angelina G.
Hicks, Mr. Clinton R.
Hicks, Master Gabriel Richard Allen
Thatcher, Lady Margaret
Tudor, Elizabeth
Zimbalist, Efram
```

How can I use this in the real world?

A C function that's capable of isolating the last name out of a full name and title entered by the user can be put to work in a number of contexts. Such a user-defined function, which might resemble the program shown in listing 19.1, could form an important part of a simple database program. Rather than relying on the user to enter a name piece by piece, the program could use its own function to isolate the parts of a name from the full line of text entered by the user. Users like programs that do most of the work for them.

Summary

In this chapter you looked at more functions for working with character strings. After reviewing some facts about how strings are stored, you looked at some string function basics. You then looked at functions to copy strings, compare strings, and search strings.

Review questions

1 What is the *null character*? Why is it important?

2 What is the difference between the maximum length and the current length of a string? How does C determine the current length? What string function returns the current length?

3 Where are the prototypes for the string functions defined?

4 What function do you use to copy the first *n* characters of one string to another?

5 What is the difference between the functions `strchr()` and `strrchr()`?

Exercises

1 Write a block of statements to look for the last comma in a given string.

2 Write a block of statements that examines a string for the first occurrence of one of the decimal digits.

3 Modify the `NameList` program given in this chapter so that, if the user enters some further designation after a trailing comma, such as **Mr. Oliver Boliver Buttes, Jr.**, the program still returns the correct answer, which in this case is

```
Buttes, Mr. Oliver Boliver, Jr.
```

20

Control a Program—Where It Goes, What It Does...

● In this chapter:

- New ways to control programs

- I'm done using this loop, but the loop isn't done doing its thing

- Go to another part of the program

- You mean C programs can deal with multiple-choice questions?

- I want to leave early, but my program's not done

Want to greatly enhance the power and flexibility of your programs? You can by using the advanced program control statements offered in C. . . . .➤

For the most part, the simpler program control statements offer an either-or choice to a program, much like a fork in the road. Even a loop can be thought of in this way: "Proceed now or go back to the beginning of this block?" Frequently, however, you're presented with more than two choices as to what to do next. Now, given enough nested if blocks, you can create any sort of decision-making apparatus, but doing so is cumbersome and produces code that isn't exactly a model of clarity. At other times, you can construct a loop that looks through a group of values for an answer that could be anywhere. Once the answer is found, there's no use proceeding with the loop; after all, the answer can only be found once. Wouldn't it be nice to be able to leave the loop early, after an answer has been located?

Can I make my programs more flexible?

Indeed you can. C has additional program control statements that address the preceding issues and more. Using these program control statements can greatly enhance the power and flexibility of your programs. They can also make your programming life a whole lot easier. The kinds of statements you look at in this chapter are mainly concerned with exiting loops and blocks early, setting up multiple-case scenarios, and interfacing with the computer world outside your program—that is, with the operating system.

I'm done using this loop!

Consider a loop that searches an array structure for a particular name. It's known that the name only occurs once in the array. The name could be anywhere; it's most likely in the middle of the array. What does your program do once the name is found?

If the program is structured the way you've been doing things until now, it continues the search until it reaches the end of the array, even though the correct item has already been found. While you could construct a while loop that only looks until the item is located, you need to make certain the loop doesn't continue executing forever in addition to stopping when the answer was located. This might call from some tricky logic on your part.

A better way is to rely on C's break statement, used in conjunction with if. When C encounters break, it immediately exits the loop it's in and executes the next executable statement after that loop. Judicious use of `break` can save your programs a good bit of processing power. Why keep looking for something once you've found it?

C has a milder form of `break` called `continue`. You can use this statement if you want, for example, to perform an operation only on selected items within an array. When a C program encounters `continue`, it skips the remainder of the loop and proceeds to the next iteration. You can use `continue` in conjunction with a test; if the item being tested (with `if`, of course) doesn't meet your criteria, you have the loop `continue` to the next item.

I have several choices, but is there an easier way to program this without `if`s?

I claimed earlier that some choices involve more than two alternatives. Suppose, for example, you add two additional capabilities to a financial program—calculating different annuities, perhaps. While it is possible to construct a set of nest `if` blocks to accommodate the additional choices, it would be nice if it could all be handled in one structure. Isn't that what structured programming is all about?

Using the C `switch()` statement, you can create just such a structure. `switch()` lets you set up a single test condition and a group of alternative statement blocks. Only one of the blocks executes, depending on the results of the test. For example, the test might determine the contents of an input variable. The different alternatives are associated with the different values a user might enter, such as "I" for interest, "P" for payment, and so on. In such a way you can construct a menuing system for your program and also handle what happens when the user presses certain function keys. `select` is probably the most powerful of the C program control statements because of all the things you can do with it.

Communicating with the operating system

At times you may need your program to interface in some manner with the outside world. From a program's point of view, the outside world means the operating system (OS). There are three main things you can do with the OS from within a C program.

The simplest one is simply to terminate executing and return control to the OS. Although all C programs do this when they encounter the terminal brace, there may be times when you want to leave a program early. In a program with a menuing system, this may just be because the user chose the program's Quit command. Or it might be the program has located the correct answer and doesn't need to continue. In any case, you can leave a program early using the `exit()` function.

For DOS systems, you can specify some tasks that need to be done before the program returns control to the OS. You've probably encountered such a situation already in your work with other programs. For example, a word processor asks if you want to save your work after you choose Quit, for instance. The C function `atexit()` lets you specify up to 32 functions that should be executed before the program actually finishes quitting. The functions, of course, need to be defined within your program as you've done before.

Finally, you can issue a command directly to your computer's OS from within a C program. One really handy use of this capability is to clear the screen before writing new output. Previous programs in this book have been a little messy in this regard. The C function `system()` lets you execute any valid OS command. You should note that using this capability requires a good bit of memory because an entirely new copy of your computer's command processor (COMMAND.COM in the case of DOS and Windows, the console in the case of UNIX) must be loaded into memory.

So there are really lots of ways you can rev up your programs and give them the capability to deal with lots of situations. The first of these you look at in detail is getting out of loops.

Getting out of loops early with...

To repeat, C has two statements that are associated with leaving a loop early or skipping part of a loop. The `break` statement leaves a loop entirely; the `continue` statement skips only that part of the loop that follows `continue`— and only for that particular pass through the loop.

...break...

When a C program encounters break, it immediately leaves the loop that it encounters break in and proceeds to execute the next executable statement following break. The general form of a break statement is simply

```
break;
```

Simply entering break like this on one line within a loop isn't useful because the program automatically leaves the loop on the first pass. Instead, it's convention to pair break with a test executed by means of an if statement, as in

```
if Input == '\0'
    break;
```

These two statements cause a break out of the loop if, for instance, the user merely pressed the Enter key without typing any data. You could use such a structure to end an input loop early, should the user not want to enter the maximum number of values. In the following section of code, I've included lines to allow the user to terminate data entry early, rather than entering all ten names called for.

```
/*Have the user input ten names*/
 for (counter = 1; counter<= 10; counter++)
     {
     puts("Enter a name, first name first,
     ➥title optional, Enter nothing to stop");
     gets(NameList[counter].FullName);
     if (strlen(NameList[counter].FullName) == 0)
         break;
     }
NumberEntered = counter-1;
```

The code looks to see if the string entered has a length of zero; if so, the user merely pressed Enter, so the loop exits. Note that this block of code preserves the value of the variable counter minus one. This lets the rest of the program know how many values were actually entered by the user. On the last pass through the loop, if no value is entered, the instance is discarded. That's why the program subtracts one from the value of counter.

TIP **If you're like me, you occasionally mix up the assignment operator (=)** with the "equal" comparison operator (==). A good way to avoid the = versus == problem is to always do your evaluation with the constant on the left of the comparison as in

```
if (0 == strlen(NameList[counter].FullName))
```

The compiler catches this if you tried

```
if (0 = strlen(NameList[counter].FullName))
```

SPEAKING C

Catch the bug

What's wrong with the following loop that uses a break statement to exit early?

```
for (counter = 1; counter<= 10; counter++)
    {
    puts("Enter a name, first name first,
    ➥title optional, Enter nothing to stop");
     (NameList[counter].FullName);
    if ( *(pInputPointer=gets(NameList
    ➥[counter].FullName)) == NULL);
        break;
    }
```

Answer: This is a tricky one. gets() *actually returns a pointer to the beginning of the input string; this value is being read into* pInPutPointer *in the* if *statement. The indirection operator then refers to the contents of the string pointed to. The value* NULL *is the null pointer valued, defined as a symbolic constant in the standard header file.*

None of this is the problem. The problem is that the if *statement terminates with a semicolon. Your C compiler won't catch this. Because the semicolon is where it is, nothing happens if the test condition is met; in other words, the* break *statement always executes. The loop allows only one value to be input. Remove the semicolon on the line with* if, *and all is well.*

...and `continue`

The form of the `continue` statement is also very simple; it's just

    continue;

As with `break`, you generally use `continue` with some form of `if` statement. Again, `continue` causes the remainder of the current pass through a loop to be skipped. Execution continues with the next iteration if there is one. Encountering `continue` on the last pass through a loop is the same as encountering `break`.

Going from one place in a program to another

I'm going to start by saying that this is a delicate subject in programming circles. This is why I haven't emphasized it very much in the opening of this chapter or elsewhere in the book. I'm referring to use of the `goto` statement to immediately transfer execution in a program from one point to another labeled point.

How can I use this in the real world?

Within a loop, you could use the `continue` statement to make sure that any special processing the loop accomplishes is only applied to those data items that need it. For example, suppose you have a function that reverses the order of a full name and title, with `Mr. Clinton R. Hicks` becoming `Hicks, Mr. Clinton R.`. Now suppose further you want to allow titles to be entered, like `Efram Zimbalist, Jr.` and `Dr. Rosa Fernandez, Ph.D.`. You could use `continue` to make sure only those names got special processing.

Within your processing loop, you search each entered name for a comma. If the name contained a comma, that would mean it had a title and required special processing. If no comma was found, you just have the program use `continue` to proceed to the next name.

The `goto` statement

When a C program encounters `goto`, it immediately and unconditionally transfers execution from that statement to the one specified by the `goto` statement.

Dos and don'ts of `goto`

In a classroom context—most especially at college—use of `goto` is almost universally discouraged. In fact, when I first took programming at college, use of a `goto` statement in any program submitted for course credit was considered immediate and sufficient grounds for the student to fail the entire course. I didn't fail a programming course.

Yet the statement also has its passionate defenders, whose hackles are definitely raised when the `goto` prohibition is brought up. These individuals claim it's absurd to forbid use of a perfectly good statement, and that if `goto` is so bad, it ought to be dropped from the language.

Why the fuss? In a nutshell, using `goto` creates programs that are difficult to read and debug. You're never really sure where the program is going to end

Speaking of `goto`

The general form of a `goto` statement is

```
goto label;
```

Here, *label* is a C identifier that is attached to a statement. A *label* consists of a name and a colon, like

```
beginning: for (counter = 0; counter<=10; counter++)
```

A *label* can appear on the beginning of a line, or it can appear on a line by itself, in which case it must be followed by a semicolon.

```
beginning: ;
```

So a statement like

```
goto beginning;
```

transfers execution to the statement labeled beginning.

up in all cases. What's more, a program retains no memory of where it came from after a goto statement is executed.

Why would you even use goto? Mainly to skip a group of statements that you don't want to execute. Clearly it's kind of dumb to always skip a block of statements—you'd just as well remove them altogether if they're never executed—so goto is frequently used with if to skip a group of statements if some condition is met.

Now, it should be clear that you can accomplish the same feat by using if blocks along with else. In fact, there's nothing you can do with goto that can't be done with some other statement. I'm not about to recommend an absolute prohibition against use of this statement; there may be strange and limited cases where it makes sense. However, do keep in mind that there's likely a better way than using goto.

Q&A *If using it is so bad, why is* goto *even in the language?*

It's a relic from earlier days. goto was about the first way available to alter program execution at all; it's very similar to an underlying machine language instruction to transfer execution. People got used to using it, and it stuck. The command has one thing going for it—it's fast.

Use switch() for several options in a program

Now, you come to one of the programming structures that has helped make goto virtually obsolete. Using a block of statements constructed with switch(), you can have a program execute one out of a number of scenarios, based on the results of a test.

You use switch() along with the keyword case to have a program switch execute to a particular block of statements. All the other blocks within a switch() structure are ignored. The handy thing about switch() is that the test condition can assume a range of values, not just 1 and 0 like an if statement. You can have a case for each possible value of the test condition.

Catch the bug

The following block of code uses a `goto` statement. Can you spot a problem?

```
start:;
puts("Input a number");
gets(Input);
ProcessInput(Input);
goto start;
```

Answer: This block of code appears to create an infinite loop. Any time you use a goto statement to transfer backward in a program, you risk creating such a loop. If the function ProcessInput() does nothing to terminate the program, the loop never stops. A better solution is to use a while loop.

```
while (Input != NULL)
{
puts("Input a number");
gets(Input);
ProcessInput(Input);
}
```

Speaking of `switch`

The form of a block using the `switch` construction is

```
switch (test_expression)
{
    case value1: statement(s);
    case value2: statements(s);
    ....
    case valuelast: statements(s);
    default: statements(s);
}
```

When a program encounters a switch statement, it tests the associated condition (*test_expression*). Based on the integer value of the *test_expression*, it then transfers execution to the case block labeled with the appropriate *value*.

Note that switch is much like goto, in that everything following the particular case statement chosen also executes. To have only the statements in that case block execute, which is what you really want, include a break statement in each case block. The following example prints a different message depending on what the user entered:

```
switch (InputValue)
{
case 1:
    {
    puts("The user entered one");
    break;
    }
case 2:
    {
    puts("The user entered two");
    break;
    }
default:
    {
    puts(The user entered something else");
    break;
    }
}
```

If, for example, the variable InputValue contains 2 when this switch block is encountered, execution transfers to case 2:. If InputValue contains 0, 3, or any other integer value besides 1 and 2, execution transfers to default:. You use this particular part of switch to handle instances in which the *test_expression* doesn't evaluate to any of the listed options.

Catch the bug

The following `switch` block is meant to call a particular function based on which number selection the user enters. Can you spot a problem?

```
puts("Enter 1 for interest,
➥2 for payment, anything else to quit");
scanf("%d", &Input);
switch (Input)
{
case 1:
    Interest(balance, rate);
case 2:
    Payment(balance, rate);
default:
    Exit();
}
```

Answer: Because break *statements are omitted from each case, every function could end up being called. This happens if the user enters 1. If the user enters 2, both* Payment *and* Exit *are called. For the construction to work properly,* break *must be added to each case, as in:*

```
puts("Enter 1 for interest, 2 for payment,
➥anything else to quit");
scanf("%d", &Input);
switch (Input)
{
case 1:
    {
    Interest(balance, rate);
    break:
    }
case 2:
    {
    Payment(balance, rate);
    break;
    }
default:
    Exit();
}
```

There's no need to add break *to the* default: *case because nothing comes after it, anyway.*

How can I use this in the real world?

While there are a number of places you can use the `switch()` construction, one good place is to create a menuing system where the user may choose from among a set of actions. It's fairly typical to provide such choices by means of the function keys. You use a `switch()` construction to define what should happen when the user presses one of the function keys shown by your menu. (Your menu consists just of a line of text defining what each available function key does; you display it with one or more calls to `puts()`.)

It's important to know that a function key (F1–F12) actually returns two values when the user presses it; 0 followed by another byte that actually refers to the key. The second-byte values for the first ten function keys and their shifted second-byte values follow:

Key	Standard	Shifted
F1	59	84
F2	60	85
F3	61	86
F4	62	87
F5	63	88
F6	64	89
F7	65	90
F8	66	91
F9	67	92
F10	68	93

To use these values within a `switch()` block, you need to retrieve both bytes using the `getch()` function. It's the value of the second byte that matters. Your `default:` block (this is what happens if the user presses any other key) could simply do nothing.

Show me an example of using `switch()`

The FINANCE program in listing 20.1 uses a `switch()` construction, along with function keys.

Listing 20.1 **The `switch()` construction in the FINANCE program**

```
/*A program to do certain financial calculations*/
#include <stdio.h>
#include <math.h>
#include <conio.h>
#include <stdlib.h>

/*Declare variables*/
/*Function Prototypes*/

float CompInt (float balance, float rate, float months);

float Payment (float balance, float rate, float months);

main()
{
char recycle;
float future, balance, rate, months, digitpower;
int digits, strpos;
char Result[12]="";
recycle = 58;
puts("A program to find either
➥compound interest or a loan payment");

while (1)
    {
    /*Have the user input the values desired
    ➥for the present balance, the rate, and the time */
    printf("\nEnter the principal: ");
    scanf("%f",&balance);
    printf("\nEnter the interest rate in percent per
    ➥year:  ");
    scanf("%f",&rate);
    printf("\nEnter the number of months: ");
    scanf("%f",&months);
    system("cls");
    /*Verify amounts entered, skip calculation if any nega-
    ➥tive*/
    if ((balance<=0)||(rate<=0)||(months<=0))
        puts("Invalid data entered");
    else
    {
        /*Have the user choose the desired calculation*/
```

```
puts("\nPress F1 for compound interest,
➥F2 for loan payment, F3 to quit ");
recycle=getch();
if (recycle == 0)
     recycle = getch();
switch (recycle)
{
case 59:
     {
     puts("\n\n\t\tCalculating compound
     ➥interest\n\n");
     future = CompInt(balance, rate, months);

     /* Convert future into Result,
     ➥a string with commas, $*/
     Result[0]='$';
     digits = log10(future);
     strpos = 1;
     for (;digits>=-2; digits--)
          {
          digitpower = pow((double) 10.0,
          ➥(double)digits);
          Result[strpos] = ((int)
          ➥(future/digitpower))+ (int)48;
          strpos++;
          future = future- (int)
          ➥(future/digitpower) * digitpower;
          if ((digits==6)||(digits==3))
               {
               Result[strpos]=',';
               strpos++;
               }
          if (digits==0)
               {
               Result[strpos]='.';
               strpos++;
               }
          }

     Result[strpos]='\0';
   puts("\t\t\t********************************");
     printf("\t\t\t* The result is %s \t*\n",
     ➥Result);
   puts("\t\t\t********************************\n");
     break;
     }

case 60:
     {
```

continues

Listing 20.1 Continued

```
                    puts("\n\nCalculating loan payment");
                    future = Payment(balance,rate,months);
                        /* Convert future into Result,
                        ➥a string with commas,$*/
                    Result[0]='$';
                    digits = log10(future);
                    strpos = 1;
                    for (;digits>=-2; digits--)
                        {
                        digitpower = pow((double)
                        ➥10.0, (double)digits);
                        Result[strpos] = ((int)
                        ➥(future/digitpower))+ (int)48;
                        strpos++;
                        future = future- (int)
                        ➥(future/digitpower) * digitpower;
                        if ((digits==6)||(digits==3))
                            {
                            Result[strpos]=',';
                            strpos++;
                            }
                        if (digits==0)
                            {
                            Result[strpos]='.';
                            strpos++;
                            }
                        }

                Result[strpos]='\0';
              puts("\t\t\t********************************");
                printf("\t\t\t* The result is %s \t*\n",
                ➥Result);
              puts("\t\t\t********************************\n");
                break;
            }


        case 61:
            exit(EXIT_SUCCESS);

        default:

        ;}
        }
    puts ("Press F3 to quit; anything else to continue");
    recycle = getch();
    if (recycle ==0)
        {
```

```
                    recycle = getch();
                    if (recycle == 61)
                         exit(EXIT_SUCCESS);
               }
          }
          return 0;
          }

          float CompInt ( float balance, float rate, float months)
          {
                    return (balance * pow(2.7183,(rate/
                    ➡1200.0*months)));
          }

          float Payment ( float balance, float rate, float months)
          {
                    return (rate/1200.) *balance* pow(2.7183,(rate/
                    ➡1200.0*months))/(pow(2.7183,(double)(rate/
          1200.*months))-1);
          }
```

This program exists in an infinite loop; it relies on the user to press F3 to exit. Within the outer loop is a `select()` construction; which of the cases is used depends on the second byte value of the function key pressed. If an undefined key—function key or otherwise—is pressed, the program does nothing and continues to wait for the user to make a selection. I cheated a little and used the `exit()` function, which is discussed later in this chapter.

There are other things you can make a program do

The last few examples of fine program manipulation you'll look at have mainly to do with the OS. They consist of quitting back to it or asking it to perform some command or other. Quitting, of course, is something you've already done in the preceding example.

Exit a program

To leave a program entirely, use the `exit()` function. This function's proto-type is defined in the header file `stdlib.h`. The prototype for this function is

```
void exit(int status);
```

The value in *status* is returned to the OS; the header file includes the symbolic constants exit_success and exit_failure for you to use. The return value is up to you to determine; it's for use by the OS but is usually ignored.

You can use the atexit() function to indicate what other functions should be run after exit() is called and before a program actually returns to the OS. I'll have more to say about atexit() in the next chapter.

C meet operating system

Finally, you can issue commands directly to your computer's OS from within a C program, presuming you've got enough memory to do so. You use the system() function to perform this valuable service.

 **CAUTION** **Using the system() command can compromise the portability of your programs.** That's because different OSs use different commands. The "clear screen" command previously shown, cls, only works for DOS; UNIX uses clear to clear the screen. A C program that uses cls in a call to system() won't work when compiled under UNIX.

If you look closely at the listing for the FINANCE program given earlier, you'll see that the program includes a call to clear the screen. (This only works on a DOS machine.) The output from this program is shown in figure 20.1.

Speaking of system()

The prototype for the system() function is included in stdlib.h. It is

```
int system(const char *command_string);
```

The *command_string* is the actual OS command you want to enter; the parameter can be a literal string constant or a pointer to a string containing a valid OS command. To issue the clear screen command to DOS, you use

```
system("cls");
```

Fig. 20.1
Clearing the FINANCE program screen after the user enters values to compute with.

```
Press F1 for compound interest, F2 for loan payment, F3 to
quit
Calculating compound interest
        ********************************
        *The result is $1,349.86        *
        ********************************
Press F3 to quit, anything else to continue
```

Summary

In this chapter you looked at ways to make your programs more powerful and flexible using advanced program control statements. You looked at exiting a loop early and at skipping the remainder of the current iteration through a loop. You also saw how to transfer execution unconditionally and set up blocks to choose one alternative from among several. Finally, you learned about exiting a program early and issuing commands to the operating system.

Review questions

1 Which statement do you use to transfer control to a labeled statement? What's wrong with using this statement?

2 What is switch() used for?

3 Indicate what happens when a program encounters break. What about continue?

4 What's the most essential thing to know about what happens when a user presses a function key?

5 Name a threat to program portability posed by use of the system() function.

Exercises

1 Write a loop that looks through an integer array for a value equal to zero. Have the program exit the loop when 0 is found, preserving the array element that 0 occurred in.

2 Write a loop that looks through another integer array and divides only the even numbers within it by two.

3 Write a short program that prints one of five different messages. Four of the messages are triggered by specific function keys—one of these messages prints if the corresponding function key is pressed. The fifth message prints if the user presses a key other than those four function keys.

What Else Can I Do with Functions?

● **In this chapter:**

- **In what other ways can I use functions?**

- **Did you know pointers can point to functions?**

- **Make functions more flexible**

- **I need this function to call itself**

Your C programs don't have to be built from the same dull, boring pieces. The topics in this chapter help you construct more flexible and more powerful building blocks for your programs . . . . ▶

Prior to this chapter, you've used quite a lot of C library functions—especially those connected with string variables—but very few functions of your own making. Now, that you've some experience with library functions and with C's more advanced data constructs like strings, structures, and pointers, it's time to return to the subject of user-defined functions.

There are ways to make functions more flexible

Remember that a function is a discrete block of C code—a small program in its own right—designed to accomplish a specific task. All C programs have at least one function, `main()`. In addition, a program may call on library functions, which are predefined blocks whose prototypes are defined in one or more header files. A program can also contain user-defined functions; these are blocks you write yourself. The code for such functions is included in the same file as the rest of the program. (In chapter 29, "Use Code That You or Somebody Else Has Already Written," you'll see how to employ user-defined functions held outside the main program source code file.)

A function communicates with the program that called it (to call a function is to run it) through its parameter list and its return value. The parameter list consists of variables whose contents are fed to the function when it's called. The return value is the answer the function sends back to the calling program. In some cases, a function may not expect any data from the program that calls it. In others, it may not return a value. Both cases are handled using the keyword `void`.

In this chapter, you expand on your current knowledge of functions. In so doing, I show you how to make your own functions work with pointers and, by extension, with strings as well. You also learn how to create flexible argument lists, something that you've seen in two of the C library functions—`printf()` and `scanf()`. You even learn about functions that call themselves—an interesting process that can be much more useful than you might think. Taken altogether, the topics in this chapter help you construct more flexible and more powerful building blocks for your programs.

Additional uses for pointers

*For more informa-
tion on strings, see
chapter 15, "String
Variables as Places
for Characters."*

If you stop to think about it, you'll agree that you've already used pointers as arguments to library functions. After all, that's just what an array's name is—a pointer constant pointing to the beginning of the array. Now, an array of char-type variables is a string, and you've used lots of string functions. So you've actually had a good bit of experience passing pointers to functions.

A function can also return a pointer. The gets() function is one example; if this function returns a null pointer, you know that the user pressed the Enter key without typing any data. You can use this fact to modify a data-entry function, so that the user can enter a variable number of data items.

As it turns out, though, there's a bit more to using pointers with functions than just passing and getting back the addresses of string variables. Passing a pointer to a variable, rather than the variable itself, allows a function to modify the original variable's contents. This is something that the standard way of passing a variable can't do. What's more, passing a pointer is the only way a function can access and work with an array variable. That's why all the string functions take pointers as arguments; after all, strings are character arrays.

You can even turn the relationship between pointer and function around, declaring a pointer that references a function. A function has an address in memory just as a variable does; you can initialize a pointer variable to reference this address. You can then call the function by using the pointer instead of the function's name. Why is this useful? Because you can then have the same section of code call a function from among several alternative functions, based on current circumstances. The exact function called depends on the pointer's contents. This, in turn, can be set according to current conditions, for example, depending on some choice made by the user.

A function can have a flexible number of arguments

Another way to make using functions more flexible is to give them argument lists that can support a variable number of arguments. You've used just such an argument list in two cases: with the scanf() and printf() functions. You can print one, two or several values with printf(); you can also have scanf() input more than one variable at a time.

Using some tools prototyped in `stdarg.h`, you can write functions of your own that accept variable numbers of arguments. Although using such a function requires you to know, when you call the function, how many arguments it actually has in that case, the resulting function is still more flexible than one expecting a fixed number of arguments.

Have a function call itself

Finally, there's absolutely nothing to prevent a function calling itself. This process is known as **recursion** and can be quite useful. In a way, a recursive function call is a lot like a loop; it performs the same calculation on data that varies until some end is reached. There are several important examples from mathematics where a recursive function call provides the easiest way to obtain the answer.

Of course, recursion has its dangers as well. You might think one danger is akin to an infinite loop, but actually, it's not possible to have infinite recursion. Here's why: each call to a function uses up a chunk of memory as all the values and operating parameters of the calling function are stored, pending return from the function that's been called. What actually happens is that eventually, as a function continues to call itself, your computer runs out of memory and crashes. That's really the main problem with recursion, but judicious programming and a little forethought helps you avoid it.

Those are the main subjects for this chapter. They do require you to be familiar with pointers, so if those little devils are still a sticky point for you, go back and review chapter 17, "How To Indirectly Access Data Storage with Pointers," where they were first introduced. For those who feel comfortable with both functions and pointers, it's time to dive right in.

How can I use functions and pointers together

The subject of functions and pointers has three logical divisions. First, there's the question of providing a function with a pointer as an argument. Next, you face having a function return a pointer as a result. Finally, you confront that most interesting case of declaring a pointer to point to a function.

Use a pointer as an argument

Again, you've seen how to pass a pointer to a function. You've done so each time you've had occasion to use a string function. To pass one or more pointers to a function of your own, you must declare them in the argument list of your function prototype. As always, you use the indirection operator to declare a pointer.

Functions can also return pointers as results; this too, you've seen when using string functions. Having a function return a pointer is no more difficult than having it pass back any other value.

You can pass a pointer to a function

For example, the following prototype declares three pointer variables: pBalance, pRate, and pMonths:

```
void InputValues(float *pBalance, float *pRate, float
➥*pMonths);
```

Why declare a pointer to a variable as a parameter instead of the variable itself? Well, C passes parameters from the calling program to a function. It might help to see the function call and the function prototype together:

```
void InputValues(float fBalance, float fRate, float fMonths);
result = InputValues(Balance, Rate, Months);
```

I've added fs to the variable names in the prototype to emphasize that these variables are quite distinct from those in the calling program. When the function InputValues is called on the second line, the contents of the three variables in the parameter list are determined; these contents are then placed into the three variables specified in the function prototype. There are actually six variables present, not three. Calling this function is a lot like saying

```
fBalance = Balance;
fRate = Rate;
fMonths = Months;
goto InputValues;
```

The important point is that nothing happens to the original variables in the calling programs. Their contents are read into the function; that's all.

Now for a function that is meant to let the user input data, this is hardly a satisfactory state of affairs. After all, a function only returns one value if any. How can a function let the program user input three values and then return all three to the `main()` function?

This is where pointers come in. Recall that the contents of a pointer are the place in memory where a variable's data are stored, and a pointer points to the variable. If you pass a function to a pointer, you're telling it where to find a specific variable from the calling function. The function can then use this information to directly modify the variable.

You use the usual way to call a function that expects pointers, invoking it by name and providing an argument list. As for the pointers in the argument list, you don't necessarily have to provide real live pointers to the variables whose values you're passing; you can actually use the address-of operator (&) and the names of the variables themselves. This saves having to declare pointers in the program that you don't intend to use. This, too, is something you've done before, namely in the `scanf()` function. The following two blocks of code do exactly the same thing; one is just much shorter:

```
/*Declare and initialize pointers, pass to function*/
float *pBalance, *pRate, *pMonths, Balance, Rate, Months;
pBalance = &Balance;
pRate = &Rate;
pMonths = &Months;
InputValues(pBalance, pRate, pMonths);
```

Contrast this to

```
float Balance, Rate, Months;
InputValues(&Balance, &Rate, &Months);
```

Clearly the second form is more compact.

Another important occasion for passing pointers, rather than variables, to a function is when you want to send the function an array; this includes sending character strings. Passing a pointer is the only way to reference an array. The following two lines first prototype a function that expects a character array (in other words, a string variable), and then call it:

```
void FormatValue(float future, char *Result);
FormatValue(future, Result);
```

For more on local variables, see chapter 13, "Some Optional Ways To Store Data. "

Again, because the name of an array is a pointer constant to its first element, you need only include the name of the array when passing it as a pointer to a function. In fact, you can subsequently use array notation—indices and all—in the function being passed to the array. You'll find this very handy indeed. Remember, however, to use the name of the array as specified in the function's header; that's the first line in the function definition. For simplicity's sake you can make all the names the same if you use only local variables.

A function can return a pointer

Functions can accept pointers, and they can also pass them back. To have a function return a pointer, include the correct type specification for the pointer to be returned and use the indirection operator in front of the function's name in the prototype. The following is a prototype for a function that returns a pointer:

```
char *FormatValues(float future, char *Result);
```

You would call such a function within an assignment statement that makes use of the pointer value returned. This pointer value is just the address of one of the parameters, as it is with several string functions. Of course, the most logical kind of pointer to return is that to a string variable; for any other sort of numeric variable you can simply pass back the numeric value itself.

A common thing to do is to test to see if a null value is returned by the function; this value is frequently used to mean some problem occurred in the function. Your program can test for the null value and, if found, deal with the consequences.

You can declare pointers to functions

You can declare pointers to just about everything else, why not declare pointers to functions? In fact, you can. Doing so can make your programs even more flexible because the same block of code can end up calling any one of a number of functions, depending on current conditions. You need only have the program set a pointer to the appropriate function and then use that pointer to call the function.

How do I declare a pointer to a function?

Declaring a pointer to a function is slightly different than declaring one to a variable. In addition to putting the indirection operator in the right place, you must also include a parameter list. A function pointer can only point to functions with the same sort of parameter list it has—the same number of variables, of the same types.

How do I point to a function?

As with any pointer, before you can use it you must initialize it. You use the address-of operator and the name of the function you want to point to. For example, the following sets the pointer pFunction to point to the function CompInt:

```
pFunction = &CompInt;
```

Catch the bug

The following short block of code includes a function prototype and a call to that function. Can you spot a problem?

```
void TruncateNumber(float *Anumber);
main()
{
float ANumber;
puts("Enter a number to truncate");
scanf("%f", &ANumber);
TruncateNumber(ANumber);
...
```

Answer: *The function expects a pointer, but the* main() *program is sending it the value in the variable* ANumber; *it should be sending a pointer to* ANumber *instead. This lets the function read and modify the contents of* ANumber *directly. You merely need to use the address-of operator. Corrected, the block reads*

```
void TruncateNumber(float *ANumber);
main()
{
float ANumber;
puts("Enter a number to truncate");
scanf("%f", &ANumber);
TruncateNumber(&ANumber);
...
```

Subsequently, to call the function associated with the pointer, you need only reference the pointer's name and provide it with arguments. For example,

```
future = pFunction(balance, rate, months);
```

The beauty of this construction is that pFunction might be set to point to any one of several functions that take the same arguments. A switch() construction, for instance, could set pFunction to point to one of several different functions, depending on a value entered by the user.

Show me an example of using pointers with functions

I had a FINANCE program lying around here (see listing 21.1), which I found had gotten to be a real mess. Aside from a couple of trivial functions, it didn't seem to follow the rules of top-down design. To tell the truth, it grew functionality like a boat grows barnacles. In the process, it became a tangled mess. Using what I know now about functions and pointers, I sat down, ripped FINANCE apart, and put it back together in functional form.

Speaking of pointer declaration statements

The general form of a declaration statement to create a pointer to a function is

```
return_type (*p_name)(type1 parm1[,...typelast
➥parmlast]);
```

Note that you must enclose the *p_name* in parentheses, with the indirection operator outside. Omit the parentheses, and you're simply prototyping a function that returns a pointer.

The following declares a pointer to a function. The pointer's name is pFunction; it supports three floating point arguments and returns a floating point value

```
float (*pFunction)(float balance, float rate, float
➥months);
```

Catch the bug

The following block of code uses a `switch()` construction to tell the program which function to call. What's the problem?

```
float Interest(float balance, float rate, float months);
float Payment(float balance, float rate, float months);
float Annuity(float balance, float rate, float months);
float *pFunction(float balance, float rate, float
➥months);
main()
{
float balance, rate, months;
int choice;
...code to input values
puts("Enter 1 for interest, 2 for loan payment, 3 for
➥annuity");
scanf("%d",&choice);
switch (choice)
    {
    case 1:
        pFunction = &Interest;
        break;
    case 2:
        pFunction = &Payment;
        break;
    case 3:
        pFunction = &Annuity;
        break;
    }
```

Answer: *The way the declaration is written, pFunction is not a pointer but a function in its own right—one that returns a pointer to a floating point variable. The name of the function pointer must be enclosed in parentheses, like so*

```
float (*pFunction)(float balance, float rate, float
➥months);
```

Listing 21.1   A more functional FINANCE program

```
/*A program to do certain financial calculations*/
#include <stdio.h>
#include <math.h>
#include <conio.h>
#include <stdlib.h>
#include <string.h>

/*Declare variables*/
/*Function Prototypes*/

float CompInt (float balance, float rate, float months);

float Payment (float balance, float rate, float months);

void InputValues (float *balance, float *rate, float *months);

char *FormatResult (float future, char *Result);

void PrintResult (char *Result, float balance,
➥float rate, float months);

float (*pFunction)(float balance, float rate, float months);

 main()
 {
 /* The main() function is contained within an infinite loop */
 /* It gives the user the choice of
➥entering new values, performing */
 /* either compound interest or loan
➥calculations with the current */
 /* values, or exiting. The choice is tied
➥to function keys F1-F4. */
 /* Pressing ESC also exits the program */
 char recycle;
 float future, balance, rate, months;
 int Function, Input = 0;
 char Result[12]="";

 while (1)
      {
      Function = 0;
      system("cls");
      puts("A program to find either compound
➥interest or a loan payment");
      puts("F1 = Enter values   F2 = Compound Interest
➥ F3 = Loan Payment F4 = Exit");
```

continues

Listing 21.1 Continued

```
/*Have the user choose the desired operation*/
recycle=getch();
if (recycle == 0)
     recycle = getch();
if (recycle == 27)
     exit(recycle);
switch (recycle)
{
case 59:
     {
     InputValues(&balance, &rate, &months);
     Input = 1;
     break;
     }

case 60:
     {
     system("cls");
     puts("\n\n\t\tCalculating compound
     ➥interest\n\n");
     Function = 1;
     pFunction = &CompInt;
     break;
     }

case 61:
     {
     system("cls");
     puts("\n\n\t\tCalculating loan payment\n\n");
     Function = 2;
     pFunction = &Payment;
     break;
     }

case 62:
     {
     exit(recycle);
     }


default:
     ;
     }

/*Perform calculation only if key pressed and there was input*/
if ((Function == 1 ¦¦ Function == 2) && Input)
     {
     future = pFunction(balance, rate, months);
```

```
                    FormatResult(future, Result);
                    PrintResult(Result, balance, rate, months);
                    puts ("Press any key to continue");
                    recycle = getch();
                    }

      }
      return 0;
      }

      float CompInt ( float balance, float rate, float months)
      {
                    return (balance * pow(2.7183,(rate/1200.0*months)));
      }

      float Payment ( float balance, float rate, float months)
      {
                    return (rate/1200.) *balance* pow(2.7183,(rate/1200.0
                    ➥*months))/(pow(2.7183,(double)(rate/1200.*months))1);
      }



      void InputValues (float *balance, float *rate, float *months)
      {
             /*Have the user input the values desired
             ➥for the present balance, the rate, and the time */
             /* Do so within a loop that
             ➥repeats if any invalid data are entered */
          char buffer;
          int DoAgain=1;
          system("cls");
          while (DoAgain)
          {
          puts("Enter values to use in subsequent calculations");
          printf("\nEnter the principal: ");
          scanf("%f",balance);
          printf("\nEnter the interest rate in percent per year:  ");
          scanf("%f",rate);
          printf("\nEnter the number of months: ");
          scanf("%f",months);
          system("cls");
          /* Verify amounts entered */
          if ((*balance<=0)||(*rate<=0)||(*months<=0))
              {
              puts("Invalid data entered; press any key to reenter");
              buffer = getch();
              }
              else
                    DoAgain = 0;
```

continues

Listing 21.1 Continued

```
        }
}


char *FormatResult (float future, char *Result)
{
/* Convert future into Result, a string with commas, $*/
int strpos, digits;
float digitpower;
                Result[0]='$';
                digits = log10(future);
                strpos = 1;
                for (;digits>=-2; digits—)
                    {
                    digitpower = pow((double)
                    ➥10.0, (double)digits);
                    Result[strpos] = ((int)
                    ➥(future/digitpower))+ (int)48;
                    strpos++;
                    future = future- (int)
                    ➥(future/digitpower) * digitpower;
                    if ((digits==6)¦¦(digits==3))
                        {
                        Result[strpos]=',';
                        strpos++;
                        }
                    if (digits==0)
                        {
                        Result[strpos]='.';
                        strpos++;
                        }
                    }

                Result[strpos]='\0';
return Result;
}


void PrintResult (char *Result, float balance,
➥float rate, float months)
{
printf("\n\tBalance = %.2f   Rate =  %.2f
➥Months = %.2f\n\n", balance, rate, months);
puts("\t\t********************************");
printf("\t\t* The result is %s \t*\n", Result);
puts("\t\t********************************\n");
return;
}
```

 First off, I isolated a couple of repeated tasks into functions; there's now a function to format a numeric result into a string. There's also a function to print this string result. I also isolated the code to input the balance, rate, and term in a function of its own.

The `main()` function is now much shorter. As before, all of the code within `main()`, aside from variable declarations, is enclosed in an infinite loop. The user is prompted to press one of four function keys; F4 quits the program. The user can also quit by pressing Esc. (The ASCII value for Esc is 27.) The principle part of `main()` is contained in a `switch()` structure; what happens depends on what key is pressed. (The program ignores any key other than the function keys listed and Esc.) A function pointer is used to generalize the code—occurring after the `switch()` block—that calls the calculation routine, the number formatter, and the printing routine. The program does not go through with a calculation unless values for `balance`, `rate`, and `months` have been input.

The `InputValues()` function also takes place within a loop; the loop continues to execute until the user has input nonzero values for all three parameters. This function has passed pointers to the variables `Balance`, `Rate`, and `Months`, so that it can read values into them and pass them back to `main()`.

The code that formats the result, `future`, into a string has been stripped out and isolated in a function called `FormatValue`. (Previously, this code was repeated for both possible calculations; it was a prime candidate for converting into a function.) `FormatValue` expects a floating point value and a pointer to a string. It returns a pointer to a string, although the program does not yet make use of it.

Finally, the program uses a function called `PrintResult` to produce output. `PrintResult` expects a pointer to a string; this is what it prints, along with some formatting stuff.

In addition to being somewhat shorter than before, the program is now more functional. It uses calls to the operating system to clear the screen at appropriate points; this keeps down the clutter. The user doesn't have to enter new values every time though; this means you can easily determine first the compound interest and then the loan payment on the same input values. Finally, and perhaps most importantly, the more functional structure of `Financsp` (the *sp* is for *structured programming*) makes the program code easier to follow and understand: discrete tasks are isolated in discrete functions. Figure 21.1 shows the results of running this new version of the FINANCE program.

Fig. 21.1
Among other things,
Financsp produces
neater output.

```
                  Calculating compound interest
        Balance: 1000.00   Rate: 5.00   Months: 60.00
                 ********************************
                 *The result is $1,284.02        *
                 ********************************
        Press any key to continue
```

A function you create can have different numbers of arguments

Forget pointers for a while. (Not a very *long* while, mind you.) Is there any other way to make functions more flexible? Well, for one thing, what about those argument lists? They always contain the same number of arguments, don't they? This seems to make functions pretty rigid with regard to their data expectations. Is it possible to break out of this rigidity?

Again, printf() and scanf() hold the answer. Setting up functions whose number of arguments is flexible can be done. In fact, printf() does just that; you can pass it as many variables to print as you want. Has C restricted this capability to its library functions, or can you get to it?

You can definitely set up functions of your own that accept variable numbers of arguments. Each such function has at least one fixed argument that must be there. scanf() and printf() have their format strings, for instance. Generally, the fixed parameter is used to determine how many actual parameters there are to the function when the program is run.

If you want to define functions with variable argument lists, you'll need to include the header file stdarg.h in your programs. The file contains prototypes for several functions that you must run to have your variable argument list work correctly.

How do I set up functions that use different numbers of arguments?

In the prototype of a function with a variable argument list, you first include all the fixed arguments; these appear no matter what. Again, in the case of the library function `printf()`, the format string is the only fixed parameter. After the last fixed argument, you include an ellipsis. It's the ellipsis that lets C know you want to use a variable number of additional arguments. The following is a prototype for such a function:

```
float MyFunc(int NumberArguments, ...);
```

Now, the tricky part is, your program must have some way of "knowing" the data type of each argument in the variable list. If all the arguments are the same, then there's no problem. Otherwise, you have to think of some clever way to specify the type of each argument. Again, `printf()` does this using the conversion specifier; the number of conversion specifiers (for example, `%f`) in the string indicates how many variables there are. The exact form of each specifier indicates the data type of the associated variable. If you want to mix types in a variable parameter list, you might use a format string like that for `printf()`. You'll need to devise code that isolates the information needed from this format string; one loop to look for the total number of variables and another to isolate and determine each conversion specifier. I'm going to leave that as an exercise for you.

I've set up my variable-argument function; now how do I use it?

There are four elements that you must call on to make a variable argument list work. These are

- `va_list` This is a special pointer type, defined in `stdarg.h`. You must declare a pointer of this type. Most programmers call the pointer `arg_ptr`.

- `va_start()` This is a function (actually this is a function macro, more on those in chapter 28; the distinction isn't important here) used to initialize the pointer `arg_ptr` (or whatever you choose to name it). You must pass the function the name of your argument pointer and the name of the last fixed argument in your function.

- `va_arg()` This function (macro) returns each argument in the variable list. You must pass it the argument pointer and the data type of the argument being retrieved. You need to call this function once for each argument in the list; you might do so using a loop.

- `va_end()` This is a clean-up function (macro) that you call when your program has retrieved all the arguments in the list.

All these items are defined or called within your variable–argument list function itself.

In essence, your variable-argument function needs to do the following:

1 Determine how many arguments were passed to it and the type of each argument. The program can assume each argument is of the same, specific type. This is the easiest and least flexible method.

2 Declare a pointer of type `va_list`.

3 Call the function macro `va_start()`, passing it the pointer declared in step 2 and the number of arguments determined in step 1.

4 Run a loop that executes the same number of times as there are arguments. Each time through, the loop calls `va_arg`. This function macro returns the value of the current parameter in the variable list. You must pass `va_arg` the argument pointer (step 2) and the data type of the current argument.

5 Call the function macro `va_end()` to clean up once all the arguments have been retrieved.

Have a function call itself

Our last topic for this chapter is the mysterious realm of recursion. Recursion refers to a function calling itself. This can be done in one of two ways. **Direct recursion** occurs when a function directly calls itself. **Indirect recursion** occurs when a function calls another function and that second function calls the first.

Why would I want a function to call itself?

If you want a function to repeat the same calculation until a certain end value is reached, recursion is the thing to do. As I said at the chapter's beginning, a recursive function call is much like a loop.

One way to use recursion is to find the factorial of a number. Factorials are only defined for integers. The factorial of a number (indicated as *number!*) is defined as that number times every other number between it and 1. So the factorial of 4 is

$$4! = 4 \times 3 \times 2 = 24$$

It's easy to define a recursive algorithm to find a factorial. The critical relationship is

$$n! = n(n-1) \times (n-2)\ldots1$$

How can I use this in the real world?

The more generalized a function is, the better it is. That's because it can be used in more places. One way to generalize functions is to remove any restrictions on how much data they can work with. You do this by defining such functions so that they feature variable argument lists.

Consider a function that performs some sort of processing on character strings— converting them to all uppercase, for instance. You might do that as part of a label-making program. You could write the function so that it expects a set number of strings or even just a single string to convert. However, if you set up the function with a variable argument list in the first place, you can pass it as many strings as you want to convert. In that way, you can make one line of code (the call to the function) do the work of an entire loop. When it comes time to reuse the function in another program, you don't need to modify it one bit in order to get it to work with a different number of arguments.

That is, the factorial of a number, n, is that number times the factorial of the next smaller number. If the function in question is called `factorial()`, the recursive definition

```
n = n × factorial(n-1);
```

actually achieves the desired results.

Some cautions about recursive functions

Recursion can take up lots of memory and lots of time. In the case of calculating a factorial recursively, you're calling the function many separate times (number − 1 times to be exact). Each call consumes a certain amount of space that the values of all variables are preserved in, along with some other important information that lets the calling function pick up exactly where it left off. If you go too many levels into recursion, you're going to run out of space.

In addition, it can be tricky to devise a recursive algorithm to accomplish all tasks. Keep in mind that your function definition should include, as a first step, what to do when the value of the parameter that's being passed to it reaches a critical value (the value 1 in the case of the factorial function). When the value of the parameter reaches this critical value, the function should stop calling itself and return a value.

Summary

In this chapter, you looked at some additional ways to make programs and their constituent functions more powerful and flexible. You learned about using pointers with functions: passing pointers as arguments, returning pointers, and creating pointers to functions. This chapter also covered the construction of functions with variable argument lists. Finally, you learned about defining a recursive function—that is, a function that calls itself.

Review questions

1 If you leave something out of the declaration of a pointer to a function, you end up with a function prototype that returns a pointer. What is that thing which you shouldn't leave out?

2 How do you pass an array to a function? Does this include a string variable?

3 How do you get multiple values back from a function?

4 What are the four important elements in creating a variable parameter list. (Hint: they all start with va_.)

5 Define *recursion*. What can it consume a lot of?

Exercises

1 Write a prototype for a function that takes one integer, one floating point, and one string parameter, and returns a pointer to a string.

2 Write a declaration statement to declare a pointer to the function from exercise 1. Assume the function does not return a value.

3 Write a short program to find the average of a list of numbers. Use a variable argument list in the function that finds the average.

22

Cool Things To Do with Pointers

● In this chapter:

- Can I have pointers to pointers, and would that be useful?

- Are there such things as arrays of pointers?

- Pass multidimensional arrays to functions

And you thought there was nothing left to learn about pointers! But wait, there's more. You'll find that each of the advanced pointer constructs described in this chapter plays a part in making your programs more useful . . . . ➤

Ｔhe preceding chapter discussed using pointers to make functions more powerful. In this chapter you're going to look at ways to make pointers more useful. I'm referring to such exotic items as pointers to pointers, arrays of pointers, and pointers to multidimensional arrays. As you gain experience programming in C, you'll find that each of these ways of using pointers plays a part in making your programs more useful. Mastery of all aspects of pointer use will also provide a firm foundation for you to begin programming graphical user interfaces such as Windows.

Can I really make pointers more powerful?

For more information on the indirection and address-of operators, see chapter 17, "How To Indirectly Access Data Storage with Pointers."

As you consider these more complicated constructs involving pointers, keep in mind what you've learned about them so far: pointers are variables whose contents specify the address in memory of some other variable's contents. A pointer points to that variable. You create pointers using the indirection operator, which can also be used to retrieve the contents of the variable being pointed to. This latter item—what's being pointed to—is set using the address-of operator in a simple assignment statement.

Can I point to pointers?

Given that a pointer is just another kind of variable, it stands to reason that pointers have what all variables have: a name, contents, and an address in computer memory where those contents are stored. Put simply, a pointer has an address and contains an address—that of another variable. Suppose that variable—the one pointed to—were itself a pointer. Nothing prevents a pointer variable from containing the address of another pointer. In this case, you have a pointer to a pointer, an example of what's called **multiple indirection**.

You can use multiple indirection to the extreme, with pointers to pointers to pointers and so on. However, seldom is multiple indirection useful beyond the first level—a pointer to a pointer. What use is even first-level indirection? I had my first exposure to them in the context of programming for the Macintosh, where pointers to pointers were called **handles**. The Macintosh has a habit of swapping programs around in memory while they're still running. Clearly this has a bad effect on the contents of pointers because they tend to point to the wrong places after memory has been adjusted.

What's worse, the pointers themselves sometimes get moved; then a program can't even find them, much less access their contents.

The solution is to keep a certain group of pointers fixed in memory, while allowing everything else to move freely when the operating system (OS) sees fit to do so. As part of the in-flight service, the Macintosh kindly takes time to update the contents of all the handles whenever what they're pointing to has moved. In this way a program's data can be shifted around in memory without crashing the program or the whole computer. The use of multiple indirection is required because it makes the Macintosh's job (not the programmer's) easier.

I'm not going to show you anything even remotely that complicated in this chapter. However, if you want to try your hand at programming for the Macintosh, Windows, or X Windows (a UNIX windowing environment), you need to know something about multiple indirection. For the present, you'll find multiple indirection a key to some other pointer constructs, especially arrays of pointers, as you'll see.

Are there really such things as arrays of pointers?

An **array of pointers** is just that: an array where each element is a pointer to some other variable. Each pointer in the array must have the same type, meaning it must point to the same sort of variable. You set and access the contents of individual pointers in the array using the array index. (Refer to chapter 14 for more information on arrays.)

Where does multiple indirection come in? Recall that the name of an array is a pointer constant, pointing to the first element in the array. The name of a pointer array is thus a pointer to the first array element, which is itself a

How can I use this in the real world?

A pointer array provides a handy way to reference a group of character strings, among other things. You might initialize such an array to point to a group of messages, any one of which might be displayed depending on what's happened in your program. One statement prints any one of the messages; all the program has to do is alter the contents of whatever index variable you are using.

pointer to some other variable. You can use multiple indirection to access that variable without even mentioning the array's index.

What about pointers to multidimensional arrays?

Another aspect of multiple indirection involves pointers and **multidimensional arrays**. Such an array has two or more indices, each specifying a dimension. The indices of a two-dimensional array can, for instance, be thought of as rows and columns.

Now, because of the way that C stores multidimensional arrays, it's necessary to use a form of multiple indirection when you want to get to the array contents in certain circumstances. This is especially true when you're attempting to pass a multidimensional array as an argument to a function. What you end up passing in such a case is a pointer to the array's final dimension, which is in turn a pointer to the array's first element. This may seem complicated, but it will become clearer later in the chapter. First, though, you need to take a closer look at multiple indirection itself.

Tell me about pointers to pointers

Again, a pointer can point to any variable, including another pointer. This represents multiple indirection. When you declare and set such a pointer, its

Speaking of declaring a pointer to a pointer

To declare a pointer to a pointer, use a statement of the form

```
variable_type **pointer_name;
```

The variable_type is that of the variable ultimately being pointed to. The pointer_name is, of course, a valid C name. The following declares a pointer named ppPointer; it points to a pointer that, in turn, points to a character variable:

```
char **ppPointer;
```

contents are the address of another pointer. As with all pointers, you declare pointers to pointers using the indirection operator and set them using the address-of operator.

How do I declare pointers to pointers?

The indirection operator (*) declares a pointer. In the case of multiple indirection, you use the operator once for each level of indirection.

How do I use pointers to pointers?

To use a pointer to a pointer, you must first initialize it. You use the address-of operator to do so, just as you do for a standard pointer. However, you use the operator on a pointer variable. The following statement sets the pointer ppPointer to point to another pointer named pCharacterPointer:

```
ppPointer = &pCharacterPointer;
```

To access the contents of the variable ultimately pointed to, use the indirection operator again. For example, the following reads the contents of a character variable—pointed to by the pointer, which is pointed to by ppPointer—into another variable:

```
Buffer = **ppPointer;
```

Catch the bug

The following statement attempts to set a pointer to a pointer. What's the problem with it?

```
ppPointer = &&CharacterVariable;
```

Answer: *You can't use the address-of operator in this way. C has no idea what you're talking about. The variable ppPointer should point to a pointer; there's no other pointer in the statement. C has no way of determining the address of a pointer to CharacterVariable, unless you explicitly set it as in the following:*

```
pPointer = &CharacterVariable;
ppPointer = &pPointer;
```

You can see that this statement is much easier to formulate than it is to describe.

What are arrays of pointers?

The next step up on the multiple-indirection ladder is working with **arrays of pointers**. You declare and work with such arrays much like regular arrays, including initializing them to specific values.

How do I create pointer arrays?

A statement to create a pointer array looks almost exactly like one to create any other array; it includes a variable type and an index. The only difference is the presence of the indirection operator.

How do I work with pointer arrays?

The ability to set pointer arrays to reference strings may be among the most important uses for such a construct now. Because of the way C handles strings, you're better off setting up the strings when creating the array in an

Speaking of creating an array of pointers

The general form of a statement creating an array of pointers is

```
variable_type *array_name[index_value];
```

variable_type is that of the variables ultimately being pointed to. array_name is the name of the pointer array; index_value is the number of pointers in the array. The following declares a pointer array with three members, each pointing to a char-type variable:

```
char *MessageArray[3];
```

You can also initialize the variables being pointed to. The following sets the three elements in MessageArray to point to three specific character strings:

```
char *MessageArray[3] = {"First Message", "Second Message",
➡"Third Message");
```

initialization statement like the final code line in the "Speaking C" section earlier in this chapter. Such a statement essentially sets up an array that points to several literal string constants, rather than to several variables.

As for setting an individual element of a pointer array within a program, that's done just the way you do with other arrays. Thus, the following statement sets the second member of pArray to point to the address of the variable Balance:

```
pArray[1] = &Balance;
```

To reference Balance's contents, you use the indirection operator. If the second member of pArray points to Balance, the following sets Balance's contents to 125:

```
*pArray[1] = 125;
```

How do I use pointers to multidimensional arrays?

The last thing you'll deal with in this chapter is using pointers with multi-dimensional arrays. You have to use such pointers if you mean to pass a multidimensional array to a function; there's no other way to use an array as a parameter except by setting and sending a pointer to it. Before you can use these kinds of pointers, you need to look further into how multidimensional arrays are built.

How are multidimensional arrays constructed?

A multidimensional array has more than one index. For example, the following statement declares a two-dimensional array to hold integer values:

```
int MyArray[2][3];
```

This array has a total of six elements. You might visualize a two-dimensional array in the manner of a checkerboard or spreadsheet, with rows specified by one index and columns specified by the other. But how is it really stored?

To C, a two-dimensional array is an array of arrays. Each index declares an array. The first index, [2] in the preceding case, declares an integer array with two members. The second index, [3], declares that MyArray is now an array of three-member arrays. At the end, MyArray is a two-member array, each of whose members is a three-member array containing integer values. You can carry this process on for each dimension you care to add; in this book you won't go beyond two.

How do I declare and use pointers to multidimensional arrays?

Now, to declare a pointer to a two-dimensional array, you need both the last index in the array and the data type of the array. This is because what you're declaring is a pointer to the first element in the array, which in its turn is an array. This is starting to sound like multiple indirection again, isn't it. Well, it is.

Here's what I mean. For the array MyArray[2][3], MyArray[0] refers to the first element in the array; itself an array with three members. MyArray[1] is the second array, MyArray[2] is the last array. MyArray[0][0] refers to the first element in the first array.

Now a pointer needs to know how "big" the variable is that it's pointing to so that it can access the next item in memory following the variable without

Speaking of declaring a multidimensional array

To declare a pointer to a multidimensional array whose last index value is n, use a statement of the form

```
variable_type (*ppointer_name)[n];
```

Note the use of parentheses; you last saw these in a pointer declaration when declaring a pointer to a function. Here, the parentheses prevent the declaration into turning into one for a pointer array. The following statement declares a pointer to an array of char-type variables. The array is two-dimensional.

```
char (*pCharacterArray)[80];
```

confusing one variable's data with another. In the case of a multidimensional array—an array of arrays—simply knowing the array data type isn't enough. The pointer must also take into account how many members the array has.

So there are two parts to declaring a pointer to a two-dimensional array: declaring the data type and declaring how many items are in the last index of the array.

A little reflection reveals that the previous "Speaking C" shows the way to pass an array of string variables to a function. An array declaration for ten such variables, each 80 characters long (plus room for the null character to terminate the string) might be

```
char LinesArray[9][81];
```

In turn, a pointer to point to such an array is declared as

```
char (*pLinesArray)[81];
```

The pointer pLinesArray "knows" that it points to an array of character variables, which is 81 units long.

Now recall how array names work. An array name points to the first element in the array. This means that LinesArray[0] points to the first element in the two-dimensional array LinesArray[][]. Why? Because the first element in a two-dimensional array is itself an array. So to set a pointer to point to a two-dimensional array, you use a statement like:

```
pLinesArray = LinesArray[0];
```

This sets pLinesArray to point to the first string variable (itself an array) within the character array LinesArray.

Once you've set a pointer to a multidimensional array, you can pass the pointer to a function. The function can use the pointer with array subscript notation to get to individual elements within the array that have been passed.

Show me an example of passing a multidimensional array to a function

I created the following short program in listing 22.1 to demonstrate passing an array of string variables to a function. Essentially, it creates a partial "screen" for the computer. This screen consists of a number of

Catch the bug

What's wrong with the following three statements?

```
char NameArray[4][25];
char (*pNameArray)[24];
pNameArray = NameArray[0];
```

Answer: *The pointer used here has the incorrect width to point to* NameArray. *Using* pNameArray *subsequently simply results in some very bad data being retrieved from—and possibly being stored into—* NameArray *because the pointer thinks each name in the array is only twenty-four characters wide. The contents of the brackets should be* 25, *not* 24. *Corrected, the block reads*

```
char NameArray[4][25];
char (*pNameArray)[25];
pNameArray = NameArray[0];
```

eighty-character lines; the computer screen is eighty characters wide on most systems. A single short routine is used to print the screen composed elsewhere.

Listing 22.1   A program that creates a screen for the computer

```
#include <stdio.h>
#include <string.h>
#include <conio.h>
#include <stdlib.h>

/*The function Screen_Paint expects a pointer
➥to a string array; each string is 80 characters*/
void Screen_Paint(char (*Screen)[81]);


main()
{
/*Variable to hold the screen*/
char ch, Screen[21][80];
/*A pointer to the screen variable; used to
➥pass it to the screen painting function*/
char (*ptr)[80];
int y, x;
```

```
            ch = getch();
            if (ch == 0)
                 ch = getch();

            switch (ch)
                 {
                 case 59:
                       {
                         for ( y = 0; y <= 20; y++)
                              {;
                              Screen[y][0] = '*';
                              for (x = 1; x <= 77; x++)
                                    {
                                    Screen[y][x] = ' ';
                                    if (y == 0 || y == 20)
                                          Screen[y][x] = '*';
                                    }
                              Screen[y][78] = '*';
                              Screen[y][79] = '\0';
                         ;}
                       ptr=Screen;
                        Screen_Paint(ptr);
                        ch = getch();
                        break;
                       }

                 case 60:
                       exit(ch);

                 default:
                       ;
                 }

      return 0;

}

void Screen_Paint(char (*Screen)[80])
{
int y;
system ("cls");
for (y = 0; y<=20; y++)
      {
      printf(" %s",&Screen[y]);
      }

}
```

 **code** The Screen_Paint routine is very simple; it just clears the screen and then prints each line of Screen, one at a time. The main() function builds the

screen to be printed. (Note that a full screen is really 40 lines high, but the way printf() works prevents more than about twenty lines from being printed in this manner.) This small program could be generalized to compose any sort of screen for Screen_Paint to produce. The screen itself appears when the user presses the F1 key.

Results of running this short program are shown in figure 22.1.

Fig. 22.1
This program is very simple, but the principle behind it is powerful; a single, short function can print the contents of the variable Screen, outputting an entire screen of data at once.

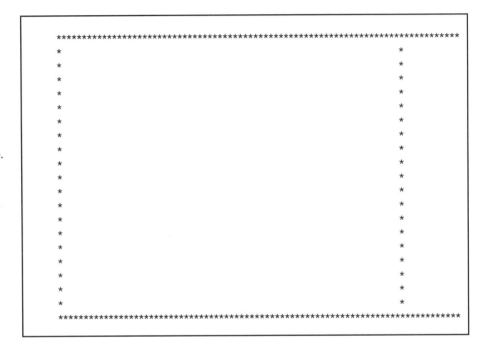

Summary

This chapter dealt with pointers and multiple indirection. After defining multiple indirection, you looked at declaring and initializing pointers to pointers. This chapter then moved on to cover arrays of pointers, looking at how to initialize such an array to reference a group of character strings. Finally, you considered pointers to multidimensional arrays, demonstrating how to pass such an array to a function using an appropriate pointer.

Review questions

1 Define *multiple indirection.*

2 What is meant by a *pointer to a pointer?*

3 What do you end up with if you leave the parentheses out of a declaration for a pointer to a multidimensional array?

4 Give a use for an array of pointers.

5 How do you pass a multidimensional array to a function?

Exercises

1 Write three statements to declare a pointer to a floating-point variable, declare a pointer to that pointer, and set the second pointer to point to the first.

2 Declare and initialize an array of pointers to point to your full name, street address, and city.

3 Make use of the `Screen_Paint` routine developed in this chapter. Create a `Screen` variable within your program's `main()` function. Have the `PrintScreen` routine modify the `Screen` to show your name and address. Pass the modified screen to `Screen_Paint`.

23

Messing Around with Bits and Bytes

● **In this chapter:**

- **What's all this about binary notation?**

- **Tell me some ways to manipulate individual bits within data**

- **Can I have single-bit variables, and if so, where?**

Want to get down to the real nitty gritty of programming? In this chapter you'll learn how to manipulate the individual bits and bytes out of which all computer data is built . . . .

I n the last several chapters, you have learned how to work with increasingly complicated data items, especially pointers in various forms. In this chapter, you will study the basic units by which the computer does its work. Any type of data that the computer processes must take the same fundamental form. You will examine and learn how to work with data in this form: single data bits.

Similar to the advanced pointer topics that the previous chapter discussed, C operations on single data bits are generally of most use when you are working with your computer's operating system (OS), most particularly when you are using a graphical flavor of that OS, such as Windows. For example, you can use these operations to make some common modifications to graphics images, such as inverting their tone. You might never use any other bit operations in C. Still, it is helpful to be familiar with them because they are fundamental to the way your computer operates.

Different ways of writing numbers

Before beginning the study of single-bit operations in C, a review of the concepts of binary numbers and binary notation, first covered in chapter 4, is helpful. Binary notation is uniquely suited for expressing numbers in the same format that a computer stores all data in.

Just as the decimal number system is based on powers of ten (10, 100, 1000, ...), binary notation is based on powers of two (2, 4, 8, ...). Each digit in a binary number represents an equivalent power of two. Therefore, the binary number 111 represents $(1 \times 2^0) + (1 \times 2^1) + (1 \times 2^2) = 7$.

The only numerals used in binary notation are zero and one. Any number system, including decimal notation, uses digits from zero up to one number less than the base. Decimal notation, therefore, uses 0 through 9. Getting back to binary, having only two numerals makes binary a useful way to conceptualize anything involving flows of electricity. The reason is that current is either flowing or not flowing. The presence or absence of current can be thought of as corresponding to a binary digit; sums of these digits make up data as a whole. Because the circuitry within your computer consists entirely of millions of tiny currents, binary notation precisely represents what is going on within it. You can think of each binary digit as representing the state of an on-off switch.

The way in which bits are grouped is entirely arbitrary. However, over the years it has become conventional to group them into eights; eight binary digits (bits, for short) taken together are said to constitute one byte. A byte can have any value from 00000000 to 11111111; in decimal notation, that is 0 to 255.

Human beings, especially ace programmers, frequently find it helpful to represent binary data in some notation other than binary or decimal. Because we are dealing with bytes and a byte is eight bits, some notation based on powers of eight is the most helpful. There are two such notations in use. **Octal notation** is indeed a base-eight number system. **Hexadecimal notation**, based on powers of sixteen (eight times two) is perhaps more widely used. Hexadecimal notation requires fifteen numerals (the base minus one, remember?). Therefore, it is conventional to represent the extra ones beyond 9 by the letters A through F. The following shows the number 255 in decimal, binary, octal, and hexadecimal notation:

255

11111111

377

FF

You might sometimes see a small O or X affixed to an octal or hexadecimal number, to distinguish it from a decimal value. To make things easier, you don't have to be concerned with both octal and hexadecimal notation; this book presents pure computer data in binary. The reason is that the discussions on this subject don't talk about more than one byte at a time.

How a byte value is interpreted depends on the context, that is, on what the computer expects to find when it looks at that byte. In some cases, the computer expects to find an instruction. Therefore, the byte value is then interpreted as a command to the microprocessor. At other times, it might expect to find a character. In this case, the ASCII convention is used to determine the appropriate character. More commonly, the computer expects to find a number. Therefore, the byte value is interpreted as such. Even in this case, though, the computer might not take the byte at face value. It might further interpret the byte's contents according to some rule, such as the one C uses for floating-point values.

A computer crash, by the way, is almost always caused by expectations conflicting with reality. A computer might expect to find an instruction in a particular byte, and interpret its contents as such. Then the computer finds that it has been told nonsense. The reason is that some program erroneously stored some other kind of data in that byte. Improper use of pointers is a common cause of such an error.

For the most part, however, your computer crunches merrily along, almost always finding exactly the sort of data it expects. You have seen the large scale ways that you can manipulate such data in C. There are also some fairly fine-grained operations, each of which has a particular use.

How does C use single bits?

Although certain operations in C are concerned with bit values, all actually operate on whole bytes at a time. Recall that the char data type represents one byte. Character data is really interpreted in integer form (the numbers from 0 to 255). This points to another characteristic of byte operations: they only work with integer data types (char, int, and long).

There is actually one place within C where you can specify data of less than a byte's length: within a structure. C structures support the use of bit fields; these are elements within structures defined as one or more bits wide. Such fields are ideal for storing yes or no values (for example, is the employee married?), especially within large databases where space is at a premium and every byte counts. You'll see how to create such bit-length fields later in the chapter.

As for byte operations, you might never need to use them. However, they are around in case you need them. Whether you find a way to employ them or not, it is beneficial to know about them. They tell you something about the way your computer works because the C byte operations are reflections on a higher scale of some very fundamental machine-language commands, as you are about to see.

Shift some bits

The first set of C byte operations to examine are the **shift operators**. These operators take a sequence of bits and move them either to the left or right within the byte that they are stored in. Under certain circumstances, you can use these operators to perform math; some deep circuitry within your computer works in much the same way.

...to the left or right

You use the shift operators with integer data types. Again, the operators move the contents within such a variable either left or right. The symbols involved are << and >>.

Any stray bits that go past the end of a variable when a shift operation is performed are lost. Therefore, shifting 11111111 to the right by one place results in 01111111; the final 1 is lost.

Speaking of the shift-left operation

The general form of an expression to perform a shift-left operation is

```
variable << n
```

The variable must be an integer variable type. The value n is an expression evaluating to an integer; it specifies how many places the data is to be shifted. Therefore,

```
Character = Character << 2;
```

shifts the contents of the variable Character left two places. If Character was of type char, and held 00100001 before, after the operation it would hold 10000100.

A shift-right operation, on the other hand, takes the form

```
variable >> n
```

The value in the variable is shifted to the right by the number of places specified by the integer expression n. If Character held 11000000 before the operation, performing

```
Character = Character >> 3;
```

shifts the contents of Character to the right three places; Character then holds 00011000.

How do I use these shift operators?

Performing a shift to the left or right is the same as multiplying or dividing by an equivalent power of two. Shifting a number one place to the left is similar to multiplying it by two; shifting it one place to the right is similar to dividing it. Any fractional result in this case (.5 in other words) is lost. Therefore, shifting right performs integer division by powers of two.

The following short program demonstrates multiplication using the shift-left operator. The affected variable is of type int.

```
#include <stdio.h>

int counter, shifted;

main()
{
puts("A program to demonstrate left-shifting a number");
puts("\nEnter an integer between 1 and 255: ");
scanf("%d",&shifted);

for (counter = 1; counter <= 4; counter++)
        {
        shifted = shifted<<1;
        printf("\nShifting left by %d results
[ic:ccc]in %d", counter, shifted);
        }

scanf("%d", &shifted);

}
```

The value in the variable shifted (counter) moves left four times, each time by one place. Figure 23.1 shows the results of running this small program.

Fig. 23.1

Shifting a value to the left is similar to multiplying it by a power of two.

```
A program to demonstrate left-shifting a number

Enter a number between 1 and 255:
25

Shifting left by 1 results in 50
Shifting left by 2 results in 100
Shifting left by 3 results in 200
Shifting left by 4 results in 400
```

You might try running this program with a large value. The results might surprise you.

CAUTION **In fact, C does not determine the value of new bits added when** a signed integer is shifted right. (The sign bit is the leftmost.) On some machines, the original contents of the sign bit are preserved; on others, the sign bit becomes a zero no matter what it held before. Thus, a program that relies on shift-right with signed integers may produce unexpected results when ported to different computer systems.

Use some logic on these bits

Other C operators perform certain logical operations on the bits within a byte. They are quite similar in principle to the logical operators introduced in chapter 9, such as && and ‖.

Get wise on the bits

The bitwise logical operators **AND** (&), **OR** (|), and **XOR** (^), which stands for *exclusive or*, take the contents of two integer-type variables and return a result based on comparing each bit of one variable with that in another. These operators are used in expressions in the same way as the shift operators are.

 Plain English, please!
Bitwise refers to operations that are applied bit-by-bit within a variable; this variable can still be one or more bytes wide, but each bit within it is affected by a bitwise operation. **99**

How to use the bitwise operators

The results depend on which of the operators you are using. Results are summarized in the following table:

Operation	Result
& (AND)	Result is 1 if corresponding bits in both variables are also 1; otherwise, result is 0.
| (OR)	Result is 0 if corresponding bits in both variables are also 0; otherwise, result is 1.
^ (XOR)	Result is 1 if one of the corresponding bits is 1, and the other is 0; if both are either 1 or 0, the result is 0.

It might be helpful to consider the effect of each of these operations on a pair of byte values:

```
        1100110011
AND     1010101010
        1000100010

        1100110011
OR      1010101010
        1110111011

        1100110011
XOR     1010101010
        0110011001
```

Speaking of the bitwise logical operators

The general form of an expression using one of the bitwise logical operators is

```
variable1 & variable2
```

for AND,

```
variable1 | variable2
```

for OR, and

```
variable1 ^ variable2
```

for XOR.

To perform an XOR operation on two variables and store the result in a third, you would use a statement such as the following:

```
Result = First ^ Second;
```

Catch the bug

The following statement compares a variable known as `Picture` with one referred to as `Mask`. Each bit in the result should be 1 if the corresponding bit in either `Mask` or `Picture` is 1. However, the result should be 0 if both are either 1 or 0. What is the problem?

```
Picture | Mask;
```

Answer: *There are two problems. First, the value of the expression is lost because it is not in an assignment statement. Second, the programming need described previously is XOR. However, the sample statement uses the OR operator. The corrected statement reads*

```
Picture = Picture ^ Mask;
```

How can I use this in the real world?

The "real world" equivalent of these operations is much harder to pin down than for the shift operators. Many times, these operators are used to work with large collections of byte values that are conceived of as representing pictures; these entities are usually referred to as bit maps. The bitwise operators are then used to combine the contents of a bitmap with another fixed bitmap called a **mask**. A mask represents some sort of overlay to be placed onto a bitmap. It might consist of a pattern, for instance, that's to be combined with a picture to reduce it to a shaded form. The XOR operator is frequently used to combine a bitmap with a mask.

If, on the other hand, a bitmap is altered using the complement operator (described in the following section, "Take a complement"), the result appears in inverse. That's because 1s become 0s and vice versa. This operator can be used to indicate that something on the screen has been selected.

Take a complement

For more informa-tion on unary oper-ators, see chapter 8, "Performing Mathematical Calculations in C."

A final bitwise operator, the **complement operator** (~), returns a value based entirely on the contents of the variable that it is attached to; therefore, it is a unary operator. The complement operator reverses a variable bit-by-bit.

What is a complement?

The complement of a number is, in a manner of speaking, its opposite; every 1 in the number's binary representation is changed to 0, and every 0 is changed to 1.

Why would I use the complement?

Similar to the binary bitwise operators, taking the complement is some-thing you will probably never do within an ordinary C program that uses character-based I/O. In the case of a simple black-and-white bit map where 1s represent black picture parts and 0s represent white, taking the comple-ment of the bit map inverts it. Much the same operation is performed on-screen when you select or highlight an item within your word processor. In general, the complement of a signed integer variable is equal to the negative of that variable minus one. (This is called the one's complement of the number.) The complement of an unsigned number is more difficult to define.

Use structures with those bits

While you might never use the bitwise operators, there is another C bit manipulation that can be much more helpful. You can combine the most

Speaking of the complement operation

The general form of an expression to perform a complement operation on a variable's contents is

    ~ variable_name

Therefore, to take the complement of Result, you use

    Result = ~Result;

complex C data constructs and structures, with the simplest, single bits. This is quite a handy space-saving hint, something perhaps not sufficiently appreciated in these days of gigabyte hard drives.

You can define elements of only a few bits in a structure

For more information on structures, see chapter 16, "Structure Storage To Meet Your Own Needs."

Recall what a structure is: a collection of variables accessed under a single name. The individual variables within a structure are sometimes referred to as fields; they have been referred to as elements or members. C enables you to define fields within a structure that occupy only one or a few bits.

To use bit fields, you've got to create them

Defining a bit field within a structure is not much more difficult than defining ordinary structure members. In the structure's definition, you provide the field with a name. You also tell C how many bits wide the bit field is.

What good are bit fields?

You can use bit fields in any place where only a limited range of data is needed. If the value you are concerned with can only be yes or no, you can store eight bit fields in the same amount of memory it takes to store one full byte. This is an eightfold reduction in memory use, which can be quite

Speaking of a bit field in a structure definition

The general form of a definition for a bit field in a structure definition is

```
unsigned field_name    :bitswide;
```

Note that all bit fields are of the unsigned data type. To create a single-bit field named Married within a structure that also includes a full name and a social security number, you use a definition similar to

```
struct name {
    char Fullname[40];
    unsigned int Married    :1;
    char SSAN[9];
    };
```

significant when you work with large array structures with many fields and numerous members.

You are not, however, limited to yes or no and true or false possibilities. You can define longer fields to hold more possibilities. If the bit field `Married` is defined with a width of two bits, for instance, you could store four possibilities: `Single`, `Married`, `Divorced`, and `Widowed`. This still saves half a byte over using a character variable and results in simpler program logic.

How to use bit fields

You read data from and store it in bit fields in the same way you do for other structure members. You use the structure instance's name, a period, and the bit field name in an assignment statement. Study the following example:

```
Names[7].Married = 0;
```

This code sets the `Married` field in the eighth member of the structure array `Names` to `0`. If this field were two bits wide, you could also set it to 3 (the fourth of the possibilities 0 through 3):

```
Names[7].Married = 3;
```

Attempting to assign a non-integer value or one that it is too small or large for the field causes an error. Of course, your code is most readable if you define symbolic constants for the possible values of a bit field. You can then use these instead of integer values. This also helps preclude attempts to put bad values into the fields.

```
const int Widowed = 3;
Names[7].Married = Widowed;
```

How can I use this in the real world?

You can use a bit field within a structure to store any sort of information in which the possible values are strictly limited. Think of someone's marriage status. A person might be single, married, divorced, or widowed. A bit field called Married, defined to be two bits wide, could hold all four of these possibilities. Using such a bit field saves space compared with storing the text values for the four marriage statuses, even if you restricted the program to using one character to represent the status.

Catch the bug

The following short section of code goes through a structure array and assigns a value to a bit field named `Married` based on a value input by the user. Can you spot a problem?

```
#include <stdio.h>
int counter;
struct name {
    char Fullname[40];
    unsigned Married     :1;
    char SSAN[9];
    };
main()
{
struct name Names[10];
for (counter = 0; counter <=10; counter++)
    {
    puts ("Enter 'y' if the employee is married);
    if ((input = getch()) == 'y')
        Names[counter].Married = Yes;
    }
...
```

Answer: You are going to get an undefined `identifier` error here; the symbolic constant `Yes` was not defined. You need the lines

```
const int Yes = 1;
const int No = 0;
```

Summary

In this chapter, you looked at operations with single bits of data. After reviewing binary notation, you examined the shift operators. You then considered the bitwise operators for AND, OR, and XOR operations, as well as the bitwise operator for taking the complement. You also learned how to define and use bit fields within structures.

Review questions

1 What is meant by *hexadecimal notation*? *Octal*? Why are they useful when expressing computer data?

2 What is the maximum integer value that can be expressed in two bytes? In four?

3 What is the shift-left operation equivalent to?

4 What is meant by the *complement* of a byte value?

5 What do you use to express the width, in bits, of a bit field in a structure. What data type do all such fields have?

Exercises

1 Write a short function to perform an integer division by four on a number. Use one of the shift operators rather than the ordinary division (/) operator.

2 Write a statement to perform the XOR operation on a number and its complement. What does this result always come out to?

3 Write a structure definition for a structure to contain a name of up to 40 characters, an employment status field to hold one of two values, a marriage status field to hold one of four values, and a department field to hold one of eight values.

What You Need To Know about Disks and Their Files

- ● **In this chapter:**

  - ● **What are disk files?**

  - ● **How do I make a disk file ready to use?**

  - ● **Functions for working with disk files**

If a thing of beauty is a joy forever, surely you'll want to find some way to keep your hard-earned data from disappearing when you turn off your computer. In this chapter, you'll see how to store it permanently . . . . ▸

What happens to the data in a computer's memory when the power is interrupted, either accidentally by a storm or on purpose through the on-off switch? Quite simply, it disappears. In the preceding chapter, you learned about data as collections of currents that are either on or off. If there's no power to drive the currents, there's no data.

The vulnerability of data in RAM is cause for occasional concern. After all, no one wants to re-enter every piece of data that is used each time the computer is turned on. What is needed is some nonvolatile way to store data. You should know by now that on most small computer systems, disks meet this need. The magnetic surface of a disk can store the same 1s and 0s that the current flows in RAM represent and can do so on a long-term basis. In this chapter, you'll see how to harness this capability for use in your own programs and to save the data they've worked so hard to process for you.

What are disk files?

You can think of a computer disk as a sort of filing cabinet. At the lowest level, it stores disk files.

 *Plain English, please!*

A **disk file** is a single, named collection of data of a certain kind.

Within a filing cabinet, a file might be several pages contained in a manila folder. On a computer, a file is a number of bytes of data referenced by a name such as myprog.c. Groups of files can be organized; just as a filing cabinet has drawers, disks have directories. A directory can contain many files. One directory can even contain other directories. A directory has a name just as a file does. The "filing cabinet" itself (disk) also has a name, to distinguish it from others that might be available. It is possible to name the disk, directory, and file name together to uniquely identify a file and its location.

So far, your C programs have completely neglected that filing cabinet that is your computer's disk filing system. Therefore, even when you have taken the trouble to enter a large amount of data with one of the example programs

(NAMELIST, for instance), all your work has been lost when the program stops running. To save such data—and retrieve it later—you need to know how to work with your computer's file system from within C. This chapter deals with this subject.

Is there a relationship between C streams and disk files?

Recall the discussion concerning data streams in chapter 12, "About Data Streams." That chapter defined a stream as a flow of data (Input/Output or simply I/O) with a given source and destination.

When you work with file data in C, you're working with streams just as you do when reading keyboard input and writing screen output. The difference is that there are no standard streams with file I/O. You must explicitly set up a stream when you want to read data from a file or write data to it.

You set up a stream by opening a file. You provide the name of the file and a pointer to store the stream's address in. This pointer becomes your program's link to the file stream. To actually access file data, you must provide the pointer to the appropriate file function.

There are several types of disk files

Although there are a variety of disk files available (documents, spreadsheets, databases, C programs), all these types boil down to two basic ones. These file types are associated with the different kinds of data streams that were introduced in chapter 12: text and binary. Recall that a text stream consists of sequences of ASCII characters organized into lines; a line is marked by the end-of-line character (escape code \n). The end of a text stream is marked by the end-of-file character. A binary stream, on the other hand, is just a long flow of bits; the data in a binary stream is meaningless outside of its role in the program which interprets it.

As you have seen, there are text files and binary files just as there are text and binary streams. **Text files**, sometimes referred to as **ASCII files**, contain simple text data. The source code for a C program is an example of such a file. A **binary file**, sometimes referred to as a **formatted file**, contains any sort of data. The way the data is interpreted depends on the program reading such a file. A document produced by a word processor is an example of a binary file. For your purposes as a C programmer, text files are useful for data you want to share among different programs; binary files are the best choice for use only within the application that created them.

Not every file name is the same

As you know, a file is a collection of data that is named. File names are among the variable parts of computer operating systems; no two systems name their files in exactly the same way. On the Macintosh, file names can be up to 32 characters long and every character except the colon is acceptable in a file name. UNIX files can also have long names, although the exact length varies among different kinds of UNIX systems. UNIX uses the slash character (/) to separate the parts of a full file name; the slash separates directory names from each other and from the file's actual name.

DOS, which also underlies all versions of Microsoft Windows up to Version 3.11, is the most limited of the systems in widespread use. A DOS file name can only be eight characters long. (File names in Windows NT and Windows 95, which don't use DOS, can be up to 255 characters long.) DOS also supports the use of an optional one to three character extension; the extension follows a period directly after the file name's last character. Although the meaning of any extension is arbitrary, it is conventional to indicate what kind of data the file contains by using an appropriate extension. C language source code files, for instance, generally get the extension .c.

DOS further differs from UNIX in that it uses the backward-slash character (\) to separate parts of the file name. (The full name of a file, including the disk it is on and the directories it appears in, is usually referred to as the **path name**.) In DOS you can also specify which disk a file appears on; the letter corresponding to the disk is shown at the beginning of the file name, followed by a colon. A complete DOS path name resembles

```
c:\myfiles\proposals\book1.doc
```

The backslash produces a minor complication in your C programming. Recall that C uses the backslash to indicate escape codes, such as that for a new line (\n). When you quote a DOS path name literally, you can end up sending escape sequences to the standard output stream. In such cases, you need to double the backslash to "quote" it, as in

```
c:\\myfiles\\proposals\\book1.doc
```

For data entered from the keyboard by a user—which file to open, for instance—you don't need to double the backslash.

The four steps for working with files

On any computer system, there are essentially four steps involved in working with files:

1 You must get a file ready for use. This is similar to locating and unlocking a file cabinet. This process is called opening the file.

2 When a file has been opened, you can read data from it. This transfers the data from your computer's disk into RAM, where it can be manipulated. Because nothing happens to the original file data on disk, this step is similar to photocopying the contents of a selected file folder within the cabinet.

3 This step is optional; if you have changed the file's data and want to preserve changes, you can write back to the original file on disk. In this step, data from RAM is transferred back to disk, changing the file's contents. In effect, you're replacing the pages from the file folder with your annotated, photocopied ones.

4 You must release a file when you're done using it. This is referred to as closing the file; here you again lock the cabinet and surrender the key.

After studying each of these steps, consider the different ways in which you can work with file data. You begin with readying a file for use. The statement you use to ready a file varies according to what your program means to do with it.

You've got to get a file ready

To work with a disk file, you must establish a data stream associated with that file. Part of this process involves setting aside an area in RAM where data on the way into or out of the file can be placed for stream processing; such an area is usually referred to as a **file buffer**. In C, you get to a file buffer by means of an address in RAM; naturally, this address is stored in a pointer, which you must supply to the statement to open the file.

Use the `fopen()` function

The C library function `fopen()` makes a file ready for use. The function establishes a data stream connected with a given file and returns the location of the file's buffer in RAM.

What do you want to do with this file?

There are several modes that you can open a file for use in; how you do so depends on what your program does with the file. You might open a file to read from if you only want to get data out of it. You can open it to write to if you only want to send data to it; this mode is also used to create a nonexistent file. There are also modes for appending data to an existing file, rather than wiping out the file's old contents. There are even mixtures of the different modes. The modes available and the letters associated with them are summarized in the following table:

Speaking of fopen()

The prototype for the function fopen() is found in stdio.h and is

```
FILE *fopen(const char *file_name, const char *mode);
```

The function expects two values to be passed to it in its argument list: a pointer to the name of the file to open and a pointer to a string containing instructions on how to open it (the *mode*; more on this in a bit).

The function returns a pointer of type FILE; this is a data type you have not yet encountered; it is really a kind of structure definition contained within stdio.h. The details needn't concern you; however, a pointer to contain the address returned by fopen() (the location of the file's buffer) must be of type FILE.

An example of a call to the fopen() function is

```
FILE *pFileOpened;
pFileOpened = fopen(FileName, "r");
```

Table 24.1   Modes to access files

Mode	Purpose
r	Read-only access. If the named file doesn't exist, using fopen() with this mode returns NULL.
w	Write-only access. If the named file doesn't exist, using fopen() with this mode creates it. If the file exists, all of its previous contents are obliterated.
a	Append data. If the named file doesn't exist, using fopen() with this mode creates it. If the file exists, new data is added to the end of its previous contents.
r+	Read and write access. If the named file doesn't exist, using fopen() with this mode creates it. If the file exists, all its previous contents are overwritten, starting at the beginning of the file.
w+	Read and write access. If the named file doesn't exist, using fopen() with this mode creates it. If the file exists, all of its previous contents are obliterated.
a+	Read and append access. If the named file doesn't exist, using fopen() with this mode creates it. If the file exists, new data is added to the end of its previous contents.

The preceding items in the table are for opening files in text mode; to open in binary mode, you append a b to the codes that the table shows.

For example, the following short section of C code prompts the user for the name of a file to enter, then attempts to open it in read-only mode, binary form:

```
FILE *pDiskFile;
puts("Enter the name of a file to load");
gets(EnteredFileName);
pDiskFile = fopen(EnteredFileName, "rb");
```

The value stored in the pointer pDiskFile must be provided to subsequent statements that attempt to read data from the newly opened file. If the named file doesn't exist, the value NULL is returned and stored in the pointer pDiskFile. NULL is also returned if the file can't be found, perhaps because there is a temporary equipment problem.

How can I use this in the real world?

Your program can also behave unexpectedly (as far as the user is concerned) when you're opening a file to write to. Recall that if the file doesn't exist, attempting to open it in write mode creates it. However, suppose your user really just wanted to save an existing file and mistyped the name. Without checking to see whether the file exists first before attempting to open it in write mode, your program creates a new file under the mistyped name. Later on, your user might think the data was lost.

In any case, your program ought to provide some sort of code to check whether a file is actually available before it attempts to use the file. You can do so by trying to open the file in read mode and then testing the pointer returned by fopen(). A pointer value of NULL means the file doesn't exist. The following short FileExists() function relies on this fact to see if a file already exists:

```
/* This short function returns NULL if the file whose name is
➡*/
/* passed to the function does not exist; */
/* otherwise it does nothing. */
FILE *FileExists(char *FileName)
{
 FILE *pDiskFile;
 pDiskFile = fopen(FileName, "r");
 fclose(pDiskFile);
 return pDiskFile;
}
```

Calling this short function has no affect on the original file. If the file is not found, the function returns NULL; otherwise, it returns the address of the file's buffer, although this information is of no use. The point is, your program can test the value returned by FileExists() to see whether it is equal to NULL; if not, the file exists. The program can then act accordingly.

Catch the bug

The following function attempts to open a file so that you can read it. Can you find a problem with it?

```
FILE *FileRead(char *FileName, char *DataBuffer)
{
 FILE *pDiskFile;
 pDiskFile = fopen(FileName, "w+");
     ...statements to read data
 fclose(pDiskFile);
 return DataBuffer;
}
```

Answer: The file is actually opened in read-write mode. This means that existing data can be read from the file. However, when the file is closed, its old data is lost. You should use r rather than w+ for the mode.

Get your data into and out of a file using...

There is a *New Yorker* cartoon where a young woman driving a small convertible has stopped to confront a dog that has been chasing her. She says to the dog, "Well, you got me. Now what are you going to do with me?" A similar situation can be drawn with the open disk file: now you have one, so what are you doing to do with it?

Depending on your program's needs, you either read data from it or write data to it. There are actually three ways that you can do this, depending on the nature of the data in the file. These ways involve working with three different kinds of I/O: direct, character, and formatted, which are similar to the formatted, string, and character I/O functions discussed in chapter 12. As you might guess, there are input and output functions associated with each; this book concentrates on direct I/O, although the other file stream I/O functions are mentioned, just so that you can recognize them.

...direct I/O...

Perhaps the most commonly used I/O method for files created and used exclusively by C programs is direct I/O. In this method, a block of bytes with a specified width is read from or written to an open file. The aforementioned byte-block must be somewhere in memory; a type `void` pointer establishes its location.

Note the use of the `sizeof` operator; this is the best way to ensure that exactly the right number of bytes are read. Recall that the name of an array or a structure is a pointer constant; therefore, you can use a structure name as the place that data should be read into.

The following short function reads data from an open file into a structure array. It then closes the file. The function uses some statements that have not yet been mentioned; the important part for now is the `fread()` function call and the statements required to support it. Note that this function calls `FileExists()` to see whether the file is really there; if not, an error message is printed and the function is terminated without reading data:

```
int FileLoad(char *FileName, struct NameRecord *pNames)
{
    FILE *pDiskFile;
    int counter = 1;
    if ((pDiskFile = FileExists(FileName)) == NULL)
        {
        puts("File Does Not Exist");
```

Speaking of `fread()`

The function to read data directly from an open file is `fread()`. This function is prototyped in `stdio.h`. Its prototype is

```
int fread(void *buffer, int blocksize, int #blocks, FILE
➥*fptr);
```

You provide this function with a pointer to a location in memory (*buffer*) where the data should be stored; this can be a pointer to a structured variable or a string. The function also expects the size, in bytes, (*blocksize*) of the block of data to read and how many such blocks it should return (*#blocks*). Also, the function expects a pointer to the open file (*fptr*); this is the pointer value returned by the `fopen()` function. The `fread()` function itself returns the number of blocks read.

The following statement reads one block of data from a file into a structure referred to as `Name`; the structure's tag is `NameDefinition`:

```
fread(&Name, sizeof(struct NameDefinition), 1, pFilePointer);
```

```
                    return 0;
                    }
                    else
                        {
                        pDiskFile = fopen(FileName, "r");
                        while (!feof(pDiskFile))
                            {
                            fread(&pNames[counter++], sizeof
                            ➥(struct NameRecord), 1, pDiskFile);
                            }
                        fclose(pDiskFile);
                        }
                return counter-1;
                }
```

The following function writes data from a structure array into a file; note that the file's previous contents are entirely obliterated. The function tests to see whether the named file actually exists. If it doesn't, the user is asked whether or not it should be created. If the file does exist, the user is prompted to indicate whether the old data should be overwritten. This last item is very important. It is a small courtesy that such a program should provide for the user.

```
        void FileSave(char *FileName, struct NameRecord
        ➥*pNames, int NumberEntered)
          {
             FILE *pDiskFile;
           int counter = 1;
```

Speaking of `fwrite()`

You use the function `fwrite()`, prototyped in `stdio.h`, to write data into an open file. Its prototype is

```
    int fwrite(void *buffer, int blocksize, int #blocks, FILE
    ➥*fptr);
```

This function writes data from the area in memory that *buffer* points to. It writes a specific number of blocks (*#blocks*) of an indicated size (*blocksize*) in bytes to an open file that *fptr* points to. The function returns the number of items written. A statement to write data from a structure referred to as Name to the file pointed to by pFilePointer resembles the following:

```
    fwrite (&Name, sizeof(struct NameDefinition), 1,
    ➥pFilePointer);
```

```
            char choice;
            if ((pDiskFile = FileExists(FileName)) == NULL)
               {
               puts("File Does Not Exist; Create New File?");
               puts("Enter 'y' if yes; anything
               ➥else to cancel save operation");
                     if ((choice = getch()) != 'y')
                         {
                         puts("File not saved");
                         return;
                         }
                     pDiskFile = fopen(FileName, "w");
                     fwrite(&pNames[counter++], sizeof(struct
                     ➥NameRecord),
                     ➥NumberEntered, pDiskFile);
                     fclose(pDiskFile);
               return;
               }
            else
               {
                   puts("File Already Exists; Overwrite existing
                   ➥file?");
                   puts("Enter 'y' if yes; anything
                   ➥else to cancel save operation");
                   if ((choice = getch()) != 'y')
                         {
                         puts("File not saved");
                         return;
                         }
                   pDiskFile = fopen(FileName, "w");
                   fwrite(&pNames[counter++], sizeof(struct
                   ➥NameRecord),
                   ➥NumberEntered, pDiskFile);
                   fclose(pDiskFile);
                   }
        return;
        }
```

...character I/O...

Less commonly used are the file stream I/O functions that deal with single characters or lines of characters. The prototypes for these functions are

```
int fgetc(FILE *file_pointer);

int fputc(FILE *file_pointer);

char *fgets(char *buffer, int numcharacters, FILE *fpointer);

char fputs(const char *str, FILE file_pointer);
```

The function fgetc() returns the value of a single character from the file pointed to; putc() writes a single character to the file. The functions fgets() and puts() are used to work with entire lines.

...and formatted I/O

Finally, there are file stream I/O functions that are counterparts to scanf() and printf(). These functions are fscanf() and fprintf(), respectively. The following are their prototypes:

```
int fprintf(FILE *file_pointer, const char *format_string,
...);
int fscanf(FILE *file_pointer, const char *format_string,
...);
```

These functions expect a *format_string* and a variable number of arguments, as do scanf() and printf(). The *format_string* has the same construction you have been using, with embedded escape codes and conversion specifiers.

Catch the bug

The following short block of code is intended to write data directly to a file. Can you spot a problem?

```
void FileWrite (struct NameRecord *pNames,
int NumberEntered, char *FileName)
{
FILE *pDiskFile;
fwrite (&pNames[counter++], sizeof(struct NameRecord),
NumberEntered, pDiskFile);
return;
}
```

Answer: The file is being written to. However, there is no evidence that it has been opened. A line should be included, such as

```
pDiskFile = fopen(FileName, "w");
```

just before the statement that calls fwrite().

Clean up when you're done

Your program has completed reading data from or writing it to a file. However, this doesn't mean the program is finished with the file. Your program should close and release the file's stream after the program is finished with it. This locks the file, and prevents any mishaps with it.

It is not absolutely necessary to close a file explicitly; C closes all file streams when it encounters the last statement of a program. If your program should crash, however, it might leave a file open. This file would then be temporarily inaccessible to other programs.

Speaking of `fclose()`

The `fclose()` function releases a file and closes the associated data stream. This function's prototype (defined in `stdio.h`) is

```
int fclose(FILE *file_pointer);
```

The function returns 0 if the close was successful, and -1 if an error occurred while attempting to close the file. The `file_pointer` required is the value returned by the original call to `fopen()` that readied the file for use. Therefore, a statement to close a file might resemble the following:

```
fclose(pFilePointer);
```

Can I poke around in a file once it's opened?

You need to be familiar with how to find your way around a file from a certain location. You also need to know how to adjust your location while searching for data. Another important part of accessing a file is finding its end. You briefly look at these and other tasks in the following sections.

Look at a file byte by byte

Normally, data from a file is accessed byte by byte, from the file's beginning to its end. As part of its definition, the FILE data type maintains a value that indicates the current position in the file from which data is read. Each call to a data reading function, such as fread(), updates the value of this file position indicator. A subsequent call to fread() gets data from the new position, and not from the file's beginning. This is referred to as **sequential access**.

If you want to reset the position indicator for a file, you can use the rewind() function. A call to rewind(), such as

```
rewind(pFilePointer);
```

sets the position indicator back to the file's beginning.

Look anywhere in a file

The capability to read data from any desired location within a file, and not just from the beginning or from the current file position, is referred to as **random access**. You use the fseek() function to set the file pointer to a specific place within the file; the place is referred to as the **offset** from the file's beginning.

Note that the fseek() function merely sets the file position indicator; a subsequent input operation would actually retrieve data from that position.

Find the end of the road... um, file

It's beneficial for you, especially when reading data, to attempt to detect the end of a file. The end of a text file is generally marked by the end-of-file character; you can simply look for it. With binary files, though, you don't have this capability. Fortunately, with respect to binary files, there is a function that tests the current position of a file and determines whether that position corresponds to the end of the file. The function is `feof()`. This function returns a `True` value if the file position indicator has reached the end of the file. Therefore, you can construct a loop beginning

```
while (!feof(pFilePointer))
```

that continues to read data until the end of the file is reached.

Speaking of `fseek()`

The prototype for the `fseek()` function is

```
int fseek(FILE *file_pointer, long offset, int origin);
```

This function moves the file position indicator for the file pointed to by *file_pointer* to a given *offset*. The *origin* value determines the starting place relative to which the position indicated is adjusted. A value of 0 calculates the offset relative to the file's beginning; 1 calculates the offset relative to the file's current position; and 2 calculates relative to the file's end. The position is changed by *offset* number of bytes. Therefore, to set the file position to two records before the file's end, you use

```
fseek(pFilePointer, 2*(sizeof(struct Record), 2);
```

What else can I do with files?

There are a few additional file operations that you need to be familiar with. These operations affect files as a whole, not just the data within them. As such, each of these operations—renaming and deleting files—has an operating system (OS) counterpart. A user can easily rename or delete a file from the OS, without having to rely on your program. In many ways, it is best to leave such tasks to the OS. You can create problems by indiscriminately renaming or deleting important files while your C programs are running. The functions do exist, however, and the following sections describe them and how they are used.

Q&A **What's so dangerous about letting the user rename or delete any file they want?**

It might very well be that they'd accidentally delete an important system file—one used by the OS. Renaming such a file is almost as bad as deleting it because doing either to such a file can crash the computer so badly that it can't be restarted without expert assistance.

Q&A **Why would I even consider using the functions to rename and delete files if they can be so dangerous within a program?**

One important use is if your program needs to open and maintain a temporary disk file. It might do so to store information while some other processing is going on. In that case, you really should delete your temporary file(s) when the program has finished with them, rather than leaving them around to clutter up the disk.

Sometimes you want to rename a file

The C function `rename()` changes the name of an existing data file. The function's prototype is

```
int rename(const char *old_name, const char *new_name);
```

Suppose that the file's existing name was stored in a string variable referred to as `OldName`. Then, assume the new name was stored in `NewName`; you can rename the file with

```
rename(OldName,NewName);
```

The function returns 0 if the renaming was successful and -1 if the renaming failed. The function can fail if the old name doesn't really exist. The function can also fail if a file with the new name already exists or if you try to cross disk boundaries. (Renaming a file on the C drive to the A drive, for instance, is moving, not renaming.)

At other times, you want to delete a file

The C function `remove()` deletes a file permanently. As such, it is perhaps the most dangerous file function of all. Its prototype is

```
int remove(const char *file_name);
```

Therefore, to delete the file whose name is contained in the string `FileName`, you use

```
remove (FileName);
```

The function returns 0 if it successfully deleted the file and -1 if it failed. It can fail because the file doesn't actually exist, is marked read-only (can't be written to), or is open and in use.

Summary

In this chapter, you explored disk files. After discussing the need for such files, and looking at how they are constructed, you moved on to C streams and their relationship to disk files. You learned how to make a file ready for use, reading from and writing to it, and closing it. You learned briefly about sequential versus random file access. You also now know how to detect a file's end. The end of this chapter discussed some file management functions.

Review questions

1 What is meant by a file's *buffer*? What is the relationship between a buffer and a data stream?

2 What function readies a file for use? What does it return?

3 Distinguish between the binary and text modes of file access.

Catch the bug

The following function is meant to delete a named file—passed to it by a pointer—after prompting the user whether to delete it or not. Can you spot a problem?

```
void DeleteFile(char *FileName)
{
char choice;
puts("Do you really want to delete the file?");
choice=getch();
remove(FileName);
if (choice == 'y')
puts("File deleted");
        return;
```

Answer: *The call to* `remove()` *comes before the user's choice is tested; this function always deletes a file, no matter what the user enters. The corrected version is*

```
void DeleteFile(char *FileName)
{
char choice;
puts("Do you really want to delete the file?");
choice=getch();
if (choice == 'y')
        {
        remove(FileName);
        puts("File deleted");
        return;
        }
else
        {
        puts("File not deleted");
        return;
        }
```

4 What C operator can you use to ensure that data read from (or written to) a file comes in blocks that are exactly the size of a particular data construct you're using to hold the blocks in memory?

5 Distinguish between sequential and random file access. Where does the file position pointer fit into this scheme? What function do you use to set the position indicator to a specific place within a file?

Exercises

1 Write a statement to prepare a file to be read from or appended to.

2 Write a short function that gives the user the opportunity to rename or delete a file whose name is held in `FileName`.

3 Write a short C program to read a specific line from a text file, and display it on-screen. Let the user specify which file to open and which line number to read. Use the `fseek()` function to set the line to be read. Assume that lines are 80 characters long and don't terminate with a null string.

25

Make Your Work Easier with the C Function Library

● In this chapter:

- What kinds of tools are there in the C function library?

- I want to give my programs the capabilities of a powerful calculator

- What else can I do with math functions?

- I need to work with times and dates; are there library functions to help?

You can compare the difference to preparing pancakes one of two ways: from scratch or from a prepackaged mix. Either way gets the job done. However, the latter is significantly less work. In the same way, using the C library functions is less work than cooking up equivalent functions from scratch . . . . ➤

Most of the C functions discussed to this point have concerned either stream operations or character strings. C supports a number of functions, however, that work with numeric data. These can be broadly grouped into those that perform mathematical calculations and the ones that work with time. This chapter considers examples of both groups.

Tell me about the C library functions

The C library functions provide you with solutions to ordinary and relatively common programming problems. In this way, they save you from having to come up with your own solutions. The difference is roughly like that between preparing pancakes entirely from scratch or using a prepackaged mix; both get the job done. However, the latter involves significantly less work.

What types of library functions are available?

Again, aside from the string and stream I/O functions that have been discussed since chapter 12, C library functions either perform mathematical calculations or provide options for working with time, except for a small minority of functions. (A small set of functions exists that work with something else—computer memory. The next chapter discusses these functions.) Of these, the math functions can themselves be divided into three functions. Some of the math functions perform trigonometric calculations—these are relationships involving right triangles, such as an angle's cosine and its tangent. Other groups of math functions work with powers, performing logarithmic and exponential calculations. You've already learned about two of these functions: `pow()` and `log10()`. The others are similar. The last group of math functions performs miscellaneous calculations.

There are basically three types of time functions. One function helps you to obtain the current time from the system clock. Then there are functions to format this value into a character string. Finally, you can use C library functions to determine the time elapsed between two dates.

How to use library functions

To use the math functions, you must include the header file `math.h` in your program. The time functions require `time.h` to be included. Omitting these header files results in an error if your program attempts to call a function that is prototyped within.

For the most part, the C math functions require and return values in type double form; that is, as double-precision floating-point values. Using an integer value for certain parameters might produce a calculation yielding zero as a result when it should be some other number. Remember that you can use type casts (such as double) to force values into the correct data type.

The time functions work with special data types and structures defined in time.h. The data types time_t and clock_t are defined in time.h as long integers; you use variables or pointers of these data types to store time values returned by certain time functions. time.h also includes a structure definition, struct tm, that contains the various parts of a date. This structure is defined as follows:

```
struct tm
{
int tm_sec,
     tm_min,
     tm_hour,
     tm_mday,
     tm_mon,
     tm_year,
     tm_wday,
     tm_yday,
     tm_isdst;
};
```

Other than knowing about the special data needs of math and time functions, all you need to do to use them is to include a call to a function within a C statement. For the most part, these function calls occur within assignment statements, so that the value returned by the function call is immediately stored in a variable of the appropriate data type. Knowing this, you can examine the available functions a bit more closely, starting with the math functions.

I want to do some math, using...

Again, there are three groups of math functions to consider here. The trigonometric functions work with the relationships among the angles of right triangles. The power functions work with exponents. The miscellaneous functions do things such as finding the absolute value of a number, locating the next integer value after a certain number, and so on.

...trigonometric functions...

You should know that the trigonometric functions in C express angles in terms of radians. A full circle contains 2π radians. Therefore, one radian is approximately equal to 57.3 degrees. You can use this value to convert degrees into radians. Table 25.1 summarizes the available C library trigonometric functions. It includes the prototype for each function.

Table 25.1   The C library trigonometric functions and their prototypes

Function purpose	Function prototype
cosine	double cos (double *angle*);
sine	double sin (double *angle*);
tangent	double tan (double *angle*);
arccosine	double acos (double *angle*);
arcsine	double asin (double *angle*);
arctangent	double atan (double *angle*);
arctangent	double atan2 (double *x*, double *y*); (second method, returns arctan *x*/*y*, which is the ratio of the angles opposite to adjacent sides, rather than relying on an angle in radians as atan2() does.)
Hyperbolic variants	
Hyperbolic cosine	double cosh (double *angle*);
Hyperbolic sine	double sinh (double *angle*);
Hyperbolic tangent	double tanh (double *angle*);

To illustrate how you can use these functions, consider the tangent of an angle. Within a right triangle—that is, a triangle with one angle equal to 90 degrees ($\pi/2$ radians)—the tangent of either of the other two angles is defined as the ratio between the side opposite the angle and the side adjacent to it. (This is the reason for the second variant of the arctangent function—to give the angle when you know the lengths of the opposite and adjacent sides.) You can use the tangent to calculate the height of an object that casts a shadow. The following explains this calculation.

If you know the angle of the sun and the length of the shadow cast by a vertical object that is known to be plumb (at 90 degrees to the earth's surface), you can calculate the object's height. The object and its shadow define a right triangle, one angle of which is equal to the sun's angle. The adjacent side of this angle is the object's shadow length; the opposite side is the object's height. Knowing that the tangent is the opposite side divided by the adjacent side, you can solve for the unknown height in this way:

$$\text{opposite} = \text{adjacent} \times \tan(\text{angle})$$

How can I use this in the real world?

Want to put the preceding to the test? The following short program calculates the height of an object, given your latitude and the length of the object's shadow at noon on the solstice. You can use it to find the height of a tree or building that you can't measure directly.

```c
#include <math.h>
#include <stdio.h>

/* A program to find an object's height */
/* The length of its shadow at noon on the first day of
➥summer, */
/* and the local latitude are required */

float length, latitude;

main()
{
puts("Enter the shadow length");
scanf("%f", &length);
puts("Enter your latitude");
scanf ("%f", &latitude);
printf ("\nThe object's height is %f units",
➥length * tan (((90.0-latitude+23.5)/57.3)));

/*pause before quitting*/
scanf ("%f", &length);
}
```

Using this program on the shadow of a tree in my front yard (and happening to be writing close to June 21), I measured a shadow of four feet and got a height of about 19 feet here at 35.5 degrees North.

To use this relationship, you have to measure the sun's angle in addition to the length of an object's shadow. On certain days of the year—the solstices and equinoxes—you can rely on known relationships between your latitude and the sun's angle at noon standard time. During the summer solstice, for example, the sun is directly overhead at the Tropic of Cancer, which is at 23.5 degrees northern latitude. For every degree of latitude you move north from this point, the sun's angle at noon decreases by one degree. Therefore, the relationship

$$90 - (\text{Your latitude} - 23.5)$$

gives the sun's angle at your location at noon on the summer solstice. (If you live in the U.S., that really occurs at 1 PM local time because of Daylight Savings Time, except in places that don't observe Daylight Savings Time, such as all of Arizona and most of Indiana.)

...power functions...

The next group of C math functions works with powers; these include logarithms. The logarithm of a number is that value which, when a base number is raised to its power, yields the original number. The base for common logarithms is 10; the base for natural logarithms is e (approximately 2.7183). Table 25.2 summarizes the power functions.

Table 25.2   The power functions and their prototypes

Function purpose	Function prototype
Antilog (natural)	double exp (double x);
Natural logarithm	double log (double x);
Common logarithm	double log10 (double x);
Normalized fraction	double frexp (double x, int *y); Returns r and assigns value to y such that $x = r - 2^y$
Normalized fraction	double ldexp (double x, int y); Returns $x - 2^y$
Power	double pow (double x, double y); Returns xy, use with 10.0 to obtain common antilog of a number;
Square root	double sqrt (double x);

Again, you have seen two of these functions used in the example programs, especially the FINANCE program.

...and the miscellaneous math functions

The following table summarizes the remaining C library math functions.

Table 25.3   Other C library math functions and their prototypes

Function description	Function prototype
Absolute value	int abs (int x);
Absolute value (long form)	long abs (long x);
Next largest integer	double ceil (double x); Returns next integer greater than x
Next smallest integer	double floor (double x); Returns next integer smaller than x
Modulus, floating point	double fmod (double x, double y); Returns the fractional remainder when x is divided by y
Modulus, floating point (2nd form)	double modf (double x, double *y); Returns the fractional remainder when x is divided by y; integer quotient returned in y.

How can I use this in the real world?

Although there is a library function to find the square root of a number, there is no function to find the nth root—the third root, fourth root, and so on. However, you can take advantage of the relationship

nth root of $x = x^{1/n}$

to construct an expression finding the nth root, using the pow( ) function. Supposing that x is a floating-point variable containing the number whose nth root you want to find and n is a floating-point variable containing the root that you want (third, fourth, etc.), you'd use a line of code like

```
root = pow(x, 1.0/n);
```

If x contains 27 and n contains 3, the result is 3. (The cube or third root of 27 is 3 because 3×3×3 = 27.)

Catch the bug

The following program uses the absolute value function abs( ) to ensure that no negative values are processed when calculating nth roots. (Negative values can cause problems.) Can you spot any problems with the program as it appears in the following listing?

```
#include <stdio.h>

/* A program to find the nth root of a number */

float number, root;

main()
{
puts("Enter a number whose nth root you want to know:");
scanf("%f",&number);
puts("Enter n:");
scanf("%f",&root);
printf("\nThe %.0fth root of %f is %f", root, number,
➥pow(abs(number), abs(1.0/root)));

/* Pause before continuing */
scanf("%f",&root);
}
```

Answer: *There are two problems. First, the header file* math.h *has been omitted. Second, recall that the* abs() *function returns an integer value. The way this program is written it wipes out the nth root value* 1.0/root *(it changes it to* 0*; the 0th root of any number is 1). If it does not matter that* abs() *wipes out the fractional parts of the values entered by the user, the offending program line could be rewritten in this way:*

```
printf("\nThe %.0fth root of %f is %f", root, number,
➥pow(abs(number), 1.0/abs(root)));
```

How to get time functions on your side

The last group of library functions that this chapter dicusses deals with time. Using these functions, you can have a program display the current time a variety of ways or calculate the elapsed time between two dates.

What time functions are there?

Table 25.4 summarizes the C library functions that deal with time.

Table 25.4 The C library functions that work with time

Function purpose	Function prototype
Current time	`time_t time(time_t *timeptr);` Returns number of seconds since 12:00 AM 1-1-1970
Format time	`struct tm *localtime(time_t *ptr);` Converts number-of-seconds value pointed to by *ptr* into a time record format; returns a pointer to a record of type *tm*
Time to number of seconds	`time_t mktime(struct tm *ntime);` Converts the time value stored in the structure pointed to by the pointer *ntime* into a number of seconds; this value is returned by the function
Time difference	`double difftime(time_t later, time_t earlier);`
Elapsed time	`clock_t clock(void);` Returns 1/100ths of a second elapsed since the current C program began running
Time to string (first)	`char *asctime(struct tm *ptr);` Returns 26-character, null terminated string corresponding to the time stored in the structure pointed to by *ptr*
Time to string (second)	`char *ctime(time_t *ptr);` Returns 26-character, null terminated string corresponding to the time stored in the elapsed time value pointed to by *ptr*
Time to string (third)	`size_t strftime(char *time_string, size_t max, char *fmt, struct tm *ptr);` Writes into the string pointed to by *time_string* up to *max* characters, consisting of a time formatted from one held in a structure pointed to by *ptr*. The string pointer **fmt* points to a format string, specifying how the time is to be formatted. (You can use a literal string constant with embedded format specifiers.) The following includes format specifiers: %a Abbreviated weekday name %A Non-abbreviated weekday name %b Abbreviated month name %B Non-abbreviated month name %c Use date and time as in 12:00:00. 1–Aug–95. %d Print day of month as decimal number 01–31 %H Use 24-hour clock and print time as decimal number 00–23 %I Use 12-hour clock and print time as decimal number 00–11

continues

Table 25.4   Continued

Function purpose	Function prototype	
	%j	Print day of year as decimal number 001–366
	%m	Print month as decimal number 01–12
	%M	Print minute as decimal number 00–59
	%p	Print AM or PM
	%s	Print seconds as decimal number 00–59
	%U	Print week of year as decimal number 00–53 with Sunday as first day of week
	%w	Print weekday as decimal number 0–6 (Sunday = 0)
	%W	Print week of year as decimal number 00–53 with Monday as first day of week
	%x	Print date representation
	%X	Print time representation
	%y	Print last two digits of year
	%Y	Print all four digits of year
	%z	Print time zone name, if known
	%%	Print a single percent sign

You use the format specifiers along with other embedded characters to construct a time string that meets the needs of your program.

How to use the time functions

A common way to use the time functions is to have a program determine the current time, then print the result in a format the programmer prefers or that meets some user need, such as knowing the current week of the year. It's also helpful to be able to determine the elapsed time between two dates for use in a subsequent calculation, such as how much vacation time an employee has accumulated.

Keep in mind that you need to use a variable of types `time_t` and `tm`; `tm` is a structure definition, while `time_t` is just a synonym for a long integer variable.

Show me an example using time functions

The following short program determines the current time and displays this in an appropriate format.

```
#include <time.h>
#include <stdio.h>

/* A program to determine and print the time */

time_t timenow;
struct tm *timestrptr;
char CurrentTime[80];

main()
{

timenow = time(0);

timestrptr = localtime(&timenow);

strftime(CurrentTime, 80, "Today is %A, the %d day of %B, %Y.
➡It is the %jth day of the year.", timestrptr);

puts (CurrentTime);

scanf("%d", &timenow);

}
```

This program relies on a call to the function time() to determine the time using the computer's system clock. It then passes the value obtained to the function localtime() to have the value converted to a structure of type tm. Finally, the pointer to this structure is passed to strftime() to create the text string that the program displays. Figure 25.1 shows the results of running this short program.

Fig. 25.1
Using a format string to print a particular representation of the time.

```
Today is Tuesday the 06 day of June, 1995.  It is the 157th
day of the year.
```

Catch the bug

The following program is supposed to print the number of months elapsed between two dates entered by the user. Then the program stores this information in structures of type tm. Can you find the reason it doesn't work as it should?

```c
#include <time.h>
#include <stdio.h>

/* A program to determine and print the elapsed months */

time_t ttimeearly, ttimelate, timediff, *timeptr;
double ttimediff;
struct tm *timestrptr, timeearlier, timelater, timeelapsed;
char ElapsedTime[80];

main()
{
 puts("Enter the former month, 0 = Jan, 11 = Dec:");
 scanf("%d", &timeearlier.tm_mon);
 puts("Enter the last two digits of the former year: ");
 scanf("%d", &timeearlier.tm_year);
 puts("Enter the later month, 0 = Jan, 11 = Dec:");
 scanf("%d", &timelater.tm_mon);
 puts("Enter the last two digits of the later year: ");
 scanf("%d", &timelater.tm_year);

 timelater.tm_mday = timeearlier.tm_mday = 1;

 ttimeearly = mktime(&timeearlier);
 ttimelate = mktime(&timelater);
 ttimediff = difftime(ttimelate, ttimeearly);
 timediff = ttimediff;
 timestrptr = localtime(&timediff);
 strftime(ElapsedTime, 80, "The number of
➡months elapsed is %m", timestrptr);

 puts (ElapsedTime);

 scanf("%d", timeearlier.tm_mon);

}
```

Answer: *Although the program calculates the elapsed time, it converts the value returned (in seconds) into a current time and displays this result. Recall, though, that the localtime function assumes that the* *number of seconds computed is the seconds elapsed since 1 Jan 1970, and converts that number of seconds to a date. The program prints an absolute date, not a date difference.*

*Instead, the program can return the whole number of months by converting the elapsed time difference into a type time structure. Then the program could multiply the number of years (*timestrptr.tm_year-70, *as 1970 is the reference date) by 12 and then add the month number (*tm_mon + 1*) to it. The new listing is as follows:*

```c
#include <time.h>
#include <stdio.h>

/* A program to determine and print the elapsed months */

time_t ttimeearly, ttimelate, timediff, *timeptr;
double ttimediff;
struct tm *timestrptr, timeearlier, timelater, timeelapsed;
char ElapsedTime[80];

main()
{
 puts("Enter the former month, 0 = Jan, 11 = Dec:");
 scanf("%d", &timeearlier.tm_mon);
 puts("Enter the last two digits of the former year: ");
 scanf("%d", &timeearlier.tm_year);
 puts("Enter the later month, 0 = Jan, 11 = Dec:");
 scanf("%d", &timelater.tm_mon);
 puts("Enter the last two digits of the later year: ");
 scanf("%d", &timelater.tm_year);

 timelater.tm_mday = timeearlier.tm_mday = 1;

 ttimeearly = mktime(&timeearlier);
 ttimelate = mktime(&timelater);
 ttimediff = difftime(ttimelate, ttimeearly);

/*Difftime returns double; force it to long */
 timediff = ttimediff;
 timestrptr = localtime(&timediff);
 timeelapsed = *timestrptr;
 printf("The number of months elapsed is %d",
➡(timeelapsed.tm_year-70)*12 + timeelapsed.tm_mon + 1);

 scanf("%d", &timeearlier.tm_mon);

}
```

Summary

In this chapter, you looked at a number of C library functions. You also studied mathematical functions, including those used to find trigonometric values, the ones that help you work with powers and logarithms, and some miscellaneous functions. The end of this chapter dealt with functions to find the system time, print a formatted version of the current date and time, and find the elapsed time between two dates.

Review questions

1 Name two different functions that can return the square root of a number.

2 Distinguish between the common and natural logarithm functions.

3 In what units do C trigonometric functions expect angles to be expressed? What is the relationship between these units and degrees?

4 What two data types are most commonly used with time functions?

5 What function do you use to build a time string formatted according to exact specifications?

Exercises

1 Write a function to find the natural logarithm of each number from 1 through 100, printing each number and its logarithm on a separate line.

2 Write a statement to convert a time value stored in a `tm` structure named `Time` to a string stored in `TimeString`. Use a maximum length of 80 and a format such as

Thursday, 8 June, 1995—12:25AM

3 Write a program to calculate the number of seconds elapsed since someone's birthday.

26

Make Memory Work for You

● In this chapter:

- Work with memory directly

- Use the program to manipulate memory to the user's needs

- Are there any C functions for working with memory?

- Help! My program is eating up my memory

C memory functions give your programs the capability to gracefully cope with a growing and changing data population. . . . .

One of the goals throughout this book has been to increase the flexibility and usefulness of your C programs. One general way of doing so is to write a program so that it accommodates itself to the user's needs and not the other way around. You can structure a data-entry function—one that accepts names and addresses, for instance—so that the user can stop entering names short of the function's capacity. Writing computer applications in this way is a hallmark of a really good programmer.

However, there is always room for improvement. A data-entry function that relies on an array to store data has a built-in limit to the amount of data the user can enter: namely, the declared size of the array. Beyond that, the program cannot accommodate any more data, even if it is running on a system with more free RAM than it knows what to do with. The best step to take under such circumstances is to annex some additional RAM as needed. This enables data constructs within your program to grow to meet changing user needs, just as a city annexes land to accommodate increases in population.

How do I work with memory in C?

There are, in fact, a group of C language library functions that let you allocate and adjust data storage from within a program. Using such functions, you can set aside new space for variables, if needed. You can also enlarge existing space—to increase the size of arrays, for example. And you can release memory you are no longer using, freeing it up for other program requirements. The C memory functions give your programs the capability to gracefully cope with a growing and changing data population. In this chapter, you examine these functions and how to use them, after starting with a closer look at the way C programs manage memory.

What you need to know about memory

Similar to the homesteaders who were granted equal-sized blocks of land on which to live and work, C programs receive an initial allocation of RAM when they are compiled and linked. It is important to note that the size of this memory block is fixed. However, its precise location is not. This is actually determined by the operating system each time a program is run. The precise memory location that a C program runs in is of no importance to the program; what matters is the amount of memory and how it is set up. This memory configuration is established by the memory model under which the program was compiled.

 Plain English, please!

> A **memory model** is a set of compiler options that determines the size and structure of computer memory (RAM) available to a program when the program is run. This includes the amount of memory available for the program's instructions and its data, including any restrictions on the size of individual data items.

When compiling under DOS, for example, available memory models range from **Tiny** to **Huge**. Under the Tiny memory model, a program receives only 64K of RAM to squeeze both its instructions and its data in; under the Huge memory model, a separate 64K segment is allocated to each function, with as many 64K segments for data as required. You should know that under any other model than Huge, individual array variables cannot be larger than 64K. You set which memory model to use within your compiler; the exact way you do this depends on the compiler. Before deciding which memory model to use, you need to closely examine your compiler's documentation to see what models are available and how to use them.

After some space is set aside for infrastructure—the names and locations of variables, for instance—a program's data segments are then divided among the declared variables in a program. Each variable occupies an unbroken sequence of bytes, with variables coming one after the other to the last variable in the program. Generally, single variables and constants come first, followed by structures and arrays. It seldom occurs that a program such as those you have studied has variables to occupy even a significant portion of the minimal 64K data segment set aside under most memory models. The remaining RAM is unused as long as the program is running.

Adjust memory as the program runs

Just as a farmer hates to see arable but uncultivated land next to his property, a good programmer dislikes having excess and unallocated RAM. While you might try to use this memory by setting aside as many variables as your program could possibly need—and making your array variables as large as possible—this is rather inefficient; it might happen that one of the program's arrays needs more space on certain occasions, while another needs more at other times. Fixing array sizes at compilation time does not allow for flexibility during program execution.

Instead, you need ways to grow or shrink arrays as a program's needs evolve. Even if you set aside space for 500 records in a database program, the program does not work if some user wants to read in 501 items. The excess space is just wasted if the user intends to read 100. Assigning computer memory to the appropriate data constructs on the fly, referred to as **dynamic allocation**, lets a program adjust its data storage to the user's needs. Variables expand out into the unused parts of RAM in their data segments, without disturbing the contents of other variables. Of course, this is not done automatically. Your program must provide the necessary functionality, using the C language memory functions that form the subject of the remainder of this chapter.

The four C memory functions are...

Four important C memory functions are available for your use; which one you use depends on exactly what your program needs to do at the time. This can be anything from setting aside space for a string, to changing the size of an array, to releasing memory that was previously allocated. A separate function exists for each such task. All of them are defined in the header file `stdlib.h`.

...`malloc()`...

The simplest of the C memory functions is `malloc()`. You pass this function a value indicating how much memory to set aside, in bytes. The function returns a pointer to the newly allocated memory.

Note that if the program cannot allocate the requested memory for any reason—usually because there is not enough of it—the function `malloc()` returns a pointer value of `NULL`. Your programs should always test the results of a call to `malloc()` to make certain `NULL` is not returned. If it is, memory was not allocated; the program should probably display an error message and quit. The reason is that further execution is probably impossible without the requested memory.

One use for `malloc()` is to assign space to character strings as a program executes, rather than all at once when the program is compiled. A really good place to do this is within functions or other program blocks that might or might not be executed every time the program is run, depending on what choices the program user makes. Space for messages and prompts and other items in such program blocks can be set aside as they are needed. This saves setting aside space for strings that you might never use. Although the amount of space saved is small and such savings might seem unrealistic in these days of multimegabytes, keep in mind the old British saying, "Take care of the pence, and the pounds take care of themselves." There is never enough RAM to go around; the less you use, the fewer problems your programs encounter with memory limitations.

 **CAUTION** When you use `malloc()` to dynamically allocate space to a string, be certain to include an extra byte for the terminating null character. If you don't terminate a string with the null character, C has no idea where it ends. It'll assume that the first null character encountered in memory is the actual end of the string. Your program will crash as a result.

Speaking of `malloc()`

The prototype for `malloc()` is

```
void *malloc(size_t size);
```

A call to this function sets aside the amount of memory (in bytes) specified in the integer expression *size*. The function returns a type `void` pointer; assigning the value to a previously declared pointer of a certain type immediately casts the pointer value to the appropriate type. Refer back to chapter 18, "Turning One Data Type into Another," for information on type casting and data conversions.

For example, the following statement sets aside storage for 25 floating-point variables; the type `void` pointer returned for the first such storage location is recast as type `float` and stored in the type `float` pointer `pFloatArray`.

```
float *pFloatArray;
pFloatArray = malloc(25 * sizeof(float));
```

The following short program uses `malloc()` to set aside space for one of three messages; which message is printed depends on what the user enters.

```c
#include <stdlib.h>
#include <stdio.h>
#include <conio.h>
#include <string.h>

/* A program to demonstrate dynamic space
➥allocation for strings, using */
/* the malloc() function   */

char *message, choice;

main()
{

while (1)
    {
    puts("Enter 1, 2, or 3; Esc to exit");
    choice = getch();

    switch (choice)
        {
        case 49:
            {
            if (message = malloc(14)!= NULL)
                {
                strcpy(message, "You pressed 1");
                break;
                }
            else
                {
                puts("Insufficient memory; cannot continue");
                exit(1);
                }
            }
        case 50:
            {
            if (message = malloc(26) != NULL)
                {
                strcpy(message, "It was 2 that you pressed");
                break;
                }
            else
                {
                puts("Insufficient memory; cannot continue");
```

```
                            exit(1);
                          }
                  }
        case 51:
            {
            if (message = malloc(24) != NULL)
                {
                strcpy(message, "This time you pressed 3");
                break;
                }
              else
                  {
                  puts("Insufficient memory; cannot continue");
                  exit(1);
                  }
            }
        case 27:
            {
            exit(0);
            }
        default:
            {
            ;
            }
        }

    puts(message);
    }

}
```

code The program uses a switch() construction to process user input. If the user presses 1, 2, or 3, the program attempts to allocate memory for a string; if no memory is available, an error message is shown. If the memory allocation (using malloc()) was successful, the program displays the string for which memory was allocated. The switch() construction is contained within an infinite loop, so the program continues to monitor input and continues to allocate new memory if the user enters 1, 2, or 3. The program actually allocates a separate pointer for every case each time through the loop; this means if you run the program and hold down one of the number keys (1, 2, or 3), the program eventually runs out of memory. This is because the program doesn't let go of any of the memory pointers it allocates. You learn how to avoid such problems later in the chapter when we talk about releasing allocated memory.

...calloc()...

As an alternative, you can allocate memory by groups of data items, as well as by bytes. You use this alternative with the calloc() function, which works just as malloc() does. However, you pass to it both the number of data storage areas you want and the size of each area. This gives you more dynamic control over the size of memory allocated.

Other than a slight adjustment in program logic, to take account of calloc()'s asking for the number of units to allocate, using calloc() and malloc() is much the same. You should note also, though, that calloc() clears the memory it's being asked to allocate, whereas malloc() does not.

...realloc()...

Perhaps the most helpful of the C memory functions is the one used to change the size of an existing data space; you use the realloc() function to

Speaking of calloc()

The prototype for calloc() is

```
void *calloc(size_t num, size_t size);
```

The function expects both the number (*num*) and *size* of data items for which it should allocate memory space. It returns a type void pointer to the first item allocated; the value NULL is returned if there is not sufficient memory available to complete the request. The following sets aside space for the number of floating-point variables indicated in integer variable NumberItems:

```
float *pFloats;
pFloats = calloc(NumberItems, sizeof(float));
```

do this. This function uses a pointer to an existing area in the memory and adjusts that area to a new size. This is done without wiping out the old data present or disturbing the contents of any other program variables.

If you pass this function a NULL pointer value, it behaves the same as malloc(), setting aside an entirely new block of memory. The function keeps reallocated memory contiguous. In other words, if the existing area cannot be expanded without overwriting some other data, the entire area is copied to a new location. The old location is freed.

...and free()

The last of the memory functions to look at releases memory that was allocated dynamically by some other function, such as malloc() or realloc(). Using the free() function, you can return memory for general use that your program no longer needs, making it available for some other program purposes. This is similar to recycling your household refuse.

Speaking of realloc() and free()

The prototype for realloc() is

```
void *realloc(void *ptr, size_t size);
```

The function expects a pointer (*ptr*) to the area of memory to be adjusted, and a new *size*, in bytes, for that area. The function returns NULL if memory cannot be allocated. The following statement adjusts the size of an array pointed to by Floats upward by one:

```
Floats = realloc(Floats, sizeof(float)*(NumberElements + 1));
```

The prototype for free() is

```
void free(void *ptr);
```

The function releases the block of memory pointed to by *ptr*; it does not return a value of any kind. To release the memory pointed to by pFloats, you use

```
free(pFloats);
```

You should note that the free() function only releases dynamically allocated memory; this means that data storage allocated at compile time using variable declaration statements cannot be let go using free().

How to use the memory functions

For more information about pointers, see chapter 17, "How To Indirectly Access Data Storage with Pointers."

Appropriate use of C memory functions requires a thorough knowledge of pointers. Keep in mind that you need a separate pointer for each block of memory you want to allocate and use dynamically at the same time; if you use the same pointer in a subsequent call to a memory function, any block previously pointed to is lost, although it remains in memory. The reason is that the old contents of the pointer are wiped out by the new contents. Use separate pointers for blocks that must be maintained simultaneously.

If you want to be able to adjust the size of an array (again, the array must be declared dynamically using a pointer; you cannot adjust an array declared in the usual way), you should maintain a separate integer variable containing the number of elements currently in the array. You can then use this variable to resize the array upward by one each time you need to add an element.

How can I use this in the real world?

One of the worst feelings a poor program user can have comes after entering a long list of data items, only to find that the program has run out of space before the user has run out of data. Of course, the program crashes, and of course, the poor user has to reenter the data.

Using realloc() in the way described in the following "Catch the bug," though, you can help get around such a problem. If you've got some kind of array that holds individual data items—names and addresses for instance—you can use realloc() to increase the size of the array by one every time the program user wants to enter an additional data item. At the end of data entry, the array is exactly the right size. Not only does this method save data-entry headaches, but it saves computer memory resources over just making the data-storage array really huge to start with and hoping the user doesn't max it out anyway.

Catch the bug

The following block of statements is meant to enable the user to enter integer variables into a block of memory that acts similar to an array. Can you spot a problem with it?

```
NumberItems = 0;
CurrentItem = 0;
while (CurrentItem != -1)
    {
    puts("Enter a positive integer value;
➥enter -1 to stop entry");
    scanf("%d", &CurrentItem);
    pNumbers = malloc(sizeof(int)*(NumberItems + 1));
    pNumbers(NumberItems++) = CurrentItem;
    }
```

Answer: This block of code uses the wrong function; it should be using `realloc()` instead of `malloc()`. As it is, the program allocates an entirely new block of memory on each pass through the `while` loop; the value entered by the user each time is put at the end of each new block. The faulty line containing `malloc()` should be changed to

```
pNumbers = realloc(pNumbers, sizeof(int)*(NumberItems + 1));
```

Summary

In this program, you looked at making adjustments to program memory requirements while a program runs. First, you learned how memory is assigned to a program, including what is meant by a memory model. You then looked at functions that assign memory as a program runs. These include `malloc()` and `calloc()`, which are used to set aside new memory blocks of a certain size; you use `realloc()` to change the size of an existing block. The `free()` function releases a previously assigned block.

Review questions

1 What is meant by *dynamic allocation of memory?*

2 Describe the feature of a memory model and its effect on a program's execution.

3 What should your program always do when attempting to use one of the memory allocation functions, other than `free()`?

4 What does the `realloc()` function do that `calloc()` and `malloc()` do not?

5 What happens if your program continues to allocate new memory without letting go of memory it no longer needs? What function can you use to remedy this?

Exercises

1 Write a function that sets a pointer to be returned to one of five possible message strings, depending on an integer value it is passed. Make the messages anything you want. However, make them of varying lengths. Use dynamic memory allocation to set the point to exactly the right size.

2 Write a program to average a group of positive integers entered by the user. Allow the user to enter as many numbers as desired. Use -1 as the tag value to end data entry. Collect the numbers entered in a dynamically sized array.

3 Modify your program from exercise 2 so that it checks to make sure memory is available before allowing the user to enter another data item. Recall that when it fails, `realloc()` returns NULL. (Don't use the same pointer to memory on each call to `realloc()`. If `realloc()` returns NULL, you'll lose your reference to existing data.) Use a separate pointer in the call to `realloc()`. Then set the existing pointer to this new pointer if the call to `realloc()` is successful.

27

How Do I Find and Fix the Errors in My Program?

● **In this chapter:**

- **What kinds of errors can occur in a program?**

- **Find and eliminate errors**

- **Protect your program from the user**

- **Hey! My program isn't running on another PC. Why?**

Some program errors are similar to structural flaws in a building; others can be compared to improper behavior on the part of the building's tenants—you can write code to handle them all . . . . ●

Things can go wrong. To paraphrase Bobbie Burns, the best-laid plans of programmers and users often go astray. Because human beings are not perfect, there is no way to prevent plans from sometimes falling through the cracks. Then you are left trying to figure out how to deal with such events when they occur.

That there are usually only a few flaws in commercial software can be attributed to the careful and time-consuming way that software developers track errors in their programs. Large software companies usually spend months working out the bugs in their software, which is the reason major projects are sometimes so late in getting on the market. For a large project such as Windows 95 (a new version of the world's leading graphical user interface), there are plenty of places for errors to lurk. Errors can lurk in your own, smaller projects as well.

How do I get rid of errors in programs?

Whether discussing a new operating system or a simple line editor, a large corporation or yourself, the process of eliminating errors is much the same. You must test a program exhaustively to make sure that no egregious errors remain in the program code. Testing also helps ensure that the program behaves as expected in all cases that can be anticipated. After testing, you should insert additional code so that the program can handle any remaining problems gracefully. In this chapter, you learn about both processes.

What kinds of errors are there?

The sorts of errors that a program can contain fall into three broad groups. Only two of these groups affect the way a program runs. The reason is that the first type of error keeps a program from running at all. As for the other error types, one group of possible errors is similar to structural flaws in a building; the other group can be compared to improper behavior on the part of the building's tenants. Both can be prevented (to a large degree, at least) by proper safeguards. Naturally, you, as programmer, must install these safeguards.

There are syntax errors...

If you have been trying out the example source code listings, attempting the exercises, and writing entirely new programs of your own as the book has progressed, you have already encountered dozens, if not hundreds, of errors in the way you have given your C code to your compiler. Leaving out the semicolon at the end of a line, omitting a closing parentheses, misspelling a keyword—all these are examples of syntax errors in using the C language itself.

 ### *Plain English, please!*

> The word **syntax** refers to the way sentences or statements in any lan-
> guage—computer or human—are constructed. For example, the rules
> governing the forms of verbs used with various pronouns constitute one
> aspect of English syntax. A statement such as "He goed to work" contains
> a syntax error. While a native speaker of English can work out the pro-
> blems in most such sentences, a C compiler cannot tolerate lapses in
> C syntax.

When you commit a syntax error within your source code and attempt to compile the offending program, your compiler gives you some sort of message regarding the error. The quality of this message depends strictly on your compiler. It is worth noting, also, that the error message you see on-screen might not clearly reveal the real trouble.

For example, some common syntax errors can include improper declara-tions and such. At times, supplying a single missing semicolon on one line has eliminated the whole crop of errors; other errors might merely be unintended consequences.

Therefore, if you submit a program for compilation, and your compiler gives you a laundry list of syntax errors, don't panic; there are most likely only a few real errors. Missing semicolons and parentheses, and misspelled key-words are among the most common. As you are probably working on a PC or workstation (most users are these days) and do not have to worry about paying for time on a mainframe, it is easy to correct the few errors that are found in the source code. Then you can submit the program for recompi-lation to see if all the problems are fixed. Generally, the number of errors returned decreases each time you repeat this process, until all syntax errors have been eliminated.

Syntax errors are not something you have to worry about in a running program. Why not? The reason is that your compiler rejects any program containing such errors; therefore, you cannot turn a syntax-error ridden program into executable form. However, this does not mean that a program that can be compiled is error free. It is just that any errors it does contain are of another sort.

...logical errors...

More insidious than syntax errors are mistakes in the way a program is constructed—mistakes that prevent the program from yielding correct results in some or even all cases. Such errors are referred to as **logical errors**; they represent flaws in the programmer's use of computer logic. Most of the "Catch the bug" sections in this book have represented errors of this sort. Programs containing logical errors run. However, they sometimes produce unexpected results that might not make sense.

Your C compiler can only translate source code into executable code; it has no way of telling whether you have constructed your program correctly. As long as there are no syntax errors, everything most likely works well. The most the compiler might do is warn you if it finds you have mixed data types in an assignment statement or used pointers in an odd way. At least half the time, such a warning is probably of no use, as it is a user error (probably typographical) and can be corrected.

If you cannot depend on the compiler to find your mistakes, what can you rely on? You must follow Henry David Thoreau: self-reliance is the key. It is up to you as programmer to track down and eliminate logical errors. You do this by testing your program—running it with a large amount of different input.

The more serious sorts of logic errors manifest themselves immediately. These cause your program to spit obvious garbage back at you almost immediately. Failing to include a terminating null character in a string is one example. If you attempt to print a string without the terminating null character with puts(), the program puts on-screen not only the string, but everything following it in memory until a null character is encountered. Your computer has no way of knowing this is wrong. However, you know right away. If such a program were a building, it would fall over immediately. Or maybe just lean a lot. Luckily, you're working with computers, which rarely fall over or burst into flames.

More subtle logic errors can be much more difficult to catch. The automatic fire doors do not really close when the boiler overheats. However, who is going to set it on fire to see? Quite simply, subtle logic errors sometimes are not caught at all. Users of most versions of Microsoft Windows can attest to that. (How many times have you heard or said, "The program MYAPP caused a general protection fault in module OMIGOSH.DLL and shut down"?) Of course, some errors can be the user's fault, as you will see.

...and user errors

"This sort of thing has happened before, and it's always been attributable to human error," said HAL, the mentally deranged computer in the movie *2001*. One of Murphy's laws puts it another way: "It's impossible to make anything foolproof because fools are too ingenious."

The users of your programs are going to try to input data or perform other processes that the program does not not expect. If a user is supposed to load a file before attempting to sort records, someone will try sorting first. If only numeric input is appropriate, someone will type in dollar signs and commas. If a program warns the user that some valuable file is about to be overwritten and destroyed, someone will choose to do so anyway—and live to regret it—and possibly blame *you* as programmer for the problem.

What should you do? To whatever extent possible, you must protect your users from themselves and any possible wrong moves they might make. You can do this by screening all user input and rejecting bad values. It is not difficult to do—have a `switch()` construction process user data and use the default condition to ignore bad values.

It is also beneficial to ensure that if some step in a program must be performed first, the user cannot choose any other step. A financial program might do this. If the user attempts to perform an interest or loan payment calculation before entering data, the program should refuse and print an error message.

Finally, there are errors that only tend to occur under certain circumstances; they are not the result of bad input by the user, but of problems with the environment that a program is running in. A lack of sufficient RAM to run in is one example. Another is the absence, through no fault of the user, of some important disk file—perhaps it is being used by some other program. Without some other provision, a program encountering such a problem merely crashes, spitting some nasty and obscure message back at the user.

You can, however, anticipate such problems. A good programmer should always do so, and provide some way for your program to exit gracefully. It might be helpful to explain in more detail what has gone wrong so that the user knows what not to do next time. Better still, it might be possible to go on running the program, simply failing to perform the requested action (but providing a message, of course).

Now you know the kinds of problems you will probably have to deal with. Keep in mind that you have been encountering them throughout the book and have been successful so far. Now, you are going to benefit from looking at some formal error-handling techniques, making use of capabilities built into C. You start this process with a look at formal ways to track down and eliminate logical errors.

How do I get rid of pesky bugs?

Programmer reactions to debugging are twofold: there are some who enjoy the challenge of problem-solving and others who find it boring. The former tend to make better programmers. The reason is that people who do not have the patience to track down all errors frequently overlook many. You are going to be introduced to a C language function that makes error-hunting easier.

Use the `assert()` function

The C programming language contains a function that you can use to hunt down logical errors. The `assert()` function lets you set up a test condition at one or many points in your program. If the program passes the test, nothing happens. If the test fails, execution stops, and a message is shown. You can use this message to help pin down what went wrong. Also, you can turn `assert()` off throughout your program very simply, without having to remove any code containing this function.

How to use assert()

The place and time to use assert() amounts to something of an art. In broad terms, you can include a call to assert() any place in a program where you suspect a variable might not contain the correct data at all times. It will probably be necessary to run through the program several times, with different input each time to determine whether or not assert() causes a failure.

If you have tested a program to your satisfaction and feel you have eliminated all logical errors, it is not necessary to go back and remove every call to assert() you included. You can simply turn the function off. Do so by including the line

```
#define NDEBUG
```

at the beginning of your program, just prior to the #include statement for assert.h. You can turn your debugging capability back on by removing this line. In this way, you preserve the option to attempt to track down more errors if a subtle problem manifests itself or if you incorporate a program or any of its functions into a new project.

Speaking of assert()

The prototype for assert(), defined in the header file assert.h, is

```
void assert(int expression);
```

The *expression* is any logical one whose contents evaluate to True or False (1 or 0). When a program encounters a statement containing assert(), it tests the *expression*. If the *expression* evaluates to True, no action is taken. If, however, the *expression* is False, assert() forces the program to terminate early. The program then displays an error message on the screen. This message includes the offending line. The following statement asserts that the value in the variable Balance should be greater than 0; if it is not, the program stops running.

```
assert(Balance > 0);
```

Here's an example of a program containing `assert()`

The following short program demonstrates how to use `assert()`. The program itself is fairly trivial. However, the kind of error it contains is more common. Can you spot the error?

```c
#include <stdio.h>
#include <assert.h>

/* A program to demonstrate use of
➥ASSERT for finding logical errors */
void IntSort(int *Array);
main()
{
int *pArray, MyArray[10]={1,2,3,4,5,6,7,8,9,0};

pArray = MyArray[0];
IntSort(pArray);

printf("The first element in the array is now %d",
➥MyArray[0]);

/* Pause before continuing */
puts("\nPress any key to continue");
scanf("%d", &MyArray[0]);
}

void IntSort(int *Array)
{
int counter1, counter2, hold;
for (counter1 = 1; counter1<=10; counter1++)
    {
    for (counter2 = counter1; counter2 <=9; counter2++)
        {
        if (Array[counter2]>Array[counter1])
            {
            hold = Array[counter1];
            Array[counter1] = Array[counter2];
            Array[counter2] = hold;
            }
        }
    }

return;
}
```

When you run the program as is, you are told the first value in the array is 1. This is clearly wrong; you are attempting to sort the array into descending order, with largest values first. The first element should be 9 after the sort. You include two calls to assert() as the following program shows. The first checks the position of the value 9 before the sort routine runs; the second checks it afterward:

```
#include <stdio.h>
#include <assert.h>

/* A program to demonstrate use of ASSERT
➥for finding logical errors */
void IntSort(int *Array);
main()
{
int   *pArray, MyArray[10]={1,2,3,4,5,6,7,8,9,0};

pArray = MyArray[0];
IntSort(pArray);

printf("The first element in the array is now %d",
➥MyArray[0]);

/* Pause before continuing */
puts("\nPress any key to continue");
scanf("%d", &MyArray[0]);
}

void IntSort(int *Array)
{
int counter1, counter2, hold;
assert(Array[9]= 0);
for (counter1 = 0; counter1<=10; counter1++)
      {
      for (counter2 = counter1; counter2 <=9; counter2++)
          {
          if (Array[counter2]>Array[counter1])
              {
              hold = Array[counter1];
              Array[counter1] = Array[counter2];
              Array[counter2] = hold;
              }
          }
      }
assert (Array[0] = 9);
return;
}
```

This time, the program fails at the first instance of assert(); the array that is passed to the function does not have the expected contents. The error must occur in the way that the array is being passed. If you have been getting a compiler warning about the statement

```
pArray = MyArray[0];
```

is the problem there? Yes, because the program is reading the contents, not the address, of MyArray[0], into the pointer. Therefore, the pointer singles out the wrong item. Now, you should change the statement to

```
pArray = &MyArray;
```

and try again. After this adjustment, you do not get an assert() failure, and the program returns the expected value of 9.

Is there more to bug catching than just assert()?

There are other methods you can use to test programs and look for logical errors. Unfortunately, they are not part of the ANSI Standard C language itself. Rather, they are capabilities supplied by the compiler package you purchased. For example, the C development tools you have might allow you to trace the execution of a program. You can execute the program line-by-line to see exactly what happens when it runs. You might also set break points; these are places where the program ceases to run when execution arrives there. You must consult your compiler documentation for information on what debugging tools you have and how to use them.

You need to protect your program from the user

You can have a fully functional and totally debugged program that still produces errors. The reason is that your program users make a wrong move. There is a computer programming expression: **garbage in, garbage out** (**GIGO**). If you supply a program, no matter how cleverly written, with garbage data, it produces garbage results. The solution is to trap and reject a bad set of data before it gets into the program and causes trouble.

You asked for a name, but the user enters a phone number

Consider the following C statements:

```
puts("Enter a positive value for the current balance:");
scanf("%f", &Balance);
```

There is nothing to prevent your program user from entering a negative number, just as a sign warning "Elevator Shaft: Do Not Enter" does not prevent someone from opening an unlocked door and dropping thirteen stories. It is up to you to lock out unwanted data.

In addition to entering values out of the acceptable range (negative or large values, for example), a user might also try to input characters in places where numbers are expected and vice versa. Such occurrences are difficult to test for. However, you can ensure that this kind of data never makes it into program variables.

There are ways of rejecting bad data

In a financial program, you can reject bad data by testing the values that the user enters. You use if statements to do this; the relevant code might look like

```
while (DoAgain)
    {
    puts("Enter values to use in subsequent calculations");
    printf("\nEnter the principal: ");
    scanf("%f",balance);
    printf("\nEnter the interest rate in percent per year:   ");
    scanf("%f",rate);
    printf("\nEnter the number of months: ");
    scanf("%f",months);
    system("cls");
    /* Verify amounts entered */
    if ((*balance<=0)||(*rate<=0)||(*months<=0))
        {
        puts("Invalid data entered; press any key to reenter");
        buffer = getch();
        }
        else
            DoAgain = 0;
    }
```

This data entry code is contained within a loop. The values the user entered are tested; if any one of them is 0 or less, the user must re-enter all values.

As for rejecting data in the wrong form—numbers in places where characters are expected, for example—certain C input functions let you do this easily. Recall that one of the conversion specifiers for scanf(), %[], lets you specify what characters constitute acceptable input. You can also use %[^], which lets you specify what characters to omit. Therefore, a call to scanf(), such as

```
scanf("%[^1234567890]", Name);
```

rejects any of the numeric digits when prompting the user to input a string.

For more information on the string-to-number functions, see chapter 18, "Turning One Data Type into Another."

Doing the opposite, rejecting any non-numeric input, using scanf() is a little more difficult. The %[] format specifier produces string input. Before you can use the results in calculations, you have to change the results into a number using one of the string-to-number functions. You can use a pair of statements, such as

```
scanf("%[1234567890.]", Input);
Balance = atof(Input);
```

This presumes that Input is a string variable and Balance is a floating-point variable.

Actually, the atof() function by itself does a fairly good job of removing unwanted characters from input that is supposed to be numeric; therefore, you can use

```
scanf("%s", Input);
Balance = atof(Input);
```

This can work better in some cases. The atof() removes commas, for instance, without losing any data that comes after them.

How can I use this in the real world?

A program that expects dollar amounts is a perfect place to use a call to atof(). People have a habit of entering dollar signs and commas when they're asked to input dollar values. The atof() function gets rid of the superfluous dollar sign and commas, so that your program can treat the entered value as a number rather than as a character string. Of course, it must be input as a string.

Run-time errors

The last class of errors to consider, a subclass of user-caused errors, are those that occur because of current operating conditions. These can be due to insufficient memory or missing files. Normally such an error can cause your programs to fail. You can, however, structure them to exit gracefully or even ignore the problem, presuming this isn't potentially fatal to subsequent program tasks. C, of course, provides an error-handling function that helps you do this. You can also write your own error-handling code.

How can I find a run-time error?

Many of the C library functions return a specific value if they encounter an error. They do this by reading a value into an external variable referred to as errno. The header file errno.h defines a number of symbolic constants for use with error codes that can be returned in errno. (You do not have to use the header file if you don't want to; you can use the direct values.) Table 27.1 summarizes the constants and associated error numbers that might occur, along with a brief description of their meaning. Note that errno.h varies from compiler to compiler; consult your compiler documentation for information on your implementation of errno.h.

Table 27.1   Typical errno.h constants and associated error numbers and what they mean

Constant	Error number	Meaning
E2BIG	1000	Argument list is too long
EACCES	5	Access to file denied
EBADF	6	Bad file description
EDOM	1002	Mathematical argument is out of range
EEXIST	80	File already exists
EMFILE	4	Too many open files
ENOENT	2	No such file or directory
ENOEXEC	1001	Format error in call to exec()

continues

Table 27.1 **Continued**

Constant	Error number	Meaning
ENOMEM	8	Insufficient memory
ENOPATH	3	Specified path not found
ERANGE	1003	Result is out of range

You can make a call to perror() at a place in which an error has occurred—for example, if an attempt to open a file returned a null pointer. This function displays to the user an optional message from you, along with a system message describing the actual error. The function's prototype is

```
void perror(char *msg);
```

The pointer *msg* is, of course, a pointer to a string variable.

The function perror() itself does nothing more than display a message; you must provide code that handles any actual error, including presenting options to the user.

How to deal with run-time errors

To handle errors that might occur when a program is run, you might want to consider adding a function that is called when an error is encountered. Such a function can display a message for the user and even present options for what to do next. You can use a call to perror() to display the message.

Listing 27.1 shows a modification to a FileLoad function, designed to open a file specified by the user. FileLoad now calls a new function referred to as error(), which the following listing also shows. The function error() makes use of perror().

Listing 27.1 **The modified Fileload function**

```
/* This function loads the named file's records into the */
/* structure pointed to by Names */
int FileLoad(char *FileName, struct NameRecord *Names)
{
    FILE *pDiskFile;
    int counter = 1, result;
    char choice;
```

```
        if ((pDiskFile = FileExists(FileName)) == NULL)
            {
            Error(FileName);
            return 0;
            }
        else
                {
                  pDiskFile = fopen(FileName, "r");
                  fread(filetag, 8, 1, pDiskFile);
                  if (result = strcmp(filetag, "FILEDATD") != 0)
                        {
                        errno=98;
                        Error(FileName);
                        return 0;
                        }
                  while (!feof(pDiskFile))
                        {
                        Names = realloc(Names, sizeof(struct
                        ➥NameRecord) * (counter + 1));
                        fread(&Names[counter++], sizeof(struct
                        ➥NameRecord), 1, pDiskFile);
                        }
                  fclose(pDiskFile);
                }
    return counter-2;
    }

    void Error(char *FileName)
    {
     char buf;
    if (errno == 98)
        {
        printf("\nFile %s has incorrect format,
        ➥cannot open", FileName);
        puts("\nPress any key to continue; Esc to quit");
        buf = getch();
        if (buf == 27)
            exit(1);
        return;
        }

    perror("Cannot open file: ");
    puts(FileName);
    puts("Press any key to continue, Esc to quit");
    buf = getch();
        if (buf == 27)
            exit(1);
    return;
    }
```

code If the specified file is found, but doesn't contain the right kind of data, then error() is called; error() displays a message that the file isn't of the right type. If the file doesn't exist, error() is also called to tell the user the file cannot be opened. If you want, you can add to the various cases possible within the error() function to display different messages; for example, if a program ran out of memory. Figure 27.1 shows the results of running a complete program with error() added and FileLoad modified.

Fig. 27.1

A somewhat more informative message now appears if a file cannot be found or is of the wrong format.

```
Enter your choice:

        1 to Enter New Data
        2 to Load a File
        3 to View Data
        4 to Sort Data
        5 to Save a File
        6 or Esc to Exit

Enter the name of a file to load:
any.dat

Cannot open file:   :No such file or directory
any.dat

Press any key to continue, Esc to quit
```

Summary

In this chapter, you considered program errors. You learned about the types of errors you might encounter, including syntax, logical, and user errors that occur at runtime. You studied using the assert() function to help track down logical errors. You then examined errno.h and the perror() function for dealing with run-time errors.

Review questions

1 What is a *syntax error*? How do you eliminate such errors from executable programs?

2 What is a *logical error*? Name two places in which errors in program logic might commonly occur.

3 What is a *run-time error*? Name two possible causes for such errors.

4 What argument does the assert() function take? How can you turn assert() off without removing it from a program's source code?

5 Is use of the errno.h file required for handling run-time errors? Why or why not?

Exercises

1 Write a program to read a number of financial values into a table. Allow the user to enter the values as dollar amounts. Store them as floating-point numbers.

2 Set up an error() function of your own that displays one of three messages when called, depending on a value passed to it by the calling function. Make the messages anything you like. Also, make use of the perror() function.

28

Programs That Update Themselves

● **In this chapter:**

- ● **Can a C program really modify its own code?**

- ● **Tell me about the #include statement**

- ● **Are there any shortcuts I can use in my source code?**

- ● **Does every statement in a C program have to be compiled every time?**

Your compound interest program is going to London, but it only uses American currency symbols. Well, C has a few special statements to help your program modify itself to be usable by both American and British companies and French and German and... . . . . ➤

Y ou have learned just about every conceivable part of a C program, except those #include statements at the very beginning. Taking a closer look at those will lead you into an entirely new arena, one that fits well with the end-of-the-book theme of increasing power and flexibility. By taking advantage of some fundamental housekeeping that C does before a program's source code is actually compiled, you can create programs that can easily be adapted to new situations. It's almost as if they rewrite themselves.

Things that happen before a program's compiled

You see, every C compiler performs certain actions on your programs before compiling them. Including certain other files is part of this process. However, there can be much more to it than that. By taking advantage of this precompilation processing, you can create programs that are compiled in different ways based on current needs. You can also use this capability for components from your own library of C language functions. (The next chapter covers this topic.) In this chapter, you learn the basics of using the C preprocessor and its directives.

There's this thing called the preprocessor

The preprocessor is part of every C compiler. It performs certain actions on your source code before it is passed along to the main compiler for conversion to object code. These actions include bringing pieces of source code into your program from an outside file, making changes to existing code based on instructions to the preprocessor embedded within the code, and substituting the longer version of shorthand expressions you have defined and used. The preprocessor, similar to a tailor, gives programs a custom fit based on current conditions.

Each of these tasks is accomplished through different commands to the preprocessor that you include within your source code. The result of all the preprocessor's work is another source code file that is then immediately compiled. As a rule, you never see this modified file, although in certain cases you can explicitly request to do so. This is something for which you will have to consult your compiler documentation.

You know those #include statements are more than decoration

The commands you issue within your source code to the C preprocessor are known as preprocessor directives. The #include statement itself is a preprocessor directive, and there are several others. Each such directive instructs the preprocessor to perform a specific action on your source code. Through the remainder of this chapter, you examine the various preprocessor directives you have at your disposal when programming in C.

Modify your source code with preprocessor directives like...

All preprocessor directives begin with the # symbol. Statements including preprocessor directives do not use a terminating semicolon; if you include one, you get an immediate error message from your compiler when you try to submit it for compilation. The first two preprocessor directives you look at are among the most important: #include and #define.

...#include...

The #include preprocessor directive tells your C compiler to bring source code from some other, specified file into the current source code file. You use it to take advantage of work that has already been done, such as using the C library functions.

The #include directive is used to include so-called header files in your source code. If you have never looked at the insides of such a file, you might try doing so using a word processor or text editor. The file stdio.h itself contains all kinds of constant and variable definitions and is about eight pages long. When your C preprocessor encounters an #include statement, it inserts all the code from the indicated file in place of the #include statement itself. Having one simple statement that inserts eight pages of existing code is a real time saver.

Files to be inserted that contain the #include directive can themselves contain #include statements. This is another example of nesting, a technique you first learned about when you studied if blocks and loops in chapter 10, "Control the Way a Program Runs." Your header files cannot go on nesting #includes forever. The exact limit depends on the compiler you are using. However, about ten levels deep is as much nesting as the typical compiler can support with #include.

...and #define

The #define directive has two uses. The first of these is to create a kind of abbreviation for a longer piece of code. Such an abbreviation is referred to as a substitution macro; it is a kind of text constant that applies only to a C source code file.

Using the #define directive can save typing if there is an expression used in many places in your program; for the expression you can define an abbreviation, then use it instead of the full form. You can also use #define to create a species of symbolic numeric constants, as in the following example for the value of PI.

For example, consider a financial program; one that works with annuities, compound interest, and the like. A program like this might use the following expression, which finds compound interest, in several places:

```
pow(2.7183,(rate/1200.0*months))
```

Speaking of #include

The syntax for the #include directive is

```
#include file_name
```

How you specify the *file_name* to include depends on its location. Enclosing the *file_name* in quotes makes the preprocessor look for the specified file in the same directory as the source code file being compiled. Enclosing the *file_name* in less-than and greater-than symbols (< and >), as you have done throughout this book, makes the preprocessor look for the specified file first in a special directory referred to as the standard directory. Which directory this is depends on and is usually set by your compiler. If the file is not found there, the directory containing the current source code file is searched. If the specified file cannot be found, you see an error message, and compilation is halted.

This expression, of course, is just C's way of saying $e^{rate/1200 \times months}$, where months is a variable that contains the term for which the money is held.

Rather than including the literal statement everywhere, you can define a substitution macro for it, as in

```
#define eRtMn pow(2.7183,(rate/1200.0*months))
```

You can then use the abbreviation eRtMn for the expression, as in the following part of a Payment() function:

```
return (rate/1200.) *balance* eRtMn/(eRtMn-1);
```

Compare this with the original version:

```
return (rate/1200.) *balance* pow(2.7183,(rate/
➥1200.0*months))
➥/(pow(2.7183,(double)(rate/1200.*months))-1);
```

That expression $e^{rate/1200 \times months}$ appears frequently in a program that does financial calculations using continuously compounded interest. Therefore, defining a substitution macro for it can be quite useful.

You should know that in C, macro names cannot come within double or single quotes; anything within quotes is supposed to be directly quoted. You should include the quotes as part of the macro definition, rather than using the macro itself inside quotes.

Speaking of #define

Using the #define processor directive to create a substitution macro involves a statement such as the following:

```
#define abbreviation full_text
```

When the C preprocessor encounters a #define directive, it immediately goes through the remainder of the program source code, replacing every *abbreviation* with *full_text*. For example,

```
#define PI 3.14159
```

substitutes the number 3.14159 every place in the program where PI is found.

Catch the bug

What's wrong with the following substitution macro created with the #define preprocessor directive?

```
#define e 2.71823
```

Answer: In #define statements, the full_text replaces every instance of the abbreviation. This #define statement replaces every e in the program's source code with 2.71823, which includes es in comments, keywords, variable names—everywhere. Obviously, this breaks the program to pieces. If you really want to use the single letter e in the manner of a constant for the natural logarithm base, use a symbolic constant definition, such as

```
const float e = 2.71823;
```

Macros in #define directives

The #define preprocessor directive is also used to create a different sort of macro—the so-called **function macros**. These entities combine, as you might guess, the features of both functions and substitution macros. In essence, they result in substitution macros that can accept arguments.

Speaking of function macros

The general form of a #define directive to create a function macro is

```
#define macro_name(parameters) expression
```

In this statement, *macro_name* refers to the name of the macro you're defining. *expression* is the actual expression being defined as a macro; *parameters* are the parameters to the expression. For example, the following statement creates a function macro referred to as Sum that accepts three parameters:

```
#define Sum(x,y,z) x+y+z
```

What good are function macros?

Function macros, similar to substitution macros, can make your source code more readable, compact, and easier to update. The reason is that you need only alter a macro definition once to have the change reflected throughout a program, wherever you use the macro. Why not just use a function instead? Function macros have one important advantage over regular C functions: their arguments are not type-sensitive. This means that you can pass a function macro any sort of data. Of course, this flexibility can present both advantages and disadvantages.

How to use function macros

When you construct a function macro, keep in mind that at compilation time the macro's name is substituted for its definition along with any arguments. Because of this, certain ways of phrasing macros can result in errors. This is especially true if you pass expressions to macros, rather than simple variable names. For example, if you had a macro named Tenth, defined in the following way:

```
#define Tenth(x) x/10
```

and you passed it the expression y + z, such as

```
Value = Tenth(y + z)
```

at compilation time, you would end up with

```
Value = y + z/10
```

If you recall the order of operations C uses in evaluating mathematical expressions, you see immediately that the expanded expression does not give the desired result. You can solve this problem if you enclose each separate parameter within parentheses in the original macro definition, as in

```
#define Tenth(x) (x)/10
```

Using y + z as a parameter as before, now a call to Tenth results in

```
Value = (y + z)/10
```

This gives the correct results.

In addition to correct phrasing with parentheses, there are some other characteristics of function macros that you should be familiar with. You can use the # sign to have a parameter print as a string; at compile time, the parameter is enclosed in quotes and appropriate escape codes are provided if the quote or backslash characters are present. For example, you can define a macro in the following way:

```
#define Banner(x) puts(#x)
```

A call to `Banner`, such as

```
Banner(A program to calculate certain values);
```

results in

```
puts("A program to calculate certain values");
```

Another handy operator is `##`. This is the **concatenation operator**. It combines two strings into one, as in

```
#define ps(x) printf("\n%f",Message##x)
```

In this way,

```
ps(3);
```

becomes

```
print("\n%s",Message3);
```

When to define your own macros

With any function macro, it only makes sense to define one if you intend to use it more than twice. Defining a macro and using it only once actually wastes space. The reason is that the definition itself is longer than the original expression. The call to the macro adds even more text to the program. Using a macro only twice does not save enough to matter. When you use it three or more times, the savings show.

There are some macros that have already been defined for you

The typical C package includes a number of predefined function macros; these include some of the functions that you have already used, for example the `feof()` function that detects the end of a file. It is actually a function macro defined in `stdio.h`. Using these macros is no different than using functions, except of course macros do not tend to be as sensitive to the type of parameters you pass them. You can consult your compiler documentation for other function macros that might be available.

Four macros that are always present are DATE, TIME, LINE, and FILE. (Their names are preceded and followed by double underscores. The reason is that if they were not, you might redefine them by using names such as DATE and FILE in your program.) The following table summarizes these four predefined macros.

Macro	Definition
__DATE__	Substitute the current date in the source code
__TIME__	Insert the current time in the source code
__LINE__	Insert the current line number into the code
__FILE__	Insert the name of the source code file into the code

You can use the last two macros during debugging to identify the file and line location of any error.

Control how your program is compiled after writing the code

Additional preprocessor directives exist that let you control how a program is compiled. Basically, these directives affect whether or not certain blocks of statements are compiled. If they are not, they do not appear in the final program. In addition to being useful during program debugging, these directives also enable one source file to produce several different programs, each adapted to special conditions—for example, use in a particular country. The whole process is referred to as **conditional compilation**.

There are three conditional directives

There are three conditional compilation directives. The four are commonly used together in a single block, although this is not mandatory. The directives are closely modeled on the standard `if` and `else` statements, covered beginning with chapter 10, "Control the Way a Program Runs."

#if

Th #if directive associates a condition with the possible compilation of a block of statements following it. The condition involved usually tests to determine whether some macro or other has been defined with a given value.

#elif

The #elif preprocessor directive is used along with #if to construct blocks of alternative conditions. The statements following #elif are compiled only if a second condition is met after the condition associated with #if fails.

Speaking of #if

The general form of a block of statements using #if is

```
#if condition
      statements
#endif
```

Note that the condition is not enclosed in parentheses, as it must be for the if statement. The following statements do not have to be enclosed in braces, although they can be. The following block of statements defines the Currency macro as a $ if the macro USA was defined as 1:

```
#if USA == 1
      #define Currency '$'
#endif
```

If USA is not defined as 1, the statement #define Currency $ does not compile.

#else

The #else preprocessor directive is used along with #if and #elif to provide an alternative to be used only if none of the other conditions are met; it is similar to the default: case used with the switch() construction.

How to use the conditional directives

You use conditional compilation in two places: during debugging and adapting a program for use in other locales. The last process is frequently referred to as **localization**. One purpose of localization is to ensure that text and other values correspond to local standards—for example, using the correct currency symbols.

Speaking of #elif

The general form of a block of statements using #elif is

```
#if condition
     statements
#elif condition2
     statements
#endif
```

There can be multiple instances of #elif within a block, each keyed to a separate condition. The following statements do not have to be enclosed in braces, although they can be. The following short listing is an example of using multiple instances of #elif within a block:

```
#if USA == 1
     #define Currency '$'
#elif BRITAIN == 1
     #define Currency 'L'
#elif FRANCE == 1
     #define Currency 'F'
#endif
```

Catch the bug

What is the problem with the following conditional compilation block?

```
#if USA == 1
      #define Yes Yes
#elif BRITAIN == 1
      #define Yes Aye
#elif FRANCE == 1
      #define Yes Oui
#else
      #define Yes OK
```

Answer: *The concluding* `#endif` *directive was omitted; it should follow the last line. Quotes should be placed around each of the definitions for* `Yes` *(except for the macro name* `Yes` *itself).*

Speaking of #else

The general form of a block of statements using #else is

```
#if condition
      statements
#elif condition2
      statements
#else
      statements
#endif
```

The following short listing is an example of using #else within a conditional compilation block:

```
#if USA == 1
      #define Currency '$'
#elif BRITAIN == 1
      #define Currency 'L'
#elif FRANCE == 1
      #define Currency 'F'
#else
      #define Currency 'M'
#endif
```

A good tool to use with any sort of conditional compilation is the defined() macro. This macro returns True if the named macro provided to it as an argument has been defined previously in the program; it does not matter where the named macro was defined. Consider the following block of statements:

```
#define BRITAIN
#if defined( USA )
    #define Currency '$'
#elif defined( BRITAIN )
    #define Currency 'L'
#elif defined( FRANCE )
    #define Currency 'F'
#else
    #define Currency 'M'
#endif
```

Note that the #define directive defining the sustitution macro BRITAIN does not define it as anything; any instance of BRITAIN in the code, if any, is replaced with nothing; in other words, the text BRITAIN is cut out altogether. This is not important if the defined macro is not likely to occur. What is important is that defining BRITAIN in this way and using defined() within each part of the conditional compilation block results in conditional compilation of one statement—that which defines the macro Currency to be equal to L.

Use conditional compilation to debug a program

During program debugging, you can include certain statements that you do not want to appear in the finished program. Rather than put the statements in only to strip them out—risking the need to reinsert them if you modify the program or incorporate it into a new one—you can use conditional compilation to create the option to retain the statements. Examples of such statements are ones that print the contents of variables at certain points, just so you can see what they are. A statement printing a simple message, such as I got to the beginning of the Format function, can also be useful; all these can be conditionally compiled.

For example, you might define a macro name, such as

```
#define YDEBUG
```

to indicate that debugging code should be compiled. Then any statements such as the following would appear in the compiled program.

```
#if defined( YDEBUG )
      puts("I got to the end of the SWITCH block");
#endif
```

If YDEBUG is defined, the call to puts() is compiled. The message is printed at the appropriate place if your program encounters it. To turn the message off in a finished program, you simply remove the line defining YDEBUG.

Use conditional compilation in localizing and customizing a program

For localizing a program, you are not so much concerned with turning certain statements on and off as you are with making sure that your program follows local conventions. In France, for instance, they use F in front of currency amounts; they also use a comma instead of a decimal point. Rather than completely rewriting a program to take such local differences into account, you can use conditional compilation to define certain values, such as what decimal symbol and currency symbol to use. These symbols can be based on whatever country macro the program defines. To change the program, only that one line containing the country macro need be altered prior to recompiling the program.

How can I use this in the real world?

To get the most mileage out of a financial program, you really ought to set it up so it will work in Britain, France, Germany, or America. These are among the biggest markets, after all. You can do this using conditional compilation. (If none of these countries are defined, an M symbol can be used for currency from other lands.) To determine which country the program should be compiled for, you include a statement at the beginning of the program—after all the #include statements—to define the appropriate country name. Your program should define macros for the currency symbol, the separator for groups of digits (that is, in America we use the comma, as in 1,000), and the symbol to indicate decimals (in America we use a period, the French use the comma).

Summary

This chapter focused on the C preprocessor and its directives that you use to issue commands. The commands you studied included #include, #define, and conditional compilation directives, such as #if and #else. You learned about how to create substitution macros and use function macros. Using conditional compilation in localization and debugging are two other processes that you learned.

Review questions

1 What output does the C preprocessor produce? How does it differ from the original source code submitted for compilation?

2 Can files included with #include statements have #include statements within them? How do you refer to this technique? Is there any limit to it?

3 Distinguish between *substitution macros* and *function macros*. What do they have in common? What advantage do function macros have over standard C functions?

4 Explain two uses for conditional compilation.

5 With what statement must a conditional compilation block always end?

Exercises

1 Write a substitution macro to define MyName as your own name, as a literal string constant.

2 Write a function macro to define a function Hypotenuse(), which returns the value of the longest side of a right triangle when the values of two shortest sides are known. Use the Pythagorean theorem: $c^2 = a^2 + b^2$.

3 Use conditional compilation to alter which strings appear in a financial program. If you know a foreign language, substitute messages in that language; if not, simply vary the English versions. Use two versions, USA and FOREIGN. Use whatever currency symbol you prefer for FOREIGN, and a comma for a decimal point. Hint: Enclose each set of `puts()` and `printf()` statements in conditional compilation blocks, as in the following:

```
#if defined( FOREIGN )
      puts("Une programme pour
      ➥calculer quelques formules financieres");
#else
      puts("A program to calculate
      ➥certain financial formulae");
#endif
```

29

Use Code That You or Somebody Else Has Already Written

● **In this chapter:**

● Is there some way I can use a function I want over and over without retyping it over and over?

● Divide your programs into pieces

● Create your own library of functions that you use again and again

● Where to find C programming written by other people

Want to get out of reinventing the wheel? Past work by you and others can form the basis of a reference library that you can return to when you want to build new programs . . . . . ⊛

f you mastered all the statements in C, you could merrily proceed, writing programs to do more and more neat things. Without knowing a little more about the language and the resources available to its programmers, however, you might find yourself unnecessarily repeating work from time to time. Engineers call this mistake **reinventing the wheel** and strongly frown upon it; you shouldn't have to redo work that you—or someone else—has already done.

If, for example, you've written a nice little function that reverses names and adds commas to them, you ought to be able to use that same work—without changes—in any other projects. And if some other programming genius has written and published a C program to make buttered toast, you ought to be able to track it down and use it, too. Given sufficient awareness of the proper C programming techniques, you can make use of any such existing code. In fact, yours and others' past work can form the basis of a **reference library** that you can return to when you want to build new programs. In this chapter, as you might suspect, I'll show you what you need to know to start building a library of your own.

To use code over again, it needs to be general

When talking about a programming reference library (usually referred to as a **code library**), you have to start with the way code within it is built. For code to be reusable, it must be written in as general and standard a way as possible. An analogous situation cropped up in the 19th century regarding machine parts. Machines and mechanical products used to be constructed more or less ad hoc, with new pieces forged from scratch for each new assembly. If a part broke, a replacement had to be created by hand; it wasn't possible to take an equivalent part from another machine because that part fit its native machine and no other.

Then some genius got the idea of creating standardized parts that could be swapped from machine to machine while still maintaining a near perfect fit. Not only did the advent of interchangeable parts make repair of existing machines easier, it also greatly enhanced the invention and creation of entirely new machines, out of the existing repertory of parts.

The advantage continues to this day. Think of how bolts and screws always come in standard sizes. You can rely on any 3/16-inch bolt to fit into any threaded 3/16-inch hole, even if the hole was bored in Detroit and the bolt was forged in Manchester. If that wasn't so, I'd never have been able to fix this office chair I'm sitting on at the moment. But it is and I was.

You can write C functions to fit existing and new situations in the same way bolts slip into any properly sized hole. Of course, a function won't work in an inappropriate context, just as a 3/8-inch bolt won't thread into a 3/16-inch hole. With care, however, you can make functions that fit a variety of situations. The key lies in how you construct them in the first place.

How is code *general*?

What distinguishes generalized code from code that is more specific? A lot has to do with what assumptions your code makes about the environment that it's running in. Many of the examples in this book have actually made some pretty specific assumptions; any program that uses the system() function to issue a cls command to the operating system (OS) is assuming that the OS is DOS—not UNIX, OS/2, or Windows NT. Any function that makes use of one or more global variables is also making assumptions about its environment. Because global variables are created outside any and all functions, a function using them is assuming that someone else is going to be nice and create them and ensure they have the right data. All such assumptions can be fatal at runtime.

It's also better to write functions that don't try to do too much. A function that formats and then sorts data may be fine in one case but won't fit the bill if all you need is something to sort some time later. Remember, good structural programming requires one function per task and one task per function. The closer you adhere to this rule, the more general and reusable your functions are.

Compare the function listing immediately following with the one after that. Both functions do the same thing; the first, however, makes some specific assumptions; the second is more general.

```
/* This function loads the named file's records into the */
/* global structure variable Names,
➥then displays the records loaded */
int FileLoad(void)
{
```

```
FILE *pDiskFile;
int counter = 1, result, counter2;
if ((pDiskFile = FileExists(FileName)) == NULL)
    {
    puts("Cannot open File");
    return 0;
    }
else
        {
        pDiskFile = fopen(FileName, "r");
        fread(filetag, 8, 1, pDiskFile);
        if (result = strcmp(filetag, "FILEDATD") != 0)
            {
            puts("File wrong type");
            return 0;
            }
        while (!feof(pDiskFile))
            {
            Names = realloc(Names, 45 * (counter + 1));
            fread(&Names[counter++], 45, 1, pDiskFile);
            }
        fclose(pDiskFile);
        }
for (counter2 = 1; counter2 <= NumberEntered; counter2++)
        {
        puts(Names[counter2].Name);
        puts(Names[counter2].Phone);
        }
        printf("Current file is: %s\n", FileName);
        puts ("Press any key to continue");
        choice = getch();
return counter - 2 ;
}
```

Note that this function is passed no parameters; thus, any variable used within it that isn't local to the function (such as the two counter variables and the file pointer) must be a global variable; the function won't work if Names, for instance, isn't declared as a global structure. The program also prints its own error messages, rather than relying on a run-time error-handling function. Finally, it displays records loaded from the file, taking on yet another task.

Contrast the preceding example with a more general version of the same function:

```
/* This function loads the named file's records into the */
/* structure pointed to by Names */
```

```
extern struct NameRecord
{
char Name[40];
char Phone[16];
};
int FileLoad(char *FileName, struct NameRecord *Names)
{
    FILE *pDiskFile;
    int counter = 1, result;
    char choice;
    if ((pDiskFile = FileExists(FileName)) == NULL)
        {
        Error(FileName);
        return 0;
        }
    else
            {
            pDiskFile = fopen(FileName, "r");
            fread(filetag, 8, 1, pDiskFile);
            if (result = strcmp(filetag, "FILEDATD") != 0)
                {
                errno=98;
                Error(FileName);
                return 0;
                }
            while (!feof(pDiskFile))
                {
                Names = realloc(Names, sizeof(struct
                ➥NameRecord) * (counter + 1));
                fread(&Names[counter++], sizeof(struct
                ➥NameRecord), 1, pDiskFile);
                }
            fclose(pDiskFile);
            }
    return counter-2;
}
```

 **co**de In the second example, error messages are left to the Error() function. What's more, the function no longer displays records; it leaves this to another function. No global variables are used; all variables used within the function are declared either in the parameter list or locally within the function. The function does expect a global structure definition (not a particular structure instance, though; just a pointer to one) called NameRecord, but this actually increases flexibility—because NameRecord isn't defined locally, the definition for the NameRecord structure type could actually be changed without breaking the function. The sizeof() operator, among other things, assures that the function always knows the size of the structure variable that it's dealing with.

Variables are a key element in general code

On a smaller level, reusable, archivable code requires care with variables, especially with variable names. It's very easy to set up conflicts if you reuse the same variable names a lot. Although this is less of a problem when you use mainly local variables, you can still experience conflicts with variable names even if all your variables are local.

I think it's worth your while at this point to review the concept of local variables. A local variable is declared and used only within a particular function. The variable can't be used by any other function, including `main()`, unless you provide a pointer to the local variable. This means you can have two local variables with the same name in two different functions; to C, the two variables are distinct, and no conflict arises.

If, however, you use the same name within a function's header or definition as you have for other variables declared locally, you can run into big trouble. And you should never use the same names for variables in an argument list as you've used for any global variables in your program; in such a case you'll find your program being passed unexpected data.

Actually, it's probably a good idea to never use global variables at all. It's with global variables that you end up with most conflicts: conflicts with local versus global variables within functions, functions that rely on global variables that might not be there, and parameter-list conflicts. As a rule, all variables should be made local; you should rely on local variables within the `main()` function to keep track of all of a program's vital data.

Comments are important for remembering what a function does

Another very important way that you can ensure that your code will be reusable is to make liberal use of comments. Recall that anything enclosed within the symbols `/*` and `*/` is a comment; the compiler ignores it. To a programmer, though, comments can be of enormous significance. They tell you what each part of a program is doing.

Catch the bug

Following are the preprocessor directives and declarations for a program. Do you see any problems with them?

```c
#include <stdio.h>
#include <conio.h>
#include <string.h>
#include <stdlib.h>

/* A short data handling program */
/* It uses functions to load and save file data */
/* Everything is designed to prevent
➥accidental overwriting of existing files */


/* Function prototypes */
int EnterData(struct NameRecord *Names, int NumberEntered);
FILE *FileExists(char *FileName);
int FileLoad(char *FileName, struct NameRecord *Names);
void FileSave(char *FileName, struct
➥NameRecord *Names, int NumberEntered);
void Error(char *FileName);
int NumberEntered;
/* Global data structure */
struct NameRecord
{
char Name[40];
char Phone[16];
} Names[100];

char *filetag[8];
```

Answer: *Two global variables are created that also appear in parameter lists: NumberEntered and Names. These should be eliminated from the declarations section and declared locally within main().*

At a minimum, each function should include a comment at the beginning that explains the function's purpose and what data it expects to be passed. Each major block of statements within a function should also be labeled with a comment, explaining what that block of statements is meant to accomplish. It's generally a good idea to use a comment to make explicit what sort of value is being returned by a function and what it means.

Including a sufficient number of comments can make it much easier for you to incorporate existing code into new projects. You'll find that memory dims, and what was obvious in a function written in March will be obscure in a function reused in September. Rather than having to pore over the function listing, puzzling out what it does and what it expects, you can just read your comments.

Of course you can carry the comment thing too far. I'm not telling you to introduce every line of every function with a separate comment; such a forest of comments probably does more to obscure a function's operation than it does to clarify it. There's an art to knowing how much information is enough, and the art of commenting is something you'll learn with experience.

Use separate and general functions to create a program

So you've got all these nicely written and commented functions that are very general and very reusable. How do you start reusing them?

I suppose you could just do it the old fashioned way—cut and paste. Some C packages let you do this within the development environment; in other cases, you have to rely on the cut-and-paste capabilities of the text editor or word processor that you're creating your source code with. This technique requires you to poke around all your source code listings looking for the right functions to copy. Still, where's there's a will, there's a way.

Although you could do it through cut-and-paste techniques, you don't have to. Although until now your programs have always been contained within a single file, it doesn't have to be this way. Just as you incorporate the C library functions, which are held separately, into your programs, you can maintain and incorporate separate functions of your own. This is called **modular programming** and is so important that it deserves a major section of its own.

How do I piece the parts together?

When you write modular code, you maintain and use each function in a separate file. When the overall project is compiled and linked, these separate files are brought together and melded into a single executable program. You must supply your compiler with the name of each file to use in the overall project. In addition, each separate source code file (**module**, for short) must be structured in a certain way.

Making a module is easy

For more information on structured programming, see chapter 2, "Specifying, Designing, and Implementing a C Program."

For your functions to be "module-ready," you need only follow the rules of structured programming that you've reviewed and expanded on in this chapter. That is, isolate your programming task into well-commented functions and restrict your use of global variables. Creating modules out of an integrated project, however, requires a little more than just good structure.

Although you can isolate the parts of a program into files in any one of several ways, it's probably best to have a separate source file for each function. However, only one function should be main() (remember that there can be only one main() function in a program). Otherwise, to make a module out of a function, you need only isolate all of the source code for the function into a text file of its own. There are some extras to add once you've done this, though.

What makes up a module?

In addition to its code, which includes any variable definitions used throughout, each module should be associated with a header file. This file has the same name as the module, but with the extension .h instead of .c. The header file includes the function prototypes for each function in the module. The header can also include constant and variable definitions. The module itself should have an #include directive specifying this header file; you'll also need to #include the header files for all modules in a project within the module for the main() function. This, the main() module, has #include directives for all functions. The other modules are referred to as secondary modules; they, too, must have #include directives for library functions if they use them.

Watch out for global variables

If any of your secondary program modules rely on global variables, you'll actually need to declare these within the secondary module(s) that they're used in. You do this using the extern keyword. Supposing the main() module contains a definition for a variable named NumberItems declared outside of main() itself, you'd need a statement like

```
extern int NumberItems;
```

in each module that the NumberItems is used.

How to compile and link a modular program

When it's time to turn a program containing modular source code files into an executable application, you'll have to provide your compiler and your linker with more than just the program file name you're used to using. In essence, you must provide the compiler with the name of each separate module used by the program. For the program contained in six modules, it is necessary to use a command like:

```
mcc filedatd.c enterdat.c errorhan.c
➥fileexis.c fileload.c filesave.c
```

If you're working within a development environment, such as that for Microsoft's Visual C, you may need to create a project file that includes the name of each separate module in your program. Your compiler's documentation will tell you how to submit multi-module programs for compilation and for linking.

Create your own code library

Once you've compiled a working module, you don't need to recompile it every time you want to use it in a new program. Recall that compiling a program—including a single or multi-function module—results in a new file called an object code file. To reuse a previously compiled module, you need only link in its object file (it will have the module's name plus an extension like .o or .obj) when you link the main module. Note that even if you use object files for previously compiled functions, you should save the original source code in case you need to modify it or use it as the basis for some new function.

As for maintaining your source and object code files, many feel it's a good idea to keep them all in one place; a single directory on your computer that constitutes your library. This can make it much easier to find parts that are otherwise apt to go missing. You might want to keep a list of all your function modules to refer to when you start a new project and are looking for code to reuse.

By the way, if you have several functions that work well and that you use a lot, you might consider placing them in a single module and compiling them together. This is how the ANSI Standard C libraries like `stdlib` and `stdio` are constructed, after all. Be sure the associated header file contains prototypes for all the functions in the library module you're creating, along with any common variable definitions.

If you want to have additional organization within your library, be sure to keep close track of how you name and refer to your different source and object code files. You don't, however, need to provide the complete path name for a file in any `#include` directive featuring the file.

If all this seems like a lot of work, remember that a good foundation greatly facilitates later building. The creation and maintenance of libraries is taken quite seriously by professional developers. A large software utility company that I once worked for (not Microsoft) took the idea so seriously they paid huge money to bring in a new executive VP whose job it was to oversee the building of a company-wide code library. They wanted a single library that could be used in new releases of all their products on all types of computers they supported.

Microsoft has taken the notion of libraries very seriously as well; in fact, they've been successful enough with the idea that they've been able to incorporate library code into products and sell it as such—two examples are Visual C and Visual Basic. While you may never achieve anything quite so grand with your own library, you'll save yourself lots of work later on.

Find and use C code written by other programmers

There's another way you can save yourself work, and that's by letting someone else do it. You'll find that programmers aren't necessarily secretive about their work; in fact, many are anxious to share their solutions with you. You can find new and interesting code to use all over the place; you just have to know where to look and what you're looking for.

 **CAUTION** **You need to make absolutely certain that you don't violate** someone else's copyright when you reuse code written by someone else. You should look for a message—probably within the code listing itself—that explicitly states you are free to use the code as you see fit. The mere absence of a copyright statement is not enough.

You can buy library files

C code written by others is frequently compiled together into library files, just like the modules you've been learning how to create. Using any such function library is no different from using the standard ones available with all C compilers. The one thing to be wary of is that not all such libraries are written in ANSI Standard C; this may mean the functions within won't link properly into programs produced with your own C compiler. The library documentation usually tells you what versions of C the library works with. You'll need to specify the library's name when you attempt to link a program that uses its functions.

If you're having problems, there are places to find the solution

There are a number of places you can go to find suggestions, source code listings, and library files. The print media, of course, are good for listings, and you can sometimes get hold of disks containing files through special offers. You can always acquire interesting libraries, however, by going online.

Magazines

There are a number of magazines devoted to computer programming. Because C is the software development language of choice, you'll find that most of the general programming magazines speak your newly acquired language. There are also magazines specific to particular operating systems, especially Unix and Windows. In any of these magazines you can find interesting new ways to solve problems. Some good ones to try are *Dr. Dobbs Journal*, *Byte*, *C/C++ Users Journal*, *PC Magazine*, *Microsoft Systems Journal*, and *Windows Tech Journal*.

Online services

If your computer is equipped with a modem, you can find even more information using the online information services, especially CompuServe and America Online. Of the two, CompuServe is perhaps the more technically oriented. I base this judgment on the fact that Los Alamos National Laboratory (birthplace of the A-bomb) has a local access number for CompuServe but not for AOL. It doesn't really matter, though—both services let you get in touch with other programmers and acquire new software development tools, including function libraries.

Both services have separate areas devoted to computer programming in general and C programming in particular. You can read messages posted by other programmers. You can also download software development tools.

 Plain English, please!

To **download** is to transfer a file from a remote computer to your local computer. Sending a file from your computer to a remote computer is called **uploading**.

Subscribing to either service is quite easy; free startup kits arrive in the mail once in a while. If the mailman isn't bringing you any such presents, you can buy a kit at your local software retailer or call the services directly to request a startup kit. The phone numbers are

| America Online | 800-827-6364 |
| CompuServe | 800-554-4079 |

Well, that wraps it up. I hope you've learned something. I hope I've taught you that programming in C, although occasionally precise and demanding, isn't necessarily difficult or time-consuming and that you can write some powerful programs. From here, the only limit on your C programming is your own imagination. Good luck!

Summary

This chapter looked at using existing C programming work, written by you or by others. You reviewed how a program needs to be built to be reusable. Then this chapter talked about modular programming. Finally, you looked at what might go into a code library and reviewed some sources for obtaining programming work done by others.

Review questions

1 What is meant by *modular programming*?

2 What should each secondary module have associated with it?

3 What are *external variables*? How can using them complicate modular programming?

4 How can you use existing functions without recompiling them?

5 What's something to be aware of when you attempt to use a function library acquired from some third party, such as through an online information service?

Exercises

1 Convert a program of your own into modular form. Use two modules; one for the `main()` function and one for all the other functions. Any program that employs user-defined functions will do.

Answers to Review Questions and Exercises

In this appendix you'll find answers to all review questions for each chapter, along with either complete answers or suggestions (as appropriate) for each chapter's exercises. For program-writing assignments in particular, I've mainly confined myself to giving hints and suggestions for how to write programs to solve the problem posed in exercises that make such requests. There is no one solution to a programming problem, unless the problem is posed very narrowly. The best indication of a program's correctness is whether it works.

Chapter 1: What Is C?

Review questions

1 In what way were the first computers programmed? Why did this method prove difficult?

Answer: The first stored-program computers were programmed in machine language in direct sequences of 1s and 0s that computers understand, with each unique sequence standing for a particular command. Such a language is very difficult for people to read.

2 Name two of the first high-level programming languages developed.

Answer: FORTRAN and COBOL were among the first languages developed.

3 Which computer operating system was rewritten entirely in C?

Answer: The operating system UNIX, developed at AT&T Bell Labs (also the birthplace of C itself) was rewritten in C.

4 What do I mean when I say that the C programming language and programs written in it are highly portable?

Answer: Portability means a program written in C can be moved to another computer—even another operating system—and compiled and run there with minimal changes.

5 Name a kind of data that is more difficult to handle in C than in BASIC.

Answer: Character-based data in the form of character strings is harder to work with in C than it is in BASIC.

Chapter 2: Specifying, Designing, and Implementing a C Program

Review questions

1 When is a problem a likely candidate for solving with a computer program? Would multiplying two specific eight-digit numbers—a process a computer can do in fractions of a second—be a good candidate?

Answer: Any problem for which a well-defined solution exists that is likely to need solving several times with many different sets of data is a good candidate for a computer program. The example given, multiplying two specific numbers, is not a good candidate. This operation could be accomplished with a decent pocket calculator in much less time than it would take to write the program.

2 Define *algorithm*.

Answer: An algorithm is an unambiguous and orderly sequence of actions that yields the solution to a specified problem.

3 In what form should a C source program be?

Answer: C source code programs take the form of unformatted text files.

4 Suppose you own an Apple Macintosh and an IBM PC-compatible. How many C compilers do you need?

Answer: You would need at least two; one for each different type of computer. If you also had access to a UNIX workstation, you'd need a third compiler for it.

5 What do you call the output from a compiler? Is this output ready to run?

Answer: The compiler takes your source code and translates it into object code. Object code is not ready to be run; it must be linked into executable form.

Exercises

1 Write an algorithm for multiplying two three-digit numbers.

Answer: You learned this algorithm back in third grade. You perform three one-digit by three-digit multiplications, adding an appropriate number of zeroes (none, then one, then two) to each result. The three results are added together. The exact form your algorithm takes isn't as important as beginning to think of problem solving in these terms.

2 Determine the data required to find the interest returned on a savings account, and the form those data should take.

Answer: You need the opening balance for the savings account, the interest rate paid on the account, and the amount of time the balance is held at that rate. Each of these constitutes a data item. The data are numeric and may contain fractional values.

3 Develop a specification, a description of the data, and an algorithm for a program that finds the volume of either a cube or a sphere, whichever is chosen by the user of the program while the program's running.

Answer: Again, the exact answer you obtain will vary. Basically, you want a program that accepts two items of input from the user. The first will be either the radius of a sphere or the side of a cube. The second represents the choice made by the user. The program takes this choice and then applies one of two formulas to the entered data item: raising it to the third power to get the cube volume or multiplying this value by 4/3π to get the volume of the sphere. This result is shown. The program needs data storage areas for the number and choice input by the user and for the result obtained from the chosen calculation.

Chapter 3: A Sample C Program

Review questions

1 What symbol should most C program statements end with?

Answer*: Any executable statement in C ends with a semicolon.*

2 At which part of a program would you find the statements marked #include?

Answer*: The #include statements are found at the beginning of the source code listing in the program header.*

3 Name two uses for comments. How would you take a line from the program specification and turn it into a comment?

Answer*: To identify the parts of a program, to make source code easier for a human to read, and to make it easy to modify a program if you come back to it after a span of time has elapsed. To turn a line for the program specification into a comment, affix the symbols /* to its beginning and add */ to it's end.*

4 What's the final step in preparing a C program to run?

Answer*: The final step occurs after compilation; it's called linking.*

Exercises

1 The following is a repeat listing of the interest.c program. However, some changes have rendered it useless. It also has changes that make it less readable. Without referring to the original program earlier in the chapter, can you spot the three errors in the new listing, as well as the changes that affect readability?

```
#include <stdio.h>
#include <math.h>
float balance, rate, future, years;
{
```

```
printf("\nEnter the opening balance: ");
scanf("%f",&balance)
printf("\nEnter the interest rate in percent per year:  ");
scanf("%f",&rate);
printf("\nEnter the number of years the balance is held: ");
scanf("%f",&years);
future = balance * (pow(2.7183,(rate/100)*years));
printf("\nThe future balance is %f",future);
```

Answer: The line main() *was left out, the semicolon that should have ended line 6 was omitted, and the concluding brace is missing. In addition, all comments have been removed; this makes the program less readable.*

2 If you haven't done so already, type in the code for the INTEREST program (that is, the example that works from earlier in the chapter) into a text editor on your computer, compile and link it, and try executing it with different values on your system. Ignore any warning messages you may receive from your compiler; they aren't important.

Answer: Did it work? If you got any error messages from your compiler, they likely resulted from typographical errors. When you begin to program in C, it's easy to omit those semicolons and braces.

3 Can you modify the INTEREST program so that the term is given in months, while keeping the interest rate entered in percent per year?

Answer: Change the variable named years *to* months, *then change line 16 as follows:*

```
future = balance * (pow(2.7183,(rate/1200)*months));
```

Note that what you're doing is dividing the interest rate, which is entered in percent per year, into a figure appropriate for months, by dividing by an additional factor of 12 (12 × 100 = 1200).

Chapter 4: Places To Store Data

Review questions

1 Define a *variable*.

Answer: A variable is a named storage location for data of a specific kind.

2 What is the purpose of initializing variables, and how is it done?

Answer: *Assignment statements are used to initialize variables. They should be initialized to eliminate any extraneous data that might be left over in your computer's memory.*

3 Where do you create variables in a program?

Answer: *You create variables at the beginning of a program, after any and all #include statements.*

4 What is meant by a *floating-point number*?

Answer: *A floating-point number is one with a decimal fraction, like 3.14159.*

Exercises

1 Find and correct the problems with the following three declaration statements:

```
int $Salary;

AvogadrosNumber float;

character Name;
```

Answer:

```
int Salary;
```
Dollar sign not allowed.

```
float AvogadrosNumber;
```
Words in reverse order.

```
char Name;
```
Wrong keyword.

2 What errors can you find in the following short program? Concentrate on the variables.

```
#include <stdio.h>

int radius;
```

```
float pi = 3.14159

main()
{
printf("Enter the circle's radius: ");
scanf("%d",Radius);
Area = (radius)^2 * pi;
printf(\n"The circle's area is %d",Area);
}
```

Answer: *Lines with errors are*

4: Semicolon missing.

9: The variable name radius *is capitalized here but was created with a lowercase first letter. C treats these as two different variables. Because* Radius *wasn't declared, an error occurs.*

10, 11: The variable Area *was not declared.*

All: None of the variables was initialized. This doesn't cause an error but is bad practice anyway.

3 Write a group of statements that creates two unsigned long integer variables named Deficit and Revenues and a character variable named YesOrNo.

Answer: *This block of statements creates the desired variables and constants:*

```
long unsigned Deficit, Revenues;
char YesOrNo;
```

Chapter 5: Paying Constant Attention to Data

Review questions

1 What is the difference between a variable and a constant?

Answer: *Their names give away the difference: the contents of a variable can change, but a constant represents the same value throughout the program in which it's declared and used.*

2 Distinguish between a symbolic constant and a literal constant.

Answer: A literal constant uses numerals or letters to represent the exact value of the constant just as we would write it down: `3.14159`, `"My Name"`, *and 5 are all literal constants. A symbolic constant represents one value by another set of symbols, such as representing the value 3.14159 by* `pi`.

3 What is required to change a statement declaring a variable into one declaring a constant?

Answer: Add the keyword `const` *to the beginning of the declaration statement.*

4 Where in a C program should symbolic constants be declared? What about literal constants?

Answer: You declare symbolic constants in the same place you declare variables. Literal constants aren't really declared; you just use them as you need them.

Exercises

1 Write three lines of C code to create three constants; an integer constant named `Weight` equal to 185, a floating-point number constant named e equal to 2.718282, and a character constant named `Ampersand` equal to &.

Answer: The relevant lines are

```
        const float e = 2.718282;
    const char Ampersand = '&';
```

2 Figure out what changes you'd make to the example program in this chapter's "How can I use this in the real world?" if you wanted to use 3.1415928 for π, rather than 3.1416.

Answer: You need only change the line declaring the constant; formerly it was

```
    const float pi=3.1416;
```

Change it to

```
    const float pi=3.1415928;
```

3   The density of water is about 62 pounds per cubic foot. Write a short program to calculate the weight of water in a circular pool with the radius and depth of the pool entered by the user. The volume of such a pool, by the way, is given by $\pi \times r^2 \times h$, where r is the radius of the pool and h is its depth. Use symbolic constants for pi and the density of water.

Hint: Find the volume of the pool and then multiply that by the density of water.

Chapter 6: Expressing Yourself with C Statements

Review questions

1   Define *expression*.

Answer: An expression is a group of symbols representing a specific value.

2   What are the three main types of expressions? What distinguishes them?

Answer: The three expression types are mathematical expressions, text expressions, and logical expressions. They're distinguished by the type of data involved.

3   What is a statement?

Answer: A statement is a single line of C programming code that accomplishes one specific task.

4   What is meant by the term *keyword*? Can a keyword also serve as the name of a variable?

Answer: A keyword is a specific word or symbol that tells C to perform one specific task. You cannot use a keyword as the name of a variable; keywords are reserved for C's use.

Exercises

1 Write a block of statements to create variables corresponding to your age, weight, and height in inches, and then use each of these in an assignment statement to give them the appropriate values.

Answer: *For yours truly, the answer is:*

```
int age, weight, height;
age = 35;
weight = 180;
height = 68;
```

2 Given the following short program, can you identify the keywords in each of the statements in that program? Ignore the lines containing `main()` or braces.

```
/* Calculating simple interest */
float AcctBalance, Rate, Term;
main()
{
puts("Enter your balance, the rate, and the term:");
scanf("%f %f %f", &AcctBalance, &Rate, &Term);
AcctBalance = AcctBalance * (1 + Rate/100) * Term;
printf("\nYour new balance is %f", AcctBalance);
}
```

Answer: *The keywords are:* `float`, `puts`, `scanf`, `=`, *and* `printf`.

3 Again referring to the example program for exercise 2, go through each line of the program and determine what kind of statement each one is. Ignore the lines containing `main()` or braces. (These can be considered program control statements.)

Answer: *The first line is a comment. The second is a variable declaration statement. All lines with* `scanf`, `puts`, *and* `printf` *are program control statements. The line containing the equal sign is an assignment statement.*

Chapter 7: Getting Information from the Keyboard and Putting It On-Screen

Review questions

1 Define *character-based I/O*.

Answer: Character-based I/O consists of inputting and outputting only those characters that can be typed in the manner of an electric typewriter.

2 What is a format string, and where and when is such a string used?

Answer: A format string specifies how data is to be input or output. You find such strings associated with the `printf()` and `scanf()` functions.

3 What are *escape sequences*? Which escape sequence do you use to sound the system beep?

Answer: An escape sequence is used to send special characters or control codes to the screen. The escape sequence for the system beep is `\a`.

4 What do conversion specifiers do?

Answer: Conversion specifiers, such as `%f`, specify the form in which data is to be written or read.

5 Name two differences in the way `printf()` and `scanf()` handle variables.

Answer: The `scanf()` function expects a variable's address as argument. You provide expressions—not just variable—to a `printf()` statement to do calculations within the statement.

Exercises

1 Write a single statement to output your name, street address, and phone number on the screen, each on a separate line.

Answer: *Use the* puts() *function along with literal string constants for your name, address, and phone number, like*

```
puts("My Name");
puts("My street");
puts("555-1111");
```

2 Modify the following program to use puts() statements instead of printf() in places where this is possible. Try to arrange it so that program output is exactly the same. (Hint: Pay attention to line spacing.)

```
#include <stdio.h>
float Age;
main()
{
printf("\nA program to find your age in days");
printf("\nEnter your age in years; fractions allowed");
scanf("%f", &Age);
printf"\nYour age in days is %f", Age*365.25);
}
```

Answer: *Use* puts() *on lines 5, 6, and 8, where the user is prompted to enter data.*

3 Write a simple C program that asks the user to input an integer and then echoes that integer back to the user with the message You entered the number. Include an opening message, Input a number, and a pause at the end, with the message Press the Enter key to quit.

Answer: *Use something like*

```
int Number;
puts("Input a number:  ");
scanf("%d", &Number);
printf("You entered the number %d", Number);
puts("Press the Enter key to quit");
scanf("%d", &Number);
```

Chapter 8: Performing Mathematical Calculations in C

Review questions

1 What does it mean to *evaluate an expression*?

   Answer: *To evaluate an expression is to determine its value.*

2 Describe the difference between unary operators and binary operators.

   Answer: *Unary operators apply to only one item, such as a variable; binary operators apply to two.*

3 What difference does it make if you place a unary operator after a variable, as opposed to before it?

   Answer: *The variable's contents are changed after the expression is evaluated, instead of before.*

4 What is meant by the phrase *order of operations*?

   Answer: *This is the way C evaluates complex expressions involving several different operators. Certain operations are performed first, regardless of their left-to-right order in the expression.*

5 What is meant by the term *modulus*? What symbol represents the modulus operator?

   Answer: *The modulus is the remainder when one number is evenly divided by another; the modulus of 7 divided by 3 is 1. The modulus operator is %.*

Exercises

1 Write two lines of C code to find the number of hours in a given number of minutes and the number of minutes left over.

   Answer: *Use the modulus operator. Assuming that Hours, Minutes, and TotalMinutes are all integer variables, you could use:*

```
Hours = TotalMinutes/60;
Minutes = TotalMinutes%60;
```

2 Write a C program to find the average of five numbers input by the user on one line. Recall that to compute the average of a set of numbers you first add all of them. Then you divided this sum by how many numbers there are.

Answer: Having five numbers input on one line means one `scanf()` *statement with five conversion specifiers. The essential code is*

```
scanf("%d %d %d %d %d", &One, &Two, &Three, &Four,
&Five);
Average = (One + Two + Three + Four + Five)/5;
printf("%d", Average);
```

3 Using the formula for the payment on a loan, write a C program to calculate and display the payment based on the loan amount, rate of interest, and length of term entered by the user. Have the term entered in months. The formula is

$$\text{payment} = (\text{rate} \times \text{amount} \times e^{\text{rate} \times \text{time}})/(e^{\text{rate} \times \text{time}} - 1)$$

Recall that e is approximately equal to 2.7183.

Answer: The most important statement looks like:

```
Payment = (((rate/1200)*months)*balance *(pow
➡(2.7183,(rate/1200)*months))/(pow(2.7183,(rate/
➡1200)*months))-1);
```

You'll need statements to prompt the user to enter values and `scanf()` *statements for the input values required.*

Chapter 9: Finding the Truth of Expressions
Review questions

1 What two results does a logical expression always evaluate to?

Answer: Conventionally, the values are called True and False; in C terms, True is 1 and False is 0.

2 What is the relational operator that expresses the concept "is less than or equal to"?

Answer: This operation is symbolized by <=

3 Which operation is performed first: ! or > ?

Answer: *Negation (!) comes first.*

4 When is an expression involving the && (AND) logical operation equal to 1? What about an expression with ¦¦ (OR)?

Answer: *An expression with && is only True when both operands are True. An expression with ¦¦ is True when either or both of the operands is True.*

5 How would you use the conditional operator to change a negative value in a variable to 0 but leave the value alone if the variable's contents are positive or equal to 0?

Answer: *Use a statement like*

```
Variable = Variable<0 ? 0 : Variable;
```

Exercises

1 Write a relational expression that asks the question: "Are the contents of the variable AccountBalance greater than or equal to an amount that's 10 times the contents of the variable BadChecks?"

Answer: *The correct expression is*

```
AccountBalance >= (BadChecks * 10)
```

2 Combine the expression from Exercise 1 with a second expression that tests whether the value in the variable BadChecks is greater than 0. Create a logical expression from these two that evaluates to 1 (True) only if both expressions are true.

Answer: *The correct compound expression is*

```
(AccountBalance >= (BadChecks * 10))&&(BadChecks>0)
```

3 Modify the program to find the payment on a loan that you created in the final exercise of the last chapter. Have the modified program print 0 for the payment if a negative loan amount is entered.

Answer: *Use a conditional assignment statement for the Payment variable, setting it to zero if* balance <= 0, *as in*

```
Payment = balance<=0 ? 0 : (((rate/1200)*months)*balance
➡* (pow (2.7183,(rate/1200)*months))/(pow(2.7183,(rate/
➡1200)*months))-1);
```

Chapter 10: Control the Way a Program Runs

Review questions

1 What does the term *conditional execution* refer to?

Answer: This refers to statements that may or may not be executed depending on the results of a logical test.

2 What is a loop? Is it possible to create a loop that never terminates?

Answer: A loop is a group of statements that are repeated until some condition is met. In a loop where the condition is never met, the block of statements is executed forever or until the program is terminated from outside.

3 What keyword is used to introduce an alternative block of statements after an if block?

Answer: Use the else keyword for such alternative blocks.

4 Distinguish between for and while.

Answer: Both create loops; for creates loops with counters, and while creates loops that execute as long as a test condition evalutes to True.

5 Define the term *nesting*.

Answer: To nest is to enclose an item within the same kind of item: a loop within a loop or an if block within an if block.

Exercises

1 Write an if block that tests the value of a variable called Age, and prints the following messages under the given conditions:

If Age is less than 18, print Child.

If Age is between 18 and 44, print Adult.

If Age is between 45 and 65, print Middle-Aged.

If Age is greater than 65, print Senior.

Try to accomplish this task in as few statements as possible.

Answer: *Use something like*

```
if (Age >= 65)
     puts("Senior");
if (Age < 65 && Age >= 45)
     puts("Middle Aged");
if (Age < 45 && Age >= 18)
     {
     puts ("Adult");
     }
else
     puts ("Child");
```

2 Write a loop that sums an input value into a variable called Sum, until the value in Sum exceeds 1000. Count the number of times the loop is executed and have a statement after the loop print this result.

Answer: *Use a while loop that executes until the value in sum is greater than 1000, like*

```
counter = 1;
while (!(Sum > 1000))
       {
       scanf("%d", &Input);
       Sum = Sum + Input;
        counter++;
       }
       printf("I went %d times through the loop",
       ➥counter);
```

3 Using while statements, modify the INTEREST program so that, if the user enters a nonpositive value for any of the variables in the program, the program displays a message indicating the value isn't appropriate and then gives the user the chance to re-enter it.

Answer: *Use a separate while loop for each data-entry point. Something like*

```
while (balance <= 0)
       {
       puts("Input the balance");
       scanf("%f", balance);
```

```
                    if (balance <= 0)
                        puts ("Invalid amount, reenter);
                }
```

Chapter 11: The Functional Structure of C Programs

Review questions

1 Define the term *top-down design*. What relationship does this concept have to structured programming?

Answer: *Top-down design means dividing a programming task into successively smaller units. Structured programs follow top-down design.*

2 What function does every C program have?

Answer: *The* main() *function.*

3 What are the parts of a function?

Answer: *The function prototype, the function definition, and the function body.*

4 What is an *argument*? What is a *parameter*?

Answer: *An argument is a variable name appearing in a function's prototype and definition, specifying what kind of data the main program hands off to the function. A parameter is the actual data passed to the function.*

5 What are library functions? What must you do to make a library function available within one of your own C programs?

Answer: *Library functions are C language programs that already exist and can be called and used within any program. To make such functions available, you must include the header file in which they're prototyped, using the* #include *directive.*

Exercises

1 Write a function to find the cube of a number; don't use the `pow()` library function.

Answer: *Try this*

```
float cube(float x)
{
return x*x*x;
}
```

2 Incorporate the function you wrote in exercise 1 into a short program that asks for a number from the user and then finds the cube of the number and the cube of half the number, printing each result on a separate line with appropriate text accompanying the result.

Answer: *You need two calls to the* `cube()` *function: one for the input value, and one for* `input/2`.

3 A close look at the output from the new FINANCE program shown in figure 11.1 reveals that this program doesn't exit as elegantly as it should; it forces the user to go through entering the balance, rate, and number of months again before allowing the user to quit. Rewrite the program so that the user is given the opportunity to quit immediately after results are displayed.

Answer: *Prompt the user if the program should continue. Test the input value, and set the value of another variable based on its value. Have the entire* `main()` *function within a* `while` *loop that executes as long as the test value remains True.*

4 Further rewrite the FINANCE program so that the input tasks are handled by a separate function.

Answer: *Remove all the* `puts()` *and* `scanf()` *statements that prompt the user for information, and put them into a separate function. Have the* `main()` *function call this function.*

Chapter 12: About Data Streams

Review questions

1 What is meant by *device independence*? How is this related to C streams?

Answer: Data that is device-independent can be prepared for use on any sort of computer system with any kind of input and output. C data streams are one way that C achieves device independence.

2 Define *echoing* and *buffering*.

Answer: To echo is to show keyboard input on the screen as it's entered. Buffering is to accumulate input or output in memory prior to sending it to its ultimate destination.

3 What is the name of the standard input stream? Of the stream connected to the system printer?

Answer: Standard input is called stdin. The standard printer is stdprn.

4 Name a function for character input and another for formatted output.

Answer: You can use getch() for character input and printf() for formatted output.

5 Define *I/O redirection*. Can you do it from within a C program?

Answer: I/O redirection refers to sending data that's intended for one destination on to another, such as redirecting screen output to the printer. Although I/O redirection is an operating system task, you can do it within a C program if you issue a call to the OS.

Exercises

1 Write a short program that reads a single character from the keyboard and writes it immediately back to the screen on a separate line, until the user enters a capital **Q**.

Answer: Try

```
while (inputch != 'Q')
    {
```

```
inputch = getch()
}
```

2 Write a `printf()` statement to output four variables: the first two unsigned integers and the last two floating point. Separate the variables with tabs. Have eight characters print for each variable, with three digits to the right of the decimal for the floating-point variables. Use a, b, c, and d for the variable names.

Answer: *The statement is*

```
printf("%8u\t%8u\t%8.3f\t%8.3f", a, b, c, d);
```

3 Write a short program that produces some sort of numerical result (calculating compound interest will do) while drawing boxes around the results using asterisks. Allow the user to repeat the program, pressing **n** to quit. Use output field widths of nine characters, and include a box around the program's title.

Hint: *Use tabs to get the necessary blank space on the line that your result is printed on. A box consists of three lines.*

Chapter 13: Some Optional Ways To Store Data

Review questions

1 Contrast an external variable with a local one. Where do you declare each?

Answer: *External variables are visible to all functions within a program; local variables can only be used in the function in which they're declared. You declare external variables outside of any and all functions; local variables are declared inside of functions.*

2 What part of a function declaration also declares variables? What scope do these variables have?

Answer: *The function definition declares variables. These variables are local to the function.*

3 What is an *automatic variable?* a *static variable?*

Answer: An automatic variable is created when declared and destroyed when the function in which it was created terminates. A static variable remains in existence when the function that created it terminates.

4 Would it make sense to have a static variable local to the `main()` function? For what reason?

Answer: No, because when the `main()` *function terminates, the whole program terminates.*

5 Name a good use for external variables.

Answer: Symbolic constants used throughout a program.

Exercises

1 Write declaration statements for a static integer variable named `Memory` and an automatic floating-point variable named `Answer`, making both local to a function named `Doodle` that accepts a single floating-point argument and returns a floating-point answer.

Answer: You can do so in one statement; the function definition for `Doodle()`, *like*

```
float Doodle(static int Memory, float Answer)
```

2 Write a short program that prints the sum of all the positive integers between zero and that number, for the integers 1 though 100. Use a nested `for` loop, with the same name for the variable counter within each loop.

Answer: Declare the counter variable local to each block in which it appears.

3 Write a function to find the fourth power of a number. Have the function check to see if it's just been called with the same value. If so, have it return the answer immediately without recalculating it.

Hint: Have a static variable hold the input value passed to it and another to hold the results of its calculation. Test the input value against the static variable; if they're equal, immediately pass the contents of the static result variable.

Chapter 14: Call Several Variables by the Same Name

Review questions

1 Define *array*. What is meant by initializing an array?

Answer: An array is a collection of variables referenced under the same name. To initialize an array is to provide each of its members with values.

2 What is an array's index?

Answer: The index is the number in brackets after the array name, used to refer to a particular array member.

3 What can go into an array's index when the array is being declared? When it's being used within a program?

Answer: At declaration time, an array's index must be an integer or a symbolic integer constant. When the array is in use, the index can be an integer expression, including the name of another variable or variables.

4 What are the limits on how many dimensions an array can have?

Answer: In theory there are no limits; in practice, it is very difficult to work with arrays having dimension greater than 2.

5 Of what use is the counter variable within a loop when working with an array?

Answer: The counter can be used as the index, to refer to each array member in turn on each pass through the loop.

Exercises

1 Write a declaration statement to create a three-dimensional array to hold an integer value for each day in each month of five consecutive years. Name the array Days.

Answer:

```
Int Days[4][11][31];
```

2 Write a short loop to print the values in a ten-member array named `Items`, printing each member in `Items` one to a line.

Answer:

```
for(counter = 0; counter <= 9, counter++)
    {
    printf("%d\n", Items[counter]);
    }
```

3 Matrices are constructs from mathematics that represent orderly collections of numbers. A three-by-three matrix of numbers looks like

```
  1     2     3
 10    -6     7
 18     0    12
```

Develop a C program that lets the user input two three-by-three matrices and adds the two matrices together to produce a third matrix. To add two matrices, you add the corresponding elements, so

```
  1    2    3        1    1    1          2    3    4
 10   -6    7    +   2    2    2     =    12   -4    9
 18    0   12        3    3    3         21    3   15
```

Have your program print out both input matrices, and print the matrix resulting from their addition.

Hint: *Store the elements of each matrix in a separate two-dimensional array. Use two nested for loops for the addition with a basic statement like the following at the heart of the loops:*

```
ResultMatr[counter1][counter2] = Matr1[counter1][counter2
↪+ Matr2[counter1][counter2];
```

Chapter 15: String Variables as Places for Characters

Review questions

1 Define *string*. What character marks the end of a string in C?

Answer: *A string is a sequence of characters. The null character \0 marks the end of a string in C.*

2 What is meant by the term *concatenation*?

Answer: *Concatenation is combining two strings into one by adding one to the end of the other.*

3 How do you designate a literal character constant? A string constant?

Answer: *A literal character constant is enclosed in single quotes—for example,* `'q'`*; a literal string constant is enclosed in double quotes—for example,* `"My Name"`*.*

4 What do you omit from a string's name when using the string as a parameter in most string functions?

Answer: *You omit the array index.*

5 Why is it important to flush the input buffer after obtaining formatted input?

Answer: *There may be excess data remaining in the buffer because the user entered too much.*

Exercises

1 Write a statement to create a string variable capable of holding 80 characters. Name the variable `Line`.

Answer:

```
char Line[80];
```

2 Write a statement to create and initialize a string variable, setting it equal to your full name. Name the variable `FullName`.

Answer: *In my case it's*

```
char FullName[12] = "Clint Hicks";
```

3 Write a program to print an address entered with last name first, followed by a comma and then the first name. Allow the user to enter an organization, such as **XYZ Co.** or **Macmillan Computer Publishing** as an optional second line. Output all four lines, omitting the organization line if it was left blank.

Hint: *You'll need to add an extra string variable for the organization. To determine whether to print it, test to see if its first character is equal to* `\0`*.*

Chapter 16: Structure Storage To Meet Your Own Needs

Review questions

1 Define a *structure*. What is meant by the structure's *tag*?

Answer: *A structure is a collection of variables defined by the user. The structure tag is the name of the structure's definition.*

2 What is the purpose of the dot operator?

Answer: *The dot operator separates the parts of a structure variable's name and is used when you access individual variables within the structure.*

3 What is the difference between using `struct` and `typedef` for defining a structure?

Answer: *There is no appreciable difference, except that when creating instances of the structure later in your code, you can omit the `struct` keyword and just use the structure tag.*

4 How do you reference a member of an array that is a structure element? a structure that is a member of an array?

Answer: *In both cases, you use the index, as in*

```
MyStructure.Numbers[3]
```

and

```
MyStructure[3].Number
```

5 What's required to incorporate a structure into a larger structure?

Answer: *You define the smaller structure first, and then include its tag and an instance name within the larger structure definition. To access parts of the smaller structure, you need to use the dot operator twice, as in*

```
MyBigStruct.MySmallStruct.Number
```

Exercises

1 Write a definition for a structure named `Collection` to hold an integer variable, `Count`, a floating-point array, `Values`, and a string variable (length 25), `Designation`. Create an instance of `Collection` named `MyCollection`.

Answer:

```
struct Collection
{
int Count;
float Values[9];
char Designation[25];
} MyCollection;
```

2 Incorporate the structure `Collection` from exercise 1 into a new structure, which also includes an integer value, `Rate`, and a floating-point value, `Time`. Give the new structure the name `BigCollection`, and create an instance of it called `MyBigCollection`.

Answer:

```
struct BigCollection
{
struct Collection MyCollection;
int Rate;
float Time;
} MyBigCollection;
```

3 Rewrite the structure definition from exercise 2 using the `typedef` keyword. Create two instances of the structure named `MBC1` and `MBC2`.

Answer:

```
typedef struct
{
struct Collection MyCollection;
int Rate;
float Time;
} BigCollection;
BigCollection MBC1, MBC2;
```

4 Write a program to input ten collections of values consisting of a balance, an interest rate, and a term. Store the results in an array of structures. Compute compound interest according to the formula and print the results, along with the input values.

Hint: Use a structure definition like

```
struct Input
{
float balance, rate, term;
} StructArray[9];
```

Chapter 17: How To Indirectly Access Data Storage with Pointers

Review questions

1 What is a *pointer*? What data does a pointer contain?

Answer: A pointer is a variable that specifies the location in memory of another variable. A pointer contains an address in memory.

2 What is the *indirection operator*? the *address-of operator*? How is each used?

Answer: The indirection operator is the asterisk. The address-of operator is the ampersand. The former is used to indicate a pointer or the contents of the variable it points to; the latter specifies the address in memory of a variable.

3 Why is the data type of a pointer important?

Answer: Different data types have different lengths in bytes. A pointer has a specific data type so that C knows how much data is being pointed to.

4 What is a *pointer constant*? Give an example of one.

Answer: A pointer constant also refers to a location in memory, but after a program is compiled and linked, the pointer constant can't be changed to point to something else. The name of an array or of a string variable is a pointer constant.

5 What arithmetic operations can be performed on a pointer variable? What use are these operations?

Answer: Pointers can be incremented, decremented, and differenced. The first two operations can be used to move among members of an array; the latter can be used to find a particular array item.

Exercises

1 Write a declaration statement to create a pointer to a string variable, and a string to which to point. Make the string 12 characters long.

Answer:

```
char *pString, String[11];
```

2 Create a pointer to a floating-point variable, and initialize it to that variable's contents. Write all the code necessary to declare the pointer and the variable.

Answer:

```
float *pVariable, Variable;
pVariable = &Variable;
```

3 Modify the averaging program from this chapter to enter the values into the table in reverse order and print them out in forward order. (Hint: use the decrement operator, discussed in chapter 8, "Performing Mathematical Calculations in C.")

Answer: What I'm asking for here is that you use pointers and pointer arithmetic to access array elements. You'll need to declare and set a pointer to the array; remember that the array's name is a pointer constant and can't be incremented or decremented.

Chapter 18: Turning One Data Type into Another

Review questions

1 A long integer and a single-precision floating-point integer (types `long` and `float`) both occupy four bytes in memory. What's the difference (if any) in how values are stored in these variables?

Answer: The byte values for a long integer are interpreted as representing a binary number; those for a floating-point number are divided into number and exponent.

2 What is meant by *type promotion* and *most inclusive type*? What are the most and least inclusive data type?

Answer: Type promotion occurs when one data type is converted, temporarily, into another that is more general. The most general data type is the most inclusive type. The most inclusive type is `float`*;* `char` *is the least inclusive.*

3 What happens when you assign a floating-point value to an integer variable?

Answer: The fractional part is lost.

4 What's a *type cast*?

Answer: An expression affixed to another to force that expression to be evaluated as a certain data type, as in

```
(double)MyFloatVariable
```

5 What's the only difference in the three string-to-number functions?

Answer: The data type of the value returned: integer, long integer, or floating point.

Exercises

1 Write an expression to convert the result of dividing two floating-point numbers by each other into an integer value. There are actually two ways of doing this; see if you can find both.

Answer: *You can divide the two numbers and assign the result to an integer variable, or you can use a type cast to force the division to type int:*

```
Integer = Float1/Float2;
```

or

```
AnyVariable = (int)(Float1/Float2);
```

2 Write a short block of statements that takes input from the keyboard in string form—use gets()—and then converts the result into an integer and prints it.

Answer: *Try something like*

```
gets(Input);
result = atoi(Input);
printf("%d", Input);
```

3 Write a short program that takes separate digits from an input number in floating-point form and prints each digit on a separate line.

Hint: *Find out how long the number is by using the log10() function; this gives the number of figures to the left of the decimal. Use a loop that executes this number of times plus six (floating-point numbers preserve six figures to the right of the decimal). To extract the digit at each position, use integer division on the input number divided by ten to the current digit's power. Subtract the digit times ten to its position's power. It might help to visualize a number like 64,328 as*

$$60,000$$
$$4,000$$
$$300$$
$$20$$
$$8$$

Chapter 19: Get Strings To Do What You Want

Review questions

1 What is the *null character*? Why is it important?

Answer: *The null character is escape sequence* \0. *It is used to mark the end of a string; most string functions take only a pointer to a string and don't care about its supposed length. They look for the null character to determine a string's end.*

2 What is the difference between the maximum length and the current length of a string? How does C determine the current length? What string function returns the current length?

Answer: *The maximum length of a string is the number of character variables in the array constituting the string; the current length is how many characters there are up to the terminating null character; the position of the null character is how C determines string length. Use the* strlen() *function to find a string's current length.*

3 Where are the prototypes for the string functions defined?

Answer: *In the header file* string.h.

4 What function do you use to copy the first *n* characters of one string to another?

Answer: *Use the function* strncpy().

5 What is the difference between the functions strchr() and strrchr()?

Answer: *The former looks for the first instance of a given character in a string, and the latter looks for the last instance of the character.*

Exercises

1 Write a block of statements to look for the last comma in a given string.

Answer: *Use a call to* strrchr(), *and then use differencing on the pointer returned to find the location of the comma within the string, like*

```
pLastPosition = strrchr(AString, ',');
position = pLastPosition - AString;
```

2 Write a block of statements that examines a string for the first occurrence of one of the decimal digits.

Answer: Use a call to the function strcspn()*, as in*

```
strcspn(AString, "1234567890");
```

3 Modify the NameList program given in this chapter so that, if the user enters some further designation after a trailing comma, such as **Mr. Oliver Boliver Buttes, Jr.**, the program still returns the correct answer, which in this case is

```
Buttes, Mr. Oliver Boliver, Jr.
```

Hint: Use strrchr() *to look for the trailing comma; if none is found (the function returns NULL), then process the name as NameList formerly did.*

Chapter 20: Control a Program— Where It Goes, What It Does...

Review questions

1 Which statement do you use to transfer control to a labeled statement? What's wrong with using this statement?

Answer: The statement is goto. *Use of this statement is to violate the rules of structured programming.*

2 What is switch() used for?

Answer: The switch() *construction is used to create blocks of alternatively executed statements in a manner easier to read and understand than using many* if *statements.*

3 Indicate what happens when a program encounters break. What about continue?

Answer: When a program encounters break, *it immediately exits the current block, which could be a loop. When it encounters* continue, *it skips the remainder of the current pass through a loop and starts on the next pass.*

4 What's the most essential thing to know about what happens when a user presses a function key?

Answer: Pressing a function key on a PC generates two bytes, not one. The first byte returned is 0.

5 Name a threat to program portability posed by use of the system() function.

Answer: Different operating systems use different commands to accomplish the same task, such as clearing the screen. If you include one such command, it won't work if the program is taken to and compiled on another type of computer with a different operating system.

Exercises

1 Write a loop that looks through an integer array for a value equal to zero. Have the program exit the loop when 0 is found, preserving the array element that 0 occurred in.

Answer: Use a loop like

```
for (counter = 0; counter <=NumberInArray; counter++)
    {
    if (Array[counter] = 0)
        {
        Position = counter;
        break;
        }
    }
```

2 Write a loop that looks through another integer array and divides only the even numbers within it by two.

Answer: Use the continue *statement on odd values; use the modulus operator while dividing by two to test for "oddness."*

```
for (counter = 0; counter <= NumberInArray; counter++)
    {
    if (Array[counter]%2 != 0)
```

```
        continue;
Array[counter] = Array[counter]/2;
}
```

3 Write a short program that prints one of five different messages. Four of the messages are triggered by specific function keys—one of these messages prints if the corresponding function key is pressed. The fifth message prints if the user presses a key other than those four function keys.

Hint: Use a while loop; each time through, use the `getch()` function and test for a byte value of zero; if zero is returned, get the next character immediately. Use a `switch()` construction to determine which message to display based on the second byte value returned. Print the error message for the `default:` case.

Chapter 21: What Else Can I Do with Functions?

Review questions

1 If you leave something out of the declaration of a pointer to a function, you end up with a function prototype that returns a pointer. What is that thing which you shouldn't leave out?

Answer: The parentheses around the pointer name and the indirection operator in its declaration statement.

2 How do you pass an array to a function? Does this include a string variable?

Answer: Provide a pointer to the beginning of the array. This includes string variables.

3 How do you get multiple values back from a function?

Answer: You must pass pointers as arguments to the function for additional values you want the function to return.

4 What are the four important elements in creating a variable parameter list. (Hint: they all start with va_.)

Answer: The elements are the pointer type va_list *and the functions* va_start(), va_arg(), *and* va_end().

5 Define *recursion*. What can it consume a lot of?

Answer: Recursion is when a function calls itself. It can consume a lot of computer memory.

Exercises

1 Write a prototype for a function that takes one integer, one floating point, and one string parameter, and returns a pointer to a string.

Answer: As an example, consider

```
char *MyFunction(int a, float b, char *c);
```

2 Write a declaration statement to declare a pointer to the function from exercise 1. Assume the function does not return a value.

Answer:

```
void (*pMyFunction)(int a, float b, char *c);
```

3 Write a short program to find the average of a list of numbers. Use a variable argument list in the function that finds the average.

Hint: This is an exercise in using va_list *along with* va_start, va_arg, *and* va_end. *Have the fixed parameter in the list be the number of values passed.*

Chapter 22: Cool Things To Do with Pointers
Review questions

1 Define *multiple indirection*.

Answer: This occurs when the address contained in a pointer refers to the address of another pointer.

2 What is meant by *a pointer to a pointer?*

Answer: *This is an example of multiple indirection.*

3 What do you end up with if you leave the parentheses out of a declaration for a pointer to a multidimensional array?

Answer: *You end up declaring an array of pointers.*

4 Give a use for an array of pointers.

Answer: *Such an array can be initialized to point to a number of literal string constants.*

5 How do you pass a multidimensional array to a function?

Answer: *You must declare a pointer in the appropriate form, using the size of the last dimension as the size of the pointer, as in*

```
float (*pArrayPointer)[80];
```

Exercises

1 Write three statements to declare a pointer to a floating-point variable, declare a pointer to that pointer, and set the second pointer to point to the first.

Answer:

```
float *pFirst;
float **pSecond;
pSecond = &pFirst;
```

2 Declare and initialize an array of pointers to point to your full name, street address, and city.

Answer: *In my case, it's*

```
char *Address[2] = {"Clint Hicks", "You don't think",
➥ "this is my address"};
```

3 Make use of the `Screen_Paint` routine developed in this chapter. Create a `Screen` variable within your program's `main()` function. Have the `PrintScreen` routine modify the `Screen` to show your name and address. Pass the modified screen to `Screen_Paint`.

Hint: Remember that you need a pointer to a multidimensional array to pass Screen to different functions. Have each part of the program that does output copy appropriate values to certain lines within Screen.

Chapter 23: Messing Around with Bits and Bytes

Review questions

1 What is meant by *hexadecimal notation*? *Octal*? Why are they useful when expressing computer data?

   Answer: *Hexadecimal is a base-sixteen notation; octal is base eight. They're useful because computer bits are grouped into eight.*

2 What is the maximum integer value that can be expressed in two bytes? In four?

   Answer: *If you ignore the sign, the maximum values are 65,536 and about 4,295,000,000.*

3 What is the shift-left operation equivalent to?

   Answer: *Multiplying by two.*

4 What is meant by the *complement* of a byte value?

   Answer: *The value that results when all 1s in the original byte value become 0s, and all 0s becomes 1s.*

5 What do you use to express the width, in bits, of a bit field in a structure. What data type do all such fields have?

   Answer: *You use the number of bits, preceded by a colon, just after the field's name. The data type of all such fields is unsigned integer.*

Exercises

1 Write a short function to perform an integer division by four on a number. Use one of the shift operators rather than the ordinary division (/) operator.

Hint: Use the shift-right operator.

2 Write a statement to perform the XOR operation on a number and its complement. What does this result always come out to?

Answer:

```
Result = Number ^ ~Number;
```

This result is always a straight string of 1s.

3 Write a structure definition for a structure to contain a name of up to 40 characters, an employment status field to hold one of two values, a marriage status field to hold one of four values, and a department field to hold one of eight values.

Answer: Use something like

```
struct Employee
{
char Name[40];
unsigned Status: 1;
unsigned Married: 2;
unsigned Dept: 3;
};
```

Chapter 24: What You Need To Know about Disks and Their Files

Review questions

1 What is meant by a file's *buffer*? What is the relationship between a buffer and a data stream?

Answer: The buffer is the place in memory where data accumulates on its way into and out of a disk file. You might say the file's data stream is connected to the buffer.

2 What function readies a file for use? What does it return?

Answer: The function is fopen( )*. It returns a pointer of type* FILE*.*

3 Distinguish between the binary and text modes of file access.

Answer: In text mode, data is organized into lines of ASCII characters with each character line assumed to be terminated with an end-of-line character. Each byte in the file is assumed to represent a character. In binary mode, there's no interpretation to the bits in the file.

4 What C operator can you use to ensure that data read from (or written to) a file comes in blocks that are exactly the size of a particular data construct you're using to hold the blocks in memory?

Answer: Use the `sizeof()` *operator along with the name of the data constuct you're using as buffer.*

5 Distinguish between sequential and random file access. Where does the file position pointer fit into this scheme? What function do you use to set the position indicator to a specific place within a file?

Answer: In sequential access, you read or write data in order from start to finish. With random access, you set the position within a file where you want to read or write. The file-position pointer indicates where data is coming from at the moment; resetting this pointer is how you accomplish random access. You do this using the `fseek()` *function.*

Exercises

1 Write a statement to prepare a file to be read from or appended to.

Answer: Use `fopen()` *with the access mode* `a+`*.*

2 Write a short function that gives the user the opportunity to rename or delete a file whose name is held in `FileName`.

Answer: Use the `rename()` *and* `remove()` *functions.*

3 Write a short C program to read a specific line from a text file, and display it on-screen. Let the user specify which file to open and which line number to read. Use the `fseek()` function to set the line to be read. Assume that lines are 80 characters long and don't terminate with a null string.

Hint: The relevant call to `fseek()` *should look like*

```
fseek(pFilePointer, 80*LineNumber, 0);
```

At this point, use fread *to put the line into an appropriate variable. You'll need to make certain the last character in the variable is a null character, by having your program put it there.*

Chapter 25: Make Your Work Easier with the C Function Library

Review questions

1 Name two different functions that can return the square root of a number.

Answer: sqr() *and* pow()*.*

2 Distinguish between the common and natural logarithm functions.

Answer: Common logs use the number 10 as base; natural logs use e, which is approximately 2.71828.

3 In what units do C trigonometric functions expect angles to be expressed? What is the relationship between these units and degrees?

Answer: Trigonometry functions expect angles to be expressed in radians. There are 2π radians in 360 degrees.

4 What two data types are most commonly used with time functions?

Answer: The type time_t *and the structure type* tm*.*

5 What function do you use to build a time string formatted according to exact specifications?

Answer: The function strftime()*.*

Exercises

1 Write a function to find the natural logarithm of each number from 1 through 100, printing each number and its logarithm on a separate line.

Hint: Use the log() *function within a loop. You'll need a type cast to force integer data into floating-point form; otherwise, the function will return zero.*

2 Write a statement to convert a time value stored in a `tm` structure named `Time` to a string stored in `TimeString`. Use a maximum length of 80 and a format such as

Thursday, 8 June, 1995—12:25AM

Hint: Use the `strftime()` function.

3 Write a program to calculate the number of seconds elapsed since someone's birthday.

Hint: Use the `mktime()` function to convert the dates—held in a type tm structure—into seconds format, and then use `difftime()` to subtract the current date from the person's birthdate.

Chapter 26: Make Memory Work for You
Review questions

1 What is meant by *dynamic allocation of memory?*

Answer: Setting aside memory for variable when a program is run; not at compile time.

2 Describe the feature of a memory model and its effect on a program's execution.

Answer: A memory model specifies how much space there is set aside for a program's instructions and for its data and how large single data items can be. It determines how much memory is available to allocate at runtime.

3 What should your program always do when attempting to use one of the memory allocation functions, other than `free()`?

Answer: The program should test to see if the memory allocation function it called was successful; if the function returns a pointer value of `NULL`, it failed.

4 What does the `realloc()` function do that `calloc()` and `malloc()` do not?

> ***Answer:*** *The* `realloc()` *function changes the size of an existing space and preserves its contents.*

5 What happens if your program continues to allocate new memory without letting go of memory it no longer needs? What function can you use to remedy this?

> ***Answer:*** *Eventually, the program may use up all available memory and crash. You can use the* `free()` *function to release memory you no longer need.*

Exercises

1 Write a function that sets a pointer to be returned to one of five possible message strings, depending on an integer value it is passed. Make the messages anything you want. However, make them of varying lengths. Use dynamic memory allocation to set the point to exactly the right size.

> ***Hint:*** *Use* `malloc()`.

2 Write a program to average a group of positive integers entered by the user. Allow the user to enter as many numbers as desired. Use -1 as the tag value to end data entry. Collect the numbers entered in a dynamically-sized array.

> ***Hint:*** *Use* `realloc()`.

3 Modify your program from exercise 2 so that it checks to make sure memory is available before allowing the user to enter another data item. Recall that when it fails, `realloc()` returns NULL. (Don't use the same pointer to memory on each call to `realloc()`. If `realloc()` returns NULL, you'll lose your reference to existing data.) Use a separate pointer in the call to `realloc()`. Then set the existing pointer to this new pointer if the call to `realloc()` is successful.

> ***Hint****: Again,* `realloc()` *returns* NULL *if insufficient extra memory was available.*

Chapter 27: How Do I Find and Fix the Errors in My Program?

Review questions

1 What is a *syntax error*? How do you eliminate such errors from executable programs?

Answer: A syntax error results from improper use of the C programming language. The second part is a trick question; executable programs cannot contain syntax errors because syntax errors prevent a program from being compiled.

2 What is a *logical error*? Name two places in which errors in program logic might commonly occur.

Answer: A logical error results from a program that isn't properly constructed. In a sense, it fails to properly reflect its underlying algorithm. Logic errors can occur when you work with pointers and when you set up if *blocks.*

3 What is a *run-time error*? Name two possible causes for such errors.

Answer: A run-time error occurs during program execution, due to some problem with current operating conditions. They can occur because the program user did something incorrectly or because the computer ran out of memory.

4 What argument does the `assert()` function take? How can you turn `assert()` off without removing it from a program's source code?

Answer: `assert()` *takes a logical test as argument. You can turn it off by defining* NDEBUG.

5 Is use of the `errno.h` file required for handling run-time errors? Why or why not?

Answer: No, `errno.h` *merely defines symbolic constants for certain error numbers.*

Exercises

1 Write a program to read a number of financial values into a table. Allow the user to enter the values as dollar amounts. Store them as floating-point numbers.

Hint: Use the atof() *function. Your input variable needs to be a string.*

2 Set up an error() function of your own that displays one of three messages when called, depending on a value passed to it by the calling function. Make the messages anything you like. Also, make use of the perror() function.

Hint: You'll need to define your own error condition.

Chapter 28: Programs That Update Themselves

Review questions

1 What output does the C preprocessor produce? How does it differ from the original source code submitted for compilation?

Answer: The preprocessor produces an expanded source code file. Among other things, in the new code, all #include statements are replaced with the contents of the files they're including.

2 Can files included with #include statements have #include statements within them? How do you refer to this technique? Is there any limit to it?

Answer: Yes, this is another example of nesting. Some compilers limit this nesting to ten levels deep.

3 Distinguish between *substitution macros* and *function macros*. What do they have in common? What advantage do function macros have over standard C functions?

Answer: Substitution macros merely insert an abbreviation for a set of symbols; function macros do the same but accept arguments. They're both created with the #define directive. Function macros don't require specific data types in their arguments.

4 Explain two uses for conditional compilation.

Answer: In debugging and localization.

5 With what statement must a conditional compilation block always end?

Answer: The directive #endif.

Exercises

1 Write a substitution macro to define MyName as your own name, as a literal string constant.

Answer: In my case, it's

```
#define MyName "Clint Hicks"
```

2 Write a function macro to define a function Hypotenuse(), which returns the value of the longest side of a right triangle when the values of two shorter sides are known. Use the Pythagorean theorem: $c^2 = a^2 + b^2$.

Answer:

```
#define Hypotenuse(a, b) pow((float)(a)*(a)+(b)*(b), 0.5)
```

3 Use conditional compilation to alter which strings appear in a financial program. If you know a foreign language, substitute messages in that language; if not, simply vary the English versions. Use two versions, USA and FOREIGN. Use whatever currency symbol you prefer for FOREIGN, and a comma for a decimal point. Hint: Enclose each set of puts() and printf() statements in conditional compilation blocks, as in the following:

```
#if defined( FOREIGN )
        puts("Une programme pour
        ➥calculer quelques formules financieres");
#else
        puts("A program to calculate
        ➥certain financial formulae");
#endif
```

Additional Hint: Put the conditional compilation directives around each statement that prints a value to the screen.

Chapter 29: Use Code That You or Somebody Else Has Already Written

Review questions

1 What is meant by *modular programming*?

Answer: This is programming with multiple source code files.

2 What should each secondary module have associated with it?

Answer: A header file.

3 What are *external variables*? How can using them complicate modular programming?

Answer: An external variable is one declared outside of any function. They complicate modular programming because you must include a declaration for each such variable in every module that uses them.

4 How can you use existing functions without recompiling them?

Answer: Maintain them as modules, compile them once, and then link in their object files when you want to use them in new projects.

5 What's something to be aware of when you attempt to use a function library acquired from some third party, such as through an online information service?

Answer: The library might not be written in an ANSI Standard C form and thus might not work with your compiler.

Exercise

1 Convert a program of your own into modular form. Use two modules; one for the `main()` function and one for all the other functions. Any program that employs user-defined functions will do.

Hint: Be sure to use #include directives in the secondary modules for all the library functions used by your program's functions.

⊘

B

ASCII Characters

The following chart shows the decimal codes associated with low ASCII (first 128) characters. High ASCII (above 127) varies from computer system to computer system. The first 32 ASCII values represent control codes.

0	NUL
1	SOH
2	STX
3	ETX
4	EOT
5	ENQ
6	ACK
7	BEL
8	BS
9	HT
10	LF
11	VT
12	FF
13	CR
14	SO
15	SI
16	DLE
17	DC1
18	DC2
19	DC3
20	DC4
21	NAK

continues

22	SYN
23	ETB
24	CAN
25	EM
26	SUB
27	ESC
28	FS
29	GS
30	RS
31	US
32	a blank
33	!
34	"
35	#
36	$
37	%
38	&
39	'
40	(
41	)
42	*
43	+
44	,
45	–
46	.
47	/
48	0
49	1
50	2
51	3
52	4
53	5
54	6
55	7
56	8
57	9
58	:
59	;
60	<
61	=

62	>
63	?
64	@
65	A
66	B
67	C
68	D
69	E
70	F
71	G
72	H
73	I
74	J
75	K
76	L
77	M
78	N
79	O
80	P
81	Q
82	R
83	S
84	T
85	U
86	V
87	W
88	X
89	Y
90	Z
91	[
92	\
93	]
94	^
95	_
96	`
97	a
98	b
99	c
100	d

continues

101	e
102	f
103	g
104	h
105	i
106	j
107	k
108	l
109	m
110	n
111	o
112	p
113	q
114	r
115	s
116	t
117	u
118	v
119	w
120	x
121	y
122	z
123	{
124	|
125	}
126	~
127	Δ (delta)

C Reserved Words

The following are reserved words in ANSI C, meaning that you can't use them as variable or function names—they're already spoken for.

Keyword	Meaning
asm	Denotes assembly-language code.
auto	Default storage type.
break	Exits a loop or block unconditionally.
case	Used with switch to create a block of statements to execute if a certain condition is met.
char	Data type to store a single byte; represents an ASCII character.
const	Declares a symbolic constant.
continue	Used to move a loop to the next iteration.
default	Used with switch to specify what happens if no cases are met.
do	Creates a loop.
double	Data type to store large floating point values.
else	Used with if to create an alternative program branch.
enum	Data type that accepts only certain (listed) values.
extern	This is a variable that is declared elsewhere.
float	Data type for numbers with fractional parts.
for	Creates a loop with a counter.
goto	Unconditional transfer to another part of a program. (Very much frowned upon by the pedantic and pedagogical.)
if	Alters program flow based on evaluation of logical expression.
int	Data type for numbers without fractional parts.
long	Data type for large integers.
register	Instructs C to store data for a variable in a processor register if it can.

continues

Keyword	Meaning
return	Exits current function and sends specified value (if any) back to the calling function.
short	Data type for small integers.
signed	Indicates data type may have positive and negative values.
sizeof	Finds the size, in bytes, of the designated item, which is generally a variable.
static	Modifies a variable so that its contents are preserved in between executions of the procedure that the variable is declared in.
struct	Creates structured variable definitions and instances thereof.
switch	Creates blocks of statements in which, depending on conditions, one choice is executed.
typedef	Creates a synonym to a data type.
union	Multiple variables share same space in RAM.
unsigned	Used in variable declaration to restrict integer variables to positive values only.
void	Used to indicate function returns or expects no values; also used with pointers to allow them to reference any data type.
volatile	Indicates variable may change and is the default.
while	Used to construct conditional loops.

C++: the Object-Oriented C

If you've had much interest in C over the last few years and have done any reading at all on the subject, you've undoubtedly run across references to C++. What is C++, and why should you care about it? In this appendix I'll give some brief answers to these questions.

C++ is an object-oriented form of C. Object-oriented programming (OOP) is a technique that has really blossomed over the last several years. In essence, OOP associates program code with certain data constructs and not just data. The functions associated with given objects are sometimes called methods; they apply only to the object that they're part of. Objects also have properties, which are data values that apply strictly to the object itself. In some ways, properties are like local variables.

One of the prime examples of an object is a window, like one you might see when you use the Macintosh or a PC with Windows 95. The functions that get a window to do things—change size, display data, scroll up and down—are the methods referred to in the previous paragraph. A window's properties might include the text to put on its title bar, the color to show it in, and its location on the screen.

OOP is the ultimate in structured programming. The properties and the methods associated with objects are kept absolutely distinct from each other. This tends to make OOP programs very modular and their components very portable.

OOP makes it easy to create new objects within your programs. All objects are created from definitions called object classes. A class definition includes an object's properties and methods. When you create an example of an object using the class definition, you create an instance of the class.

Classes can be organized by relying on a feature called **inheritance**. It's possible to define a new class that inherits many of the properties of another class. The new class can have properties and methods of its own. By creating several such classes, you can end up with a class hierarchy. There might be one "master class" at the top of the hierarchy—windows, for instance. Below this class you might have program windows and document windows. Below document windows you could have word processor document windows, spreadsheet document windows, and so on.

In an object-oriented version of a language, the library functions that you may have relied on the non-object version may come in a special form. That is, functions may have been converted into objects in their own right. This process is called **encapsulation**. We say that an object encapsulates a function when it converts that function to object form.

There are a number of excellent versions of C++ available for sale. Among the most widely used are Borland's Turbo C++ and Microsoft's Visual C++. The latter contains a number of important development tools, including the Microsoft Foundation Classes (MFC). This is the entire set of class definitions that Microsoft uses with Windows. You can use MFC to create any Windows object. They also make it much simpler to develop a complete Windows application.

The good news about C++ is that you don't have to unlearn anything you've just learned; C++ is a superset of the C language, which means that everything in regular C is in C++. If you're content with the kinds of programs you've learned to write in this book, you don't need to worry about C++. If, on the other hand, you program for graphical user interfaces like Windows, branching out into the wider version of C that is C++ is a great idea. For information, you might want to consult a book about C++: Que offers *Turbo C++ by Example*, *Visual C++ by Example*, and *Using Borland C++ 4*, Special Edition.

Index

PLUG YOURSELF INTO...

THE MACMILLAN INFORMATION SUPERLIBRARY™

Free information and vast computer resources from the world's leading computer book publisher—online!

FIND THE BOOKS THAT ARE RIGHT FOR YOU!

A complete online catalog, plus sample chapters and tables of contents give you an in-depth look at *all* of our books, including hard-to-find titles. It's the best way to find the books you need!

- **STAY INFORMED** with the latest computer industry news through our online newsletter, press releases, and customized Information SuperLibrary Reports.

- **GET FAST ANSWERS** to your questions about MCP books and software.

- **VISIT** our online bookstore for the latest information and editions!

- **COMMUNICATE** with our expert authors through e-mail and conferences.

- **DOWNLOAD SOFTWARE** from the immense MCP library:
  - Source code and files from MCP books
  - The best shareware, freeware, and demos

- **DISCOVER HOT SPOTS** on other parts of the Internet.

- **WIN BOOKS** in ongoing contests and giveaways!

TO PLUG INTO MCP: ➔

GOPHER: gopher.mcp.com
FTP: ftp.mcp.com

WORLD WIDE WEB: **http://www.mcp.com**

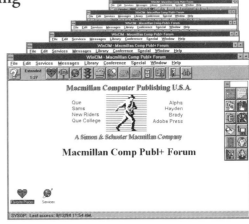

Complete and Return this Card
for a *FREE* Computer Book Catalog

Thank you for purchasing this book! You have purchased a superior computer book written expressly for your needs. To continue to provide the kind of up-to-date, pertinent coverage you've come to expect from us, we need to hear from you. Please take a minute to complete and return this self-addressed, postage-paid form. In return, we'll send you a free catalog of all our computer books on topics ranging from word processing to programming and the internet.

Mr. ☐   Mrs. ☐   Ms. ☐   Dr. ☐

Name (first) ☐☐☐☐☐☐☐☐☐☐☐☐   (M.I.) ☐   (last) ☐☐☐☐☐☐☐☐☐☐☐☐☐☐☐☐☐

Address ☐☐☐☐☐☐☐☐☐☐☐☐☐☐☐☐☐☐☐☐☐☐☐☐☐☐☐☐☐

City ☐☐☐☐☐☐☐☐☐☐☐☐☐   State ☐☐   Zip ☐☐☐☐☐ ☐☐☐☐

Phone ☐☐☐ ☐☐☐ ☐☐☐☐   Fax ☐☐☐ ☐☐☐ ☐☐☐☐

Company Name ☐☐☐☐☐☐☐☐☐☐☐☐☐☐☐☐☐☐☐☐☐☐☐

E-mail address ☐☐☐☐☐☐☐☐☐☐☐☐☐☐☐☐☐☐☐☐☐☐☐☐

1. Please check at least (3) influencing factors for purchasing this book.

Front or back cover information on book .... ☐
Special approach to the content .... ☐
Completeness of content .... ☐
Author's reputation .... ☐
Publisher's reputation .... ☐
Book cover design or layout .... ☐
Index or table of contents of book .... ☐
Price of book .... ☐
Special effects, graphics, illustrations .... ☐
Other (Please specify): _____ ☐

2. How did you first learn about this book?

Saw in Macmillan Computer Publishing catalog .... ☐
Recommended by store personnel .... ☐
Saw the book on bookshelf at store .... ☐
Recommended by a friend .... ☐
Received advertisement in the mail .... ☐
Saw an advertisement in: _____ ☐
Read book review in: _____ ☐
Other (Please specify): _____ ☐

3. How many computer books have you purchased in the last six months?

This book only .... ☐   3 to 5 books .... ☐
2 books .... ☐   More than 5 .... ☐

4. Where did you purchase this book?

Bookstore .... ☐
Computer Store .... ☐
Consumer Electronics Store .... ☐
Department Store .... ☐
Office Club .... ☐
Warehouse Club .... ☐
Mail Order .... ☐
Direct from Publisher .... ☐
Internet site .... ☐
Other (Please specify): _____ ☐

5. How long have you been using a computer?

☐ Less than 6 months   ☐ 6 months to a year
☐ 1 to 3 years   ☐ More than 3 years

6. What is your level of experience with personal computers and with the subject of this book?

	With PCs	With subject of book
New	☐	☐
Casual	☐	☐
Accomplished	☐	☐
Expert	☐	☐

Source Code ISBN: 0-7897-0267-3

Which of the following best describes your job title?

Administrative Assistant .... ☐
Coordinator .... ☐
Manager/Supervisor .... ☐
Director .... ☐
Vice President .... ☐
President/CEO/COO .... ☐
Lawyer/Doctor/Medical Professional .... ☐
Teacher/Educator/Trainer .... ☐
Engineer/Technician .... ☐
Consultant .... ☐
Not employed/Student/Retired .... ☐
Other (Please specify): _____ ☐

8. Which of the following best describes the area of the company your job title falls under?

Accounting .... ☐
Engineering .... ☐
Manufacturing .... ☐
Operations .... ☐
Marketing .... ☐
Sales .... ☐
Other (Please specify): _____ ☐

9. What is your age?

Under 20 .... ☐
21-29 .... ☐
30-39 .... ☐
40-49 .... ☐
50-59 .... ☐
60-over .... ☐

10. Are you:

Male .... ☐
Female .... ☐

11. Which computer publications do you read regularly? (Please list)

_____
_____
_____
_____
_____
_____
_____
_____
_____
_____
_____

Comments: _____
_____
_____

Fold here and scotch-tape to mail.